The Future of E-Mobility

David D'Acunto

The Future of E-Mobility

Investigating the Role of Electric Mobility for Consumers and Industries

palgrave
macmillan

David D'Acunto
Department of Management
University of Verona
Verona, Italy

ISBN 978-3-031-65052-9 ISBN 978-3-031-65053-6 (eBook)
https://doi.org/10.1007/978-3-031-65053-6

This Palgrave Macmillan imprint is published by the registered company Springer Nature Switzerland AG
The registered company address is: Gewerbestrasse 11, 6330 Cham, Switzerland

Foreword—Navigating the Electric Horizon

Electric vehicles are about to change the game, and David D'Acunto's book explores deep into what that means for everyone. The book studies how electric vehicles (EVs) will impact how we drive, businesses operate, and even governments make decisions. It is not just a deep dive into electric vehicles, it is a guide to how they are reshaping our lives, businesses, and even the decisions governments are making.

Thus, I am pleased to introduce "The Future of E-Mobility - Investigating the Role of Electric Mobility for Consumers and Industries," in which the author comprehensively looks at electric mobility and its potential to transform consumer behavior and industry practices.

One major hurdle? Making EVs affordable and practical for everyone. Many electric cars today are pricey and beyond the average buyer's reach. Furthermore, a concern regarding the availability of charging stations during long journeys is a common one among electric vehicle drivers. In Europe, there is a significant need for an expansion of the charging infrastructure.

Consequently, this book investigates into the intricate dynamics of the energy transition, highlighting challenges and potential consequences such as the increased demand for rare earth elements essential for EV batteries. The research positions e-mobility as a catalyst for profound changes within supply chains, introducing new efficiencies and demanding innovative approaches to logistics and manufacturing, especially within the context of the European Union. This is not just about technology; it is about making life better.

Despite technological progress, the book addresses current market challenges, noting the tendency of automakers to focus on more extensive and expensive electric models, which limits the availability of affordable EV options for the mass market. There is a noticeable trend toward electric vehicles as part of a broader push for sustainability. However, challenges such as the need for extensive EV charging infrastructure remain critical in Europe, particularly in some countries, where significant build-out of charging stations is required to meet future demand. This focus may hinder broader EV adoption and delay the transition toward a more sustainable automotive industry. But the book is not all about problems. The author also shows how EVs can be a major force for good. They can help reduce pollution, conserve resources, and create new jobs.

The empirical research underpinning this book provides valuable insights into the factors influencing Italian consumers' intentions to purchase electric vehicles. These findings, though not conclusive, reveal the complex interplay of economic variables, informational levels, perceived obstacles, and benefits in shaping consumer attitudes toward EVs. They emphasize the importance of transparent information dissemination and infrastructure development in accelerating the adoption of electric mobility in Italy and suggest further research to elucidate varying perceptions beyond the Italian context as changes continue.

This book is not just an academic text; it is a roadmap. "The Future of E-Mobility" serves as a critical resource, dissecting the multifaceted impacts of e-mobility from its environmental benefits to its economic ramifications and the necessary policy frameworks. It presents beyond the analysis of consumer behaviors, the industry shifts beyond traditional automotive boundaries, and the critical influence of regulatory landscapes in shaping the future of e-mobility. The debate on electric vehicles in Europe is sparking diverse views on the proposed ban of combustion engine cars. While different objections have been raised, a nuanced understanding of the topic remains crucial.

In his analysis, D'Acunto offers advice for everyone wanting to join the electric vehicle revolution. For consumers, he underscores the importance of practical considerations such as affordability, accessibility, and sustainability in adopting e-mobility solutions. Industries are encouraged to embrace innovation and adaptability to stay competitive in a rapidly evolving market. For policymakers, he outlines strategies for fostering e-mobility, including implementing supportive regulations and incentives that facilitate this transition.

The book also identifies areas where more research is needed. Looking ahead, the author identifies critical areas for future research that promise to deepen our understanding and enhance the implementation of e-mobility solutions. These areas include advancements in battery technology, integrating e-mobility with renewable energy sources, influencing consumer adoption, and the broader socioeconomic impacts of transitioning to e-mobility. Each of these topics is poised to contribute significantly to the overarching goal of sustainable development to achieving the United Nations Sustainable Development Goals (SDGs), specifically Goals 7, 9, 11, 12, and 13.

In summary, this book section provides actionable insights for all stakeholders and a comprehensive roadmap for future research endeavors, underscoring the pivotal role of e-mobility in achieving sustainable development goals. By addressing these recommendations and future research directions in the preface, readers are primed to explore the transformative potential of e-mobility detailed throughout the book. It is evident that no single strategy can universally address the diverse challenges of achieving sustainability through mobility.

Finally, what excites me is the book's focus on how EVs will transform supply chains and the logistics industry. This is a fascinating area, and that is one of the reasons that I find this book resonates deeply with my interests, mainly in its focus on supply chain transformations. It provides a baseline to understand how this industry is changing and the need for innovative approaches, especially in project design, strategic sourcing of critical materials, manufacturing and assembly of diverse components, changing how products are delivered and sold, and organizing tailored after-sales strategies.

I invite you to engage with this research, reflect on its extensive analyses, and consider the broader implications of e-mobility in our collective pursuit of sustainable development, industry organization, and effective climate action. This topic is appealing and demands further exploration; this is a good start. While unquestionably important, the full scope of its impact remains uncertain. "The Future of E-Mobility" is a springboard for this ongoing journey.

Ivan Russo, Ph.D.
Full Professor of Business
Logistics & Supply Chain
Management
Department of Management
University of Verona
Verona, Italy

Contents

List of Figures

List of Tables

1

Introduction to Electric Mobility

Abstract This chapter introduces the concept of electric mobility, emphasizing its necessity in contemporary transportation, and discusses the urgent need for electric mobility due to environmental concerns and resource depletion. A comparative analysis of traditional and electric vehicles highlights the benefits of the latter in terms of efficiency and sustainability. The chapter then discusses the significance of electric mobility for both consumers and industries, detailing how it empowers consumer choices and offers economic advantages for organizations. The chapter closes by examining the role of electric mobility in fostering the transition from linear to circular economies, illustrating how it supports sustainable development and resource efficiency. This comprehensive overview underscores the pivotal role of electric mobility in driving a greener and more resilient future.

Keywords electric vehicles · sustainability · consumer empowerment · circular economy · transition · economic advantages · environmental impacts

D. D'Acunto, *The Future of E-Mobility*,
https://doi.org/10.1007/978-3-031-65053-6_1

The modern world is at a pivotal juncture in its ongoing battle against climate change and environmental degradation. As the global population continues to swell, the demand for energy and transportation grows in tandem, making it challenging to reduce greenhouse gas emissions and mitigate the impacts of a rapidly changing climate. Amid these pressing concerns, the emergence and rapid adoption of electric mobility present a glimmer of hope on the horizon. Electric mobility, encompassing electric vehicles (EVs), e-bikes, and other electric modes of transportation, has the potential to revolutionize not only how we move but also how industries function and how consumers engage with transportation.

The importance of electric mobility cannot be understated, as it offers a compelling solution to the dual crises of environmental sustainability and the need for efficient transportation systems. This comprehensive exploration aimed to investigate the multifaceted role of electric mobility in shaping the future of transportation, both for consumers and industries. By delving into the various dimensions of this emerging phenomenon, we aimed to highlight the opportunities and challenges it presents, the implications for different sectors, and the potential for electric mobility to drive a more sustainable and accessible future (Calise et al., 2019).

Electric mobility marks a profound shift from traditional combustion engine vehicles to cleaner, more sustainable alternatives. The development and mass adoption of EVs, in particular, represent a transformative force in the automotive industry. These vehicles are powered by electricity stored in batteries, which eliminates tailpipe emissions and reduces the carbon footprint of transportation (Kumar & Alok, 2020). As a result, electric mobility aligns with global efforts to combat climate change, improve air quality, and reduce dependence on fossil fuels. From the perspective of consumers, electric mobility offers a compelling array of benefits. EVs are not just an eco-conscious choice but also provide cost savings in the long run due to their lower operating and maintenance costs compared to traditional vehicles. Moreover, they offer a smoother, quieter, and more technologically advanced driving experience. Yet, barriers such as range anxiety and the lack of availability of charging infrastructure must be addressed to encourage a wider adoption of EVs (Calise et al., 2019). Investigating consumer perceptions, preferences, and behaviors is crucial to understanding how electric mobility can become more accessible and appealing.

Electric mobility has far-reaching implications for various industries. Automakers are investing heavily in EV technology to remain competitive in a rapidly changing market. Beyond the automotive sector, the electric mobility ecosystem extends to energy providers, charging infrastructure companies, and battery manufacturers. The transition to electric mobility necessitates significant shifts in business strategies, supply chains, and regulatory frameworks. This work explores the strategies industries are adopting to navigate this transformation and seize new opportunities (Sæther, 2022). One of the key advantages of electric mobility is its potential to significantly reduce greenhouse gas emissions. The shift from internal combustion engines (ICEs) to electric motors can lead to substantial reductions in carbon dioxide emissions, provided that electricity generation comes from cleaner sources. Analyzing the environmental benefits and challenges associated with electric mobility is vital for assessing its overall impact on sustainability and climate change mitigation (Rauh et al., 2015).

The success of electric mobility hinges on the development of a robust charging infrastructure. The availability, accessibility, and convenience of charging stations are critical factors influencing consumer adoption. Investigating the expansion of charging networks, the emergence of fast-changing technologies, and the role of public and private stakeholders in building this infrastructure is essential to understanding the future of electric mobility. Government policies and regulations play a pivotal role in shaping the trajectory of electric mobility. Subsidies, incentives, emissions standards, and urban planning decisions all directly impact the adoption and growth of EVs and other electric transportation modes (Kumar & Alok, 2020). Analyzing the evolving policy landscape at the local and national levels will help to elucidate the dynamics of electric mobility development.

According to Wang et al. (2020), electric mobility is not only about sustainability but also about economic opportunities. This shift has the potential to create jobs, stimulate innovation, and drive market growth. Investigating the economic implications of electric mobility, including the emergence of new industries and the impact on traditional sectors, offers insights into the broader socioeconomic effects of this transformation. While electric mobility holds great promise, it is not without its challenges and barriers. Range limitations, battery technology constraints, charging infrastructure gaps, and consumer hesitations pose hurdles to the widespread adoption of electric mobility. Understanding these challenges and exploring potential solutions are essential for ensuring the success of electric mobility initiatives (Rauh et al., 2015).

Electric mobility extends beyond passenger vehicles and encompasses e-bikes, electric scooters, and electric public transportation systems. Investigating the role of electric mobility in its diverse forms highlights how it can reshape urban transportation, improve last-mile connectivity, and enhance the overall quality of life in cities (Li et al., 2017). The integration of electric mobility into mainstream transportation systems is an ongoing process that requires collaboration among governments, industries, and consumers. This investigation seeks to provide a comprehensive overview of the current state of electric mobility, the challenges it faces, and the opportunities it offers. By understanding the multifaceted role of electric mobility for consumers and industries, we can chart a path toward a more sustainable, efficient, and accessible future for transportation.

In the pages that follow, we will delve into each of these dimensions, exploring the intricate tapestry of electric mobility and its potential to transform the way we move, live, and interact with our environment. Through rigorous analysis and insightful discussion, we aim to equip readers with a deeper understanding of the significance of electric mobility and its implications for consumers and industries alike (Liu et al., 2022).

1.1 Need for Electric Mobility

In the wake of the twenty-first century, the need for electric mobility has become increasingly apparent as we confront the complex challenges of environmental sustainability, urbanization, and the quest for cleaner, more efficient transportation. This section explores the factors that have catalyzed the transition to electric mobility and set the stage for its transformative potential.

The foremost driver behind the emergence of electric mobility is the urgent need to combat climate change. The transportation sector is a major contributor to global greenhouse gas emissions, primarily due to the widespread use of internal combustion engine vehicles powered by fossil fuels (Van Fossen et al., 2022). Electric mobility, with its inherently lower carbon footprint, offers a viable solution to reduce emissions and mitigate the impacts of climate change. Furthermore, EVs produce zero tailpipe emissions, which not only helps reduce carbon dioxide emissions but also significantly improves air quality. In urban areas, where air pollution poses a grave threat to public health, the transition to electric mobility can result in cleaner air and a reduction in respiratory illnesses, demonstrating its immediate benefits to society (Wang et al., 2020).

The need for electric mobility extends beyond environmental concerns. Fossil fuel dependency raises issues of energy security, as nations often rely on imported oil, subjecting their economies to price volatility and geopolitical tensions (Li et al., 2017). In contrast, electric mobility reduces dependence on finite and geopolitically sensitive resources, such as oil, by utilizing electricity, which can be generated from diverse and domestically available sources, including renewable energy. Moreover, EVs are inherently more energy-efficient than their gasoline or diesel counterparts. They convert a higher percentage of the energy from the grid to power at the wheels, reducing overall energy consumption and resource waste. This heightened efficiency is critical for reducing energy demand and minimizing the environmental impact of transportation (Wang et al., 2020).

The world is experiencing rapid urbanization, with more people moving to cities than ever before. This demographic shift has led to increased congestion, longer commute times, and a strain on transportation infrastructure. Electric mobility, especially in the form of electric public transportation, offers a means to address these challenges. Electric buses and trains can provide cleaner and more efficient mass transit options, reducing the number of private vehicles on the road and alleviating traffic congestion. Furthermore, electric micro-mobility solutions, such as e-scooters and e-bikes, are well-suited for urban environments, offering flexible and sustainable transportation alternatives for short trips and last-mile connectivity (Lipu et al., 2018).

The rapid advancement of EV technology has made electric mobility more viable and attractive than ever before. Innovations in battery technology have led to increased energy density, longer ranges, and faster charging times. Additionally, economies of scale in manufacturing have contributed to cost reductions, making EVs more accessible to consumers. As the cost of batteries continues to decline, electric mobility will become a financially competitive option for consumers, further incentivizing its adoption (Lipu et al., 2018). Moreover, ongoing research and development efforts promise even more efficient and affordable EVs in the future, solidifying the role of electric mobility in the global transportation landscape. Governments and regulatory bodies worldwide have recognized the need for electric mobility and have implemented a range of policies and incentives to accelerate its adoption. These measures include subsidies, tax incentives, emissions standards, and the promotion of charging infrastructure development. For instance, countries like Norway have successfully incentivized EV adoption through a combination of tax breaks and other benefits, resulting in a high percentage of EVs on their roads. In the United States, federal- and state-level incentives encourage consumers to purchase EVs and promote investment in EV charging infrastructure. These policy initiatives play a crucial role in creating an enabling environment for electric mobility (Sæther, 2022).

Beyond the practical considerations, there is a growing cultural shift toward sustainable and eco-conscious living. Many consumers are becoming more environmentally aware and are seeking ways to reduce their carbon footprint. Electric mobility aligns with these changing values, allowing individuals to make environmentally responsible choices in their transportation decisions. Additionally, electric mobility is often associated with innovation and modernity, appealing to a younger generation of consumers who are both tech-savvy and environmentally conscious. This cultural shift toward sustainability and innovation further bolsters the need for electric mobility as a preferred mode of transportation (Van Fossen et al., 2022).

In conclusion, the need for electric mobility arises from a confluence of factors, including environmental imperatives, energy security concerns, urbanization challenges, technological advancements, policy incentives, and evolving cultural values. As we move forward, it is imperative to recognize and respond to these needs by embracing electric mobility as a transformative solution that not only addresses pressing global issues but also enhances the quality of life for individuals and communities worldwide. In the subsequent sections in this paper, we will delve deeper into the various facets of electric mobility, examining its impact on consumers, industries, and the environment (Liu et al., 2022).

1.2 Comparison Between Traditional and Electric Vehicles

To comprehend the significance of electric mobility, it is essential to compare and contrast traditional ICE vehicles with their electric counterparts. This section aims to provide a comprehensive analysis of the key differences between these two vehicle types, highlighting the advantages and disadvantages of EVs. Several examples, including Tesla, will be referenced to illustrate these distinctions.

According to the Ravi and Aziz (2022), traditional cars are equipped with ICEs that rely on the combustion of gasoline or diesel fuel to generate power. These engines are known for their mechanical complexity, consisting of hundreds of moving parts, and the energy they produce is transmitted to the wheels through a multi-speed transmission system. In contrast, EVs are driven by electric motors powered by batteries, which convert electrical energy into mechanical motion. This electric powertrain is inherently simpler, with fewer components and moving parts, leading to reduced maintenance requirements and higher efficiency.

Tesla, a prominent example, has garnered acclaim for its electric powertrain technology. The Tesla Model S, for instance, employs an electric motor at each axle, providing all-wheel drive and precise control of power distribution for enhanced performance and stability (Turner et al., 2020). Traditional cars rely on fossil fuels, such as gasoline and diesel, which are combusted in the engine to produce energy. This combustion process releases carbon dioxide (CO_2) and other pollutants, contributing to air pollution and climate change. EVs, in contrast, draw power from electricity, which can be generated from various sources, including renewables like solar and wind. As a result, EVs produce zero tailpipe emissions, making them a cleaner and more environmentally friendly option (Sæther, 2022).

Tesla's commitment to sustainability is exemplified by their emphasis on electric power. The company's gigafactories are designed to produce EVs as well as batteries and solar products, promoting a holistic approach to reducing carbon emissions. One of the primary concerns regarding EVs is their range, i.e., the distance they can travel on a single charge. Traditional cars, especially those with ICEs, typically offer longer ranges than most EVs. However, EV ranges have been steadily improving due to advancements in battery technology. High-end EVs like the Tesla Model S and Model X can now travel over 300 miles on a single charge, rivaling the ranges of many gasoline-powered vehicles (Turner et al., 2020). The availability of charging infrastructure is crucial to addressing range anxiety. Tesla, recognizing this need, has developed a comprehensive network of supercharger stations across the globe. These fast-charging stations can replenish a significant portion of a Tesla vehicle's battery in a short time, making long-distance travel in EVs more practical (Omahne et al., 2021).

EVs are renowned for their impressive acceleration and torque. Unlike traditional cars, which require time to build up engine power, EVs provide instantaneous torque, resulting in rapid acceleration from a standstill. Tesla, in particular, has set a high standard for EV performance. For example, the Tesla Model 3 can accelerate from 0 to 60 miles per hour in just a few seconds, comparable to some high-performance gasoline-powered sports cars (Omahne et al., 2021).

This acceleration is achieved through the precise control of electric motors and the elimination of gear shifting, characteristics that set EVs apart from their traditional counterparts.

EVs generally have lower operating and maintenance costs compared to traditional vehicles. Traditional cars require regular oil changes, transmission fluid replacements, and exhaust system repairs, all of which contribute to ongoing expenses. In contrast, electric cars have fewer moving parts, reducing the need for maintenance and the associated costs. They also benefit from regenerative braking systems that extend the life of brake pads.

Tesla's EVs exemplify these cost advantages. With no ICE, there is no need for oil changes or complex exhaust systems. Moreover, Tesla's over-the-air software updates provide enhancements and fixes, reducing the necessity for physical service appointments (Ravi & Aziz, 2022).

EVs, by virtue of their reduced emissions and reliance on cleaner energy sources, have a lower environmental impact than traditional vehicles. Tesla, as a company, places a strong emphasis on sustainability. In addition to producing EVs, Tesla manufactures energy storage products like the Powerwall and Powerpack and offers solar energy solutions. This holistic approach aligns with the broader goal of reducing the carbon footprint of both transportation and energy generation (Llopis-Albert et al., 2021).

The initial purchase price of EVs is often higher than that of traditional vehicles due to the cost of batteries and electric powertrain technology. However, this difference can be mitigated by government incentives, such as tax credits and rebates, offered to encourage EV adoption. Tesla buyers in the United States, for instance, are eligible for federal tax incentives that reduce the effective purchase price of their EVs (Liang et al., 2020).

Furthermore, the lower operating and maintenance costs of EVs can offset the higher upfront price over time. Reduced fuel costs, fewer maintenance visits, and potential savings on insurance premiums make EVs an economically attractive option in the long run.

EVs are primarily charged at home, where owners can use standard electrical outlets or dedicated home chargers. This convenience allows EV owners to start each day with a full charge, eliminating the need for frequent visits to gas stations. Tesla offers home charging solutions, such as the Tesla Wall Connector, which provide faster charging capabilities.

In addition to home charging, Tesla has developed a network of supercharger stations strategically located along highways and major travel routes. These fast-charging stations enable long-distance travel and reduce charging time, further enhancing the convenience of electric mobility (Liang et al., 2020).

In summary, a comprehensive comparison between traditional and electric vehicles reveals distinct advantages associated with electric mobility. EVs offer a cleaner and more environmentally friendly alternative, with reduced operating costs, impressive performance, and the potential for government incentives. Tesla, a pioneer in the EV market, exemplifies many of these advantages through its innovative electric powertrain technology and commitment to sustainability. As the automotive industry continues to evolve, the transition to electric mobility is poised to reshape the way we perceive and engage with transportation.

1.3 The Importance and Relevance of Electric Mobility for Consumers and Industries

Electric mobility is not only a technological evolution in the automotive sector but also a paradigm shift with profound implications for both consumers and industry business models (Fig. 1.1). This section elucidates the importance and relevance of electric mobility in the contemporary context, dissecting its transformative impact on a spectrum of consumer experiences and industrial domains (Secinaro et al., 2022).

In an era marked by growing environmental concerns, consumers are increasingly seeking eco-friendly alternatives in their daily lives. Electric mobility aligns perfectly with this shift in consumer values. The choice to drive an EV is considered a tangible commitment to reducing one's carbon footprint. This environmental consciousness resonates with consumers who aspire to live sustainably and mitigate their contribution to climate change. Electric mobility offers tangible economic advantages to consumers (Suman et al., 2020). Although the upfront cost of

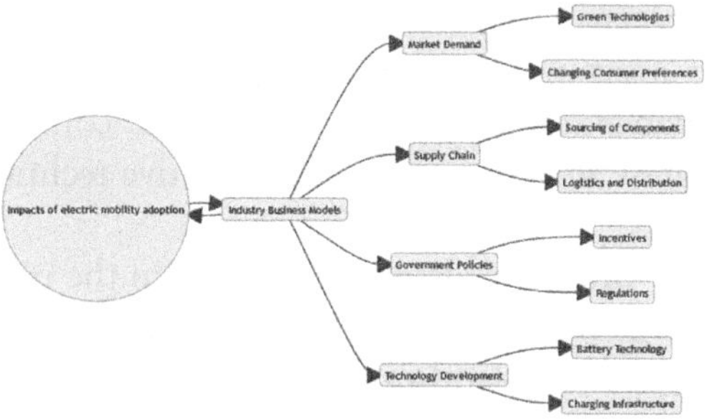

Fig. 1.1 Main areas of impact of EM adoption on industry business models (personal elaboration)

EVs may be higher than that of traditional vehicles, the total cost of ownership is often lower with EVs due to reduced fuel and maintenance expenses. Additionally, government incentives and tax credits aimed at promoting EV adoption can make them an even more economical choice (Huang & Ge, 2019).

EVs deliver a unique driving experience characterized by smooth, quiet, and instantaneous acceleration. The absence of a traditional ICE results in reduced noise and vibration, creating a serene driving environment. This enhanced experience appeals to consumers seeking a more comfortable and refined driving experience (Liang et al., 2020). As concerns about energy security and the volatility of fossil fuel prices persist, electric mobility offers consumers a degree of independence from the fluctuations in the oil market. By relying on electricity, which can be generated from diverse sources including renewable energy, EV owners are less vulnerable to the geopolitical and economic factors that affect fuel prices (Secinaro et al., 2022).

Charging EVs can be incredibly convenient for consumers. With home charging options, EV owners can start each day with a fully charged vehicle, eliminating the need for frequent trips to the gas station. Moreover, the expansion of public charging infrastructure, exemplified by Tesla's supercharger network, provides reassurance for long-distance travel, making electric mobility a practical choice for a wide range of consumers (Llopis-Albert et al., 2021). Electric mobility is at the forefront of technological innovation in the automotive industry, with features such as regenerative braking, over-the-air software updates, and advanced driver assistance systems being commonplace in EVs. These innovations enhance safety, convenience, and connectivity, offering consumers the latest advancements in automotive technology (Mesch & Dodel, 2022).

The automotive industry, historically rooted in the production of ICE vehicles, is undergoing a seismic transformation. Electric mobility is reshaping the competitive landscape, prompting traditional automakers to invest heavily in EV development. This shift is evident in the portfolios of companies like Ford, Volkswagen, and General Motors, which are increasingly prioritizing electric models (Liu et al., 2022). Furthermore, electric mobility necessitates changes in manufacturing processes, supply chains, and workforce skills, leading to a broader industrial transformation. Automakers and their suppliers are adapting to the demand for EV components, such as batteries and electric drivetrains, creating new economic opportunities and job markets (Secinaro et al., 2022).

Electric mobility is intrinsically linked to the growth of clean energy industries. The production of lithium-ion batteries, a critical component of EVs, has led to the emergence of battery manufacturing facilities worldwide (Mesch & Dodel, 2022). These facilities not only support EV production but also provide energy storage products for renewable energy sources, such as solar and wind. Tesla's gigafactories are prominent examples of this integration. These massive facilities produce both batteries for EVs and energy storage products for residential and commercial use. This convergence of clean energy and electric mobility creates synergies that benefit industries and consumers alike (Secinaro et al., 2022).

The expansion of electric mobility is driving the development of charging infrastructure, representing a significant industrial opportunity. Companies specializing in charging technology, such as Charge Point and EVgo, are capitalizing on the increasing demand for charging solutions. This growth extends to the construction and maintenance of charging stations, creating jobs and stimulating economic activity (Casals et al., 2019). Additionally, the deployment of charging infrastructure is not limited to traditional fueling stations; industries such as the hospitality, retail, and real estate industries are recognizing that offering charging facilities will attract customers and residents. Electric mobility is thus influencing the design and development of various business sectors (Suman et al., 2020).

Electric mobility is reshaping the landscape of urban transportation. The rise of electric scooters, e-bikes, and electric ridesharing services is altering the way people move within cities. Companies like Lime and Bird have introduced electric scooters as convenient and sustainable options for short trips, reducing congestion and air pollution in urban areas. Moreover, electric public transportation systems, including buses and trains, are gaining momentum. The electrification of public transit contributes to cleaner and more efficient urban mobility while reducing the environmental impact of city transportation networks. The proliferation of electric mobility has fostered innovation ecosystems that extend beyond traditional automotive companies. Startups specializing in EV components, battery technologies, and mobility solutions are thriving. Venture capital firms and technology incubators are actively investing in these startups, catalyzing innovation and driving the development of cutting-edge technologies. Tesla's meteoric rise as an EV manufacturer, energy company, and technology innovator epitomizes this phenomenon. The company's EVs, energy products, and software innovations have helped to position it as a global leader in multiple industries, demonstrating the transformative potential of electric mobility (Ravi & Aziz, 2022).

Electric mobility has implications for global supply chains. The production of EVs relies on a complex web of suppliers, including those providing battery components, electric motors, and specialized materials. As EV adoption grows, supply chain dynamics will keep evolving, with new players emerging and established suppliers diversifying their portfolios.

For instance, the demand for lithium, a critical component of lithium-ion batteries, has surged. Thus, lithium mining and processing industries are expanding to meet this demand, impacting global commodity markets and trade relationships (Apostolou & Welcher, 2021).

In conclusion, the importance and relevance of electric mobility extend far beyond its function as a mode of transportation; it embodies a shift in consumer values, economic advantages, and technological innovation. For industries, electric mobility represents a transformative force that is reshaping the automotive sector, fostering clean energy industries, and driving innovation ecosystems. As electric mobility continues to gain traction, its impact on consumer lifestyles and industrial landscapes will only grow, solidifying its position as the cornerstone of the twenty-first-century mobility revolution (Turienzo et al., 2022).

1.4 The Role of Electric Mobility for Consumers and Industries

The role of electric mobility in contemporary society is multifaceted, encompassing a broad spectrum of implications and opportunities for both consumers and industries. This section examines the intricate dynamics of electric mobility, dissecting its evolving role and the transformative impact it exerts on consumer behaviors and industrial landscapes (Huang & Ge, 2019).

Electric mobility plays a pivotal role in reshaping the way consumers approach transportation. It goes beyond mere conveyance to transform the very fabric of mobility patterns and behaviors. Several factors contribute to this transformation.

EVs, including electric cars and e-bikes, are increasingly becoming the preferred choice for daily commuting and urban travel. The reduced operating costs of EVs, in terms of both fuel and maintenance, make them an attractive option for urban dwellers. This shift toward electric mobility aligns with the global trend of urbanization, where sustainable and efficient transportation solutions are paramount (Apostolou & Welcher, 2021).

Electric mobility solutions such as e-scooters and e-bikes are redefining last-mile connectivity. These micro-mobility options provide a convenient and eco-friendly means of bridging the gap between public transportation hubs and final destinations. For consumers, this means greater ease in navigating urban environments, reducing the reliance on personal vehicles and mitigating traffic congestion (Krishnan & Butt, 2022).

The rise of electric mobility is intertwined with the emergence of ridesharing and mobility-as-a-service (MaaS) platforms. Companies like Uber and Lyft have incorporated EVs into their fleets, offering consumers the choice to ride in an eco-conscious manner. Such platforms not only reduce the environmental impact of transportation but also cater to the preferences of a growing demographic of consumers seeking sustainable travel options (Ravi & Aziz, 2022). The electrification of public transportation with the introduction of electric buses and trams has had a profound impact on consumer mobility. Electric public transit systems offer quieter and cleaner alternatives to traditional diesel buses, improving the quality of life of urban residents. Consumers are increasingly choosing these services for their reduced emissions and enhanced comfort (Casals et al., 2019).

1.4.1 Empowering Consumer Choice

Electric mobility empowers consumers by providing various options to cater to their specific needs and preferences. This empowerment is exemplified through the following mechanisms:

Consumers now have access to a wide range of EVs, from compact electric cars (for urban commuting) to high-performance electric sports cars. Electric SUVs and crossovers offer spaciousness and versatility, addressing the needs of families and adventure enthusiasts. The availability of diverse vehicle types ensures that consumers can find an electric mobility solution tailored to their lifestyle (Liang et al., 2020). EV manufacturers recognize the importance of personalization and customization to consumer preferences. Many electric car manufacturers, including Tesla, offer various configurations and options for consumers to tailor their vehicles to their liking (Huang & Ge, 2019). This approach enhances the overall ownership experience and fosters brand loyalty. Electric mobility also provides consumers with various charging options. Home charging solutions, such as Level 2 chargers, enable consumers to conveniently charge their EVs overnight, while public charging infrastructure, including fast-charging networks, offer flexibility for long-distance travel. Consumers can choose the charging option that best suits their needs, enhancing the practicality of electric mobility (Krishnan & Butt, 2022).

1.4.2 Economic Implications for Consumers

Electric mobility bears significant economic implications for consumers, contributing to both short-term savings and long-term financial sustainability:

The lower operating costs of EVs are a major financial incentive for consumers. EVs are more energy-efficient, resulting in lower electricity costs compared to gasoline or diesel fuel. Additionally, EVs have fewer moving parts, reducing maintenance expenses over the lifetime of the vehicle (Bösehans et al., 2023). Many governments worldwide are offering incentives, including tax credits, rebates, and access to high-occupancy vehicle lanes, to encourage EV adoption. Such measures offset the initial purchase price of EVs, making them more affordable for consumers. While EVs may have a higher upfront cost, the total cost of ownership over the lifetime of the vehicle can be lower than that of traditional vehicles. The reduced operating costs combined with potential incentives contribute to long-term financial savings for consumers.

The role of electric mobility extends beyond consumer choices to reverberate throughout industrial ecosystems, stimulating innovation, job creation, and economic growth. The automotive industry is undergoing profound transformation due to electric mobility. Traditional automakers are investing heavily in EV development and production, accelerating the transition away from ICEs. This shift impacts manufacturing processes, supply chains, and workforce skills, creating new opportunities and challenges for the industry (Bösehans et al., 2023). Battery manufacturing is a critical component of the electric mobility ecosystem. The growth of EVs has driven the demand for high-capacity lithium-ion batteries, and battery manufacturers are expanding their operations, creating jobs, and contributing to the development of advanced energy storage solutions beyond transportation (Liang et al., 2020).

The development of charging infrastructure is a thriving industry within the electric mobility ecosystem. Companies that design, build, and operate charging networks play a vital role in facilitating the widespread adoption of EVs. This sector generates employment opportunities and fosters competition, driving advancements in charging technology (Turienzo et al., 2022). The electric mobility industry intersects with clean energy industries, creating synergies that benefit both sectors. The production of EVs and batteries aligns with the growth of renewable energy sources such as solar and wind, and this integration contributes to sustainability and energy independence. The electric mobility revolution has spawned a robust innovation ecosystem, and startups specializing in EV components, mobility solutions, and battery technologies are flourishing. These companies receive investment from venture capital firms and contribute to the development of cutting-edge technologies that extend beyond the automotive sector (Casals et al., 2019).

Electric mobility is influencing urban planning and development, as cities are adapting to accommodate electric public transportation systems and micro-mobility solutions. This shift toward sustainable urban planning has the potential to improve quality of life, reduce congestion, and enhance the overall sustainability of urban environments. Electric mobility's role transcends consumer choices and industrial dynamics, with far-reaching societal implications—the adoption of electric mobility contributes significantly to reducing greenhouse gas emissions and improving air quality. This reduction in pollution benefits public health and mitigates the effects of climate change, aligning with global sustainability goals. Electric mobility reduces dependence on fossil fuels, enhancing energy security (Pelletier et al., 2016). By diversifying the energy mix and promoting renewable energy sources, electric mobility contributes to a more stable and resilient energy infrastructure. Electric mobility initiatives, such as electric public transportation, have the potential to enhance transportation equity. Furthermore, accessible and efficient electric transit systems can bridge transportation gaps in underserved communities, improving mobility and access to opportunities. The development and adoption of electric mobility have driven technological advancement across multiple sectors, fostering innovation and creating a ripple effect of progress in areas such as energy storage, smart infrastructure, and data analytics (Jie et al., 2019).

In summary, the role of electric mobility in contemporary society is multifaceted, encompassing consumer mobility patterns, economic implications, and societal impacts. It empowers consumers by offering diverse choices and economic advantages while driving transformations across industrial ecosystems. Beyond these immediate effects, electric mobility contributes to broader societal goals, including environmental sustainability, energy security, and transportation equity. As it continues to evolve, electric mobility will shape the way we move, live, and interact with our environment in the years to come (Bösehans et al., 2023).

1.5 The Role of Electric Mobility in the Transition Toward a Circular Economy

The transition toward a circular economy, an economic model focused on minimizing waste and maximizing the reuse of resources, has gained prominence in recent years as a sustainable alternative to traditional linear economic systems. Electric mobility plays a pivotal role in advancing this transition, offering a multifaceted approach to circularity that addresses various aspects of resource efficiency and environmental sustainability (Schwabe, 2020).

EVs embody circular design principles that reduce waste and extend product lifecycles.

EVs often have longer lifespans than traditional ICE vehicles due to the simplicity of electric powertrains, fewer moving parts, and less wear and tear. EVs are also well-suited for second-life applications, where batteries removed from retired vehicles can find new purposes, e.g., as energy storage solutions (Schwabe, 2020).

Many EV manufacturers have adopted modular design strategies, allowing for easier component replacement and repair. This approach minimizes the need for complete vehicle replacements when certain components, such as batteries or electric motors, reach the end of their useful life. The modular design encourages efficient resource utilization (Tian et al., 2018).

Manufacturers often incorporate recyclable and sustainable materials in their construction of EVs. Automakers increasingly use recycled plastics and metals, reducing the demand for virgin materials. Additionally, the recycling potential of lithium-ion batteries in EVs is being explored, further contributing to circularity. Electric mobility extends beyond the design of EVs to encompass innovative mobility services that support circularity (Pelletier et al., 2016).

Car-sharing and ride-hailing platforms that integrate EVs into their fleets promote shared mobility, reducing the number of privately owned vehicles on the road. This reduction aligns with circular economy principles by maximizing resource use and minimizing waste associated with vehicle production. MaaS platforms, which integrate various transportation options into a single, user-friendly service, facilitate efficient travel planning and resource optimization. By promoting the use of electric mobility solutions within their offerings, MaaS providers contribute to circularity by reducing congestion and environmental impact (Jayakumar et al., 2021). Electric micro-mobility solutions, such as e-scooters and e-bikes, offer sustainable and efficient modes of transportation for short trips. These services, often available on-demand through mobile apps, encourage users to embrace eco-friendly alternatives, reducing the need for personal vehicle ownership and production (Bissell et al., 2020).

Electric mobility relies heavily on advanced battery technologies, and circular practices are increasingly being integrated into battery design and management—the recycling of lithium-ion batteries from retired EVs is a crucial aspect of circularity. Recycling facilities can recover valuable materials such as lithium, cobalt, and nickel from used batteries, reducing the environmental impact of mining and refining these resources. Moreover, retired EV batteries can find second-life applications as stationary energy storage systems, further extending their utility (Saw et al., 2016). Research and development efforts are focused on finding sustainable, abundant materials for battery production. Innovations in material science aim to reduce the reliance on rare and environmentally damaging elements, further aligning electric mobility with circular economy principles (Schwabe, 2020).

The principles of circular economy are influencing supply chain practices in the electric mobility sector, with automakers and battery manufacturers exploring closed-loop supply chains, where materials are sourced from recycled and reclaimed sources (Bissell et al., 2020). This approach minimizes the extraction of raw materials, reduces waste, and lessens the environmental footprint of production processes. Supply chain sustainability involves responsible sourcing practices, ensuring that raw materials used for producing EV components are obtained in an environmentally and socially responsible manner. Sustainable sourcing reduces the negative impacts associated with resource extraction and promotes circularity (Liu et al., 2022).

Remanufacturing and refurbishment practices in the electric mobility industry extend the lifecycle of products and reduce waste. These processes involve restoring used components and vehicles to almost-new conditions, reducing the need for a fresh production. Governments and regulatory bodies are introducing policies and regulations that support circular practices in electric mobility; for instance, extended producer responsibility (EPR) policies shift the responsibility of the end-of-life management of products, including EVs and batteries, from consumers to manufacturers. This incentivizes manufacturers to design products with circularity in mind, as they become accountable for the recycling and disposal of their products (Saw et al., 2016).

Some regions have set recycling targets for EV components and materials. These targets encourage the development of recycling infrastructure and promote circular practices within the electric mobility industry. Government incentives and subsidies may be responsible for the increased circularity noted among EV manufacturers. Incentives could be linked to the use of recycled materials, extended product warranties, and the implementation of closed-loop supply chains observed in the electric mobility sector. The adoption of circular economy principles in electric mobility has several noteworthy benefits. Circularity maximizes the use of resources, reducing the environmental impact of EV production and operation (Jie et al., 2019). This efficiency is crucial in a world where resource scarcity and sustainability are growing concerns. Circular practices significantly reduce the waste generation associated with electric mobility, including the disposal of end-of-life vehicles and batteries. This aligns with global efforts to minimize landfill waste and reduce environmental pollution. By reducing the demand for raw materials and promoting responsible sourcing, circularity in electric mobility contributes to preserving ecosystems and protecting biodiversity (Tian et al., 2018).

Circular practices can enhance the resilience of the electric mobility industry by reducing its vulnerability to resource price fluctuations and supply chain disruptions.

In conclusion, electric mobility serves as a powerful catalyst in the transition toward a circular economy. The industry's adoption of circular design principles, promotion of shared mobility services, integration of circular practices in battery technology, and influence on supply chains contribute to resource efficiency, waste reduction, environmental preservation, and economic resilience. As electric mobility continues to evolve and expand, its alignment with circularity will play an increasingly crucial role in addressing the global challenges of resource scarcity and environmental sustainability (Jayakumar et al., 2021).

2

Literature Review

Abstract This chapter presents a comprehensive literature review on electric mobility, focusing on the examination of current marketing and consumer research in the field. It provides an overview of the latest technologies and advancements in electric mobility, highlighting key innovations. The chapter delves into consumers' perceptions and the barriers to adopting electric vehicles (EVs), offering insights into the challenges faced by potential users. The chapter also reviews policy and regulatory frameworks designed to promote electric mobility, analyzing their effectiveness and impact. Additionally, it discusses the crucial role of innovative aspects (e.g., lithium batteries) that drive the advancement of electric mobility. This review offers a foundational understanding of the multifaceted landscape of electric mobility.

Keywords marketing research · consumer research · consumer adoption · policy framework · technological advancements · lithium batteries

D. D'Acunto, *The Future of E-Mobility*,
https://doi.org/10.1007/978-3-031-65053-6_2

2.1 State-of-the-Art Marketing and Consumer Research on Electric Mobility

The integration of electric mobility into marketing represents a paradigm shift and reflects a response to evolving consumer preferences and environmental imperatives. Marketing electric vehicles (EVs) goes beyond traditional automotive strategies; it necessitates a nuanced understanding of consumer psychology, environmental awareness, and technological advancements. This realm of marketing is not only about selling a product but also about advocating for a shift in mobility culture (Pandey et al., 2020). While electric mobility presents a compelling proposition for reducing carbon emissions, marketers are struggling to translate these environmental benefits into compelling value propositions for a diverse consumer base. EV marketing is not just about highlighting technical specifications but also about addressing broader concerns such as range anxiety, charging infrastructure, and the total cost of ownership. This necessitates a multifaceted approach that combines education, engagement, and an understanding of the evolving narrative around sustainability and technology in the automotive sector. As such, marketing in the realm of electric mobility is as much about driving a cultural and behavioral shift as it is about promoting a new class of vehicles.

In recent years, consumer research on EVs has highlighted several trends that are critical for understanding the market dynamics and future trajectory of EV adoption.

Growing Environmental Consciousness

A prominent trend is the increasing environmental awareness among consumers. Driven by concerns about climate change and pollution, a proportion of consumers is showing more interest in EVs due to their lower carbon footprint compared to traditional internal combustion engine (ICE) vehicles. Yet, this environmental awareness is not consistent across all demographics or regions, pointing to a diverse market penetration (Jones et al., 2016).

Perception of Technological Sophistication

EVs are often perceived as more technologically advanced than conventional vehicles. This viewpoint holds a dual nature: it magnetizes tech-savvy individuals and early adopters while simultaneously triggering concerns among others regarding the intricacies of usage, upkeep, and the perceived novelty of the technology (Lieven, 2015).

Range Anxiety and Charging Infrastructure

One of the most significant barriers to EV adoption remains "range anxiety"—the fear of running out of battery without access to charging facilities. Despite enhancements in EV charging infrastructure, the uneven geographical spread of charging stations and the time needed for charging still discourage potential buyers, particularly in regions lacking adequate infrastructure (Rezvani et al., 2015).

Cost Considerations

Initially, the higher upfront cost of EVs compared to traditional vehicles was a significant deterrent. However, costs are now gradually declining, despite technological advancements and growing production scales. Nevertheless, for a complete market transition, EVs must attain cost parity with traditional vehicles without depending on government subsidies (Wu et al., 2015).

The Role of Government Policies and Incentives

Government initiatives and incentives play a crucial role in shaping consumer attitudes toward EVs. Positive policies could significantly accelerate EV adoption, while the absence of supportive measures or the existence of prohibitive regulations could impede market growth.

These trends reflect a complex and evolving landscape in consumer research on EVs. While there is a clear trajectory toward increased interest and acceptance, numerous challenges remain that must be addressed to fully harness the benefits of electric mobility.

The impact of marketing strategies on EV adoption is a multifaceted issue that warrants critical examination. The influence of marketing on consumer attitudes and behaviors is crucial, yet its effectiveness within the context of EVs is influenced by several factors (Requia, 2018).

Targeted Marketing and Consumer Segmentation

Effective marketing strategies for EVs often involve targeted approaches that cater to specific consumer segments. For instance, marketing campaigns highlighting the environmental benefits of EVs may resonate well with environmentally conscious consumers (Gionfriddo et al., 2023) but may be less effective for cost-conscious buyers or those primarily concerned with performance and convenience. The challenge lies in crafting messages that appeal to a diverse consumer base and address varied motivations and barriers.

Educational and Informational Campaigns

A significant hurdle in EV adoption is the lack of consumer awareness and understanding of EVs. Marketing strategies that focus on educating consumers about the benefits of EVs, such as their lower operating costs and reduced emissions, can be instrumental. However, these campaigns must also address common misconceptions and concerns, such as range anxiety and charging infrastructure availability. Merely focusing on the positives without addressing these concerns may lead to skepticism and reduce the effectiveness of the campaigns.

Brand Positioning and Partnerships

The position of EVs in the market significantly influences their adoption. High-profile collaborations and partnerships (e.g., between automotive manufacturers and technology companies) can elevate the status of EVs, presenting them as cutting-edge solutions. However, if not managed carefully, such positioning can alienate potential buyers who might perceive EVs as luxury items or niche products, thus limiting broader market appeal.

Influence of Social Norms and Visibility

Marketing strategies that leverage social norms and visibility, such as showcasing EVs being used by relatable figures or within familiar contexts, can be potent. However, excessive dependence on celebrity endorsements and the production of exclusive high-end models can foster perceptions of inaccessibility (Dwivedi et al., 2021).

In conclusion, while marketing strategies have a significant impact on EV adoption, their success largely depends on how well they are aligned with the diverse needs, expectations, and concerns of potential consumers. Balancing educational content with aspirational messaging and addressing specific barriers to adoption is crucial for these strategies to effectively foster EV adoption.

The progression of EV technology has been defined by notable strides forward as well as concurrent hurdles, showcasing an innovation journey propelled by both necessity and opportunity (Berkeley et al., 2017).

Early Developments and Decline

The history of EVs dates back to the nineteenth century, with early models offering a quiet and smoke-free alternative to their gasoline counterparts. However, the advent of the mass-produced Ford Model T and the discovery of cheap petroleum sources led to the decline of EVs in the early twentieth century. These initial electric models, though innovative, suffered from limited range, low top speeds, and lengthy charging times, factors that contributed to their eclipse by gasoline vehicles.

Resurgence in the Late Twentieth Century

The oil crises of the 1970s and growing environmental concerns reignited interest in EVs. However, this resurgence was tempered by technological limitations, particularly in battery technology. Early EVs in this era, although more advanced than their predecessors, still struggled with issues of range, performance, and cost. It was not until the late 1990s and early 2000s, with the introduction of vehicles like the Toyota Prius, that EVs began to gain a foothold in the market.

Recent Technological Advancements

The last decade has witnessed remarkable advancements in EV technology, with lithium-ion batteries emerging as a game-changer, offering higher energy densities, longer lifespans, and shorter charging times. Developments in power electronics, electric motor technology, and regenerative braking systems have further enhanced the efficiency and performance of EVs (Ullah et al., 2021). Modern EVs now boast ranges and speeds comparable to, and in some cases exceeding, their gasoline counterparts.

Challenges and Future Directions

Despite these advancements, challenges remain. The high cost of advanced batteries, although decreasing, still impacts the overall affordability of EVs. Moreover, the environmental impact of battery production and disposal and the reliance on critical materials like lithium and cobalt pose sustainability concerns. Ongoing innovations in battery technology, coupled with progress in domains such as solid-state batteries, wireless charging, and enhanced infrastructure, are pivotal for the next substantial leap in EV evolution (Axsen et al., 2016).

In conclusion, the journey of EV technology has been one of remarkable transformation, driven by evolving societal needs and technological breakthroughs. While significant progress has been made, ongoing research and development are essential to address the remaining challenges and fully realize the potential of electric mobility.

The state-of-the-art in marketing and consumer research on electric mobility extends beyond the introductory aspects, trends, and impacts of marketing strategies to delve into deeper realms such as market segmentation, consumer behavior theories, digital marketing innovations, and the role of branding and public perception in the adoption of EVs.

Market Segmentation and Targeting

Advanced market segmentation plays a crucial role in electric mobility marketing. Unlike traditional vehicles, EVs appeal to various consumer segments not only based on demographic factors like age and income but also on psychographic factors such as environmental consciousness, technological affinity, and lifestyle choices. Understanding these consumer segments—from early adopters and tech enthusiasts to environmentally conscious consumers and pragmatic users looking for cost efficiency—is crucial for tailoring marketing messages. This segmentation enables marketers to develop more focused and effective strategies, ensuring that the right messages reach the right audience.

Consumer Behavior Theories in EV Adoption

The application of consumer behavior theories is fundamental in understanding and influencing the adoption of EVs. For instance, the theory of planned behavior can be employed to understand how attitudes, social norms, and perceived behavioral control influence EV adoption decisions. Similarly, the Diffusion of Innovation theory helps in understanding how EVs are perceived as innovative products and how they can achieve mass adoption over time. Leveraging these theories allows marketers to devise strategies that resonate with consumers' logical decision-making and also tap into emotional and social influences (Kumar & Alok, 2020).

Digital Marketing Innovations

The rise of digital marketing has opened new avenues for promoting EVs. Social media campaigns, influencer partnerships, and targeted online advertising play a significant role in shaping public perception and awareness regarding EVs. Interactive tools like virtual test drives and augmented reality experiences are being used to engage potential customers, offering them a virtual taste of EV technology. Moreover, leveraging big data and analytics helps in understanding consumer preferences and behavior, enabling more personalized and effective marketing efforts.

The Role of Branding and Public Perception

Branding is a powerful tool in the EV market. Companies are not just selling cars; they are selling a vision of the future. Strong branding that aligns with sustainability, innovation, and forward-thinking can significantly influence consumer perceptions and decisions. Public perception, fueled by media representation, word-of-mouth, and societal trends, also plays a crucial role. Challenging stereotypes and misunderstandings regarding EVs, such as worries about range limitations and the accessibility of charging stations, represents a crucial challenge for marketers. Crafting strong branding and fostering positive public perceptions can notably reduce these psychological hurdles (Liao et al., 2017).

Educational Marketing and Community Engagement

Since EV technology is relatively new to many consumers, educational marketing becomes essential. This involves providing clear, accessible information about the benefits and practicalities of EVs, dispelling myths, and addressing common questions and concerns. Community engagement through events, workshops, and partnerships with local organizations can also play a vital role in building trust and acceptance.

Global Market Dynamics and Cultural Sensitivity

The global landscape of electric mobility presents diverse challenges and opportunities. Therefore, marketing strategies need to be adapted to different cultural, economic, and regulatory environments. Moreover, understanding local attitudes toward sustainability, technology, and mobility is key to crafting messages that resonate with different audiences. This global perspective is crucial for international players in the EV market.

In conclusion, the state-of-the-art in marketing and consumer research on electric mobility is a dynamic and multifaceted field that goes beyond conventional marketing approaches. It requires a deep understanding of market segmentation, consumer behavior, digital innovations, effective branding, educational outreach, and global market dynamics. As the EV market continues to evolve, these aspects will play a critical role in shaping the future of electric mobility and its adoption on a global scale.

2.2 An Overview of Electric Mobility Technologies and Advancements

Recent advancements in electric mobility underscore a rapidly evolving landscape characterized by technological innovation and market shifts; however, they also highlight persisting challenges and emerging concerns.

Battery Technology and Energy Density

A critical area of advancement has been in battery technology, particularly lithium-ion batteries. Modern EVs benefit from higher energy densities, allowing for longer ranges and reduced weight. However, the reliance on materials like lithium, cobalt, and nickel raises sustainability and ethical sourcing concerns (da Silva Lima et al., 2023). Innovations such as solid-state batteries promise higher energy densities and safety, but their commercial viability and scalability remain under scrutiny.

Charging Infrastructure and Speed

The development of faster and more accessible charging infrastructure has been pivotal in addressing range anxiety. Ultra-fast-charging stations can now recharge batteries to a significant level in minutes, not hours. However, the implementation of this infrastructure varies, leaning more toward urban locales than rural ones, and the potential grid impact of widespread fast charging remains a concern that has not been completely resolved (Martin et al., 2017).

Integration of Renewable Energy

There is an increasing emphasis on integrating EVs with renewable energy sources. Innovations in solar-powered charging stations and vehicle-to-grid (V2G) technologies, where EVs can feed energy back into the grid, are promising. However, the practical implementation of these technologies is complex and fraught with regulatory, technical, and economic challenges.

Autonomous and Connected EVs

Advancements in autonomous driving and connected vehicle technologies are transforming EVs into smart, self-driving machines. However, although this integration could revolutionize mobility, it raises issues around data security, privacy, and the readiness of infrastructure and regulatory frameworks (Martins et al., 2021).

Material Efficiency and Recycling

Progress has been made in improving material efficiency and the recyclability of EV components, particularly batteries. However, the recycling infrastructure is still nascent, and the environmental impact of battery production and disposal remains a significant challenge.

In summary, while recent advancements in electric mobility mark significant strides toward cleaner, more efficient transportation, they also bring to light new challenges. Sustainable material sourcing, equitable infrastructure development, and integrating these advancements with existing energy and transport systems are essential considerations for the future trajectory of electric mobility.

Comparing electric mobility technologies with traditional vehicle technologies involves assessing various dimensions, including energy efficiency, environmental impact, performance, and overall lifecycle costs. Each option has its unique strengths and limitations, shaped by technological progressions and market dynamics (Hagman et al., 2016).

Energy Efficiency and Emissions

EVs are inherently more energy-efficient than ICE vehicles, as they convert a higher percentage of electrical energy from the grid to power at the wheels. This efficiency translates to lower operational costs per mile and reduced greenhouse gas emissions, assuming the electricity is sourced from low-emission or renewable sources. However, the environmental benefits of EVs are somewhat offset by the carbon-intensive battery manufacturing process, and the emissions benefits vary significantly based on the electricity mix of a given region.

Performance and Maintenance

Regarding performance, modern EVs have demonstrated capabilities comparable to, or even surpassing, traditional vehicles, especially in relation to acceleration and torque. The simplicity of EV powertrains generally leads to lower maintenance requirements and costs, seeing as it lacks components like exhaust systems, radiators, and fuel injection systems. Yet, EVs face challenges in weight due to heavy batteries and can have diminished performance in extreme weather conditions which affect their range and battery efficiency.

Cost Considerations

The upfront cost of EVs remains higher than that of ICE vehicles, primarily due to expensive battery packs, although the gap is narrowing with advancements in battery technology and economies of scale (Costa et al., 2021). The total cost of ownership over time can be lower for EVs due to lower operating and maintenance costs and potential tax incentives. Yet, this hinges on factors such as electricity expenses, vehicle usage behaviors, and the accessibility of incentives (Palmer et al., 2018).

Infrastructure and Range

While ICE vehicles benefit from having a mature, widespread refueling infrastructure, the EV charging network is still expanding. This disparity contributes to the range anxiety present among potential EV users despite improvements in battery range and charging technology. The advancement of fast-charging infrastructure and battery swap technology stands as a critical focal point in bridging this gap (Hardman et al., 2018).

In summary, while electric mobility technologies offer significant advantages in terms of efficiency, emissions, and performance, they are still catching up to traditional vehicle technologies in terms of cost parity and infrastructure support. The transition to electric mobility is ongoing, and its pace will be hastened with continued technological advancements, supportive policies, and changing consumer perceptions.

Additionally, electric mobility technologies have advanced beyond the core developments in EV technology, embracing a broader spectrum of innovations that are reshaping the landscape of personal and public transportation. These advancements, while interlinked with the evolution, recent progress, and comparison to traditional vehicle technologies, extend into various aspects including autonomous driving, integration with smart-city infrastructure, advancements in alternative electric mobility modes, and the development of supportive software and services.

Autonomous Driving Integration

A significant advancement in electric mobility is the integration of autonomous driving technologies. EVs are increasingly being equipped with advanced sensors, cameras, and artificial intelligence (AI) systems that enable varying levels of autonomy. This integration is not just about reducing driver intervention but also about increasing efficiency. Autonomous EVs can optimize energy use, reduce traffic congestion, and improve overall road safety. The convergence of electrification and autonomy promises to transform the very essence of vehicle use, shifting the focus from ownership to mobility-as-a-service.

Smart City and Internet of Things (IoT) Connectivity

Electric mobility is intrinsically linked with the development of smart cities and the IoT. EVs are becoming part of a larger, interconnected urban ecosystem, where real-time data exchange between vehicles, infrastructure, and grid systems can optimize energy consumption and traffic flow. Features like smart charging (where EV charging can be scheduled during off-peak hours) and V2G technologies (which allow EVs to return energy to the grid) are pivotal in this integration. This connectivity enhances the efficiency of urban transportation systems and supports the broader objectives of sustainability and reduced environmental impact.

Alternative Electric Mobility Modes

Beyond cars, the electric mobility sector is witnessing growth in various other areas such as bikes, scooters, buses, and even aircraft. These modes of transport are catering to various needs, from last-mile connectivity to mass transit solutions. The proliferation of these alternatives is essential in addressing urban mobility challenges, reducing reliance on personal vehicles, and mitigating traffic congestion and pollution.

Supportive Software and Services

The ecosystem supporting EVs has grown to include an array of software and services—advanced navigation systems that provide real-time information on charging stations and route optimization, apps for seamless access to public EV charging networks, and platforms for EV car-sharing and ride-hailing services. These digital tools enhance user experience, increase accessibility, and encourage the adoption of EVs by making their use more convenient and adaptable to various lifestyles.

Energy Storage and Management Systems

Advancements in energy storage and management are critical in supporting the broad adoption of electric mobility. Energy storage systems, both stationary and in-vehicle, are crucial in balancing grid loads, especially with the increasing integration of renewable energy sources. Efficient energy management systems ensure that the energy demands of EVs are met without overburdening the electrical grid, paving the way for a more sustainable energy ecosystem.

Materials Science and Sustainability

Innovations in materials science are playing a pivotal role in enhancing the sustainability of electric mobility. Research into more sustainable and efficient battery materials, lighter and more durable vehicle components, and recyclable materials is driving the development of greener and more sustainable EVs. These advancements are not only critical in reducing the environmental footprint of EVs but also important in ensuring their long-term viability and acceptance.

In summary, the advancements in electric mobility technologies extend well beyond the vehicles themselves to encompass a holistic transformation of transportation, blending autonomy, connectivity, diverse mobility modes, supportive digital infrastructure, and sustainable practices. This broad spectrum of innovations is essential in realizing the full potential of electric mobility, not just as an alternative to traditional vehicles but as a cornerstone of a more efficient, sustainable, and interconnected transportation future.

The widespread adoption of EVs is considered a pivotal step toward a more sustainable transportation future. However, several barriers, ranging from technological limitations to economic and infrastructural challenges, hinder this transition. Understanding and addressing these barriers is crucial for the successful integration of EVs into the mainstream automotive market.

Technological Challenges

A primary barrier to EV adoption is the current limitations in battery technology. While there have been significant advancements in lithium-ion batteries, concerns such as limited range, long charging times, and battery degradation over time persist for potential buyers. Although the average daily commute is well within the range of most modern EVs, the concept of "range anxiety"—the fear of running out of power before reaching a destination or charging point—is a significant psychological barrier. Additionally, the performance of EV batteries can be adversely affected by extreme temperatures, which impact their range and efficiency.

High Upfront Costs

Despite the decreasing cost of batteries, EVs generally have higher upfront costs than traditional ICE vehicles. This price differential is a significant barrier for many consumers, especially in the absence of substantial government incentives and subsidies. The total cost of ownership may be lower for EVs in the long run due to reduced fuel and maintenance costs, but the initial price remains a prohibitive factor for widespread adoption.

Charging Infrastructure Deficit

The availability and convenience of charging infrastructure are crucial for EV adoption. Many regions, especially rural and less developed areas, lack sufficient public charging facilities. Moreover, existing charging infrastructure often do not support fast charging, leading to extended charging times compared to the convenience of quickly refueling a gasoline vehicle. Home charging is a viable alternative, but it is not feasible for individuals living in apartments or homes without a garage.

Consumer Awareness and Perception

Awareness regarding the capabilities and benefits of EVs is lacking among many consumers. Misconceptions about range, cost, and performance persist, often fueled by a lack of clear and accessible information. This challenge is compounded by the fact that numerous consumers have never driven an EV, resulting in uncertainty and reluctance toward adopting this new technology (Zhou et al., 2015).

Economic and Policy Factors

The pace of EV adoption is heavily influenced by government policies and economic factors. EV adoption rates are higher in countries where policies strongly support EVs through incentives, infrastructure investment, and stringent emissions regulations. Conversely, in regions lacking such support, the transition to EVs is much slower. Additionally, the economic environment, including fuel prices and the overall cost of living, plays a significant role in consumer decisions regarding EVs.

Supply Chain and Manufacturing Constraints

The EV industry is facing supply chain and manufacturing challenges, particularly concerning the sourcing of raw materials for batteries. The concentration of critical minerals like lithium and cobalt in only a few countries creates supply vulnerabilities and ethical concerns related to mining practices. Additionally, the EV manufacturing sector is still scaling up, and there are concerns regarding its ability to meet the rapidly growing demand.

Recycling and End-of-Life Management

The recycling and disposal of EV batteries pose significant environmental challenges. The current recycling rates for lithium-ion batteries are low, and the processes are complex and expensive. As the number of EVs on the road increases, so will the volume of batteries reaching the end of their life, necessitating the establishment of effective recycling and disposal practices to mitigate environmental impacts.

Market Diversity and Consumer Choice

Finally, fewer EV models are available in the market compared to conventional vehicles. As the quantity of models expands, consumers will encounter fewer choices regarding size, style, and brand, which can dissuade those considering a switch to EVs (Jaiswal et al., 2021).

In conclusion, while the transition to EVs offers immense potential for reducing carbon emissions and fostering sustainable transportation, overcoming the barriers to their widespread adoption is essential and requires concerted efforts in technological innovation, policy support, infrastructure development, consumer education, and addressing the environmental and ethical concerns associated with battery production and disposal. Only through a comprehensive and multifaceted approach can these barriers be effectively addressed, paving the way for a more widespread adoption of EVs.

2.3 Consumers' Perception and Adoption of EV and Barriers to EV Adoption

Consumer perception and adoption of EV and barriers to EV adoption encompass a complex interplay of factors that influence how individuals and the broader society view and engage with this emerging form of transportation. Understanding these elements is key to addressing the challenges and harnessing the opportunities in the journey toward widespread EV adoption.

Consumers' Perceptions and EV Adoption

Consumers' perceptions of EVs are influenced by a myriad of factors including environmental concerns, technological advancements, economic considerations, and social influences. Numerous consumers view EVs as a positive step toward curbing carbon emissions and addressing climate change. This environmental advantage significantly motivates a segment of the market, especially individuals prioritizing sustainability (Tarei et al., 2021).

However, the perception of EVs is not uniformly positive, as range anxiety, the fear of running out of battery power without access to a charging station, remains a major concern. Although the range of modern EVs is sufficient for most daily needs, the fear of being stranded continues to influence consumer attitudes negatively. Additionally, the perception of EVs as expensive, despite decreasing battery costs and total cost of ownership, further impacts consumer attitudes, particularly in the price-sensitive segments of the market.

Technological Advancements and Consumer Trust

Technological advancements in EVs, such as improved battery life, faster charging times, and enhanced performance, are gradually changing consumer perceptions. However, trust in new technology takes time to build, and consumers accustomed to traditional ICE vehicles may be skeptical about the reliability and longevity of EVs. Thus, fostering consumer trust through transparent information, education, and first-hand experience is essential.

Economic Considerations

The economic aspect of EV ownership plays a critical role in consumer decision-making. Despite the appealing long-term cost benefits of EVs, such as reduced fuel and maintenance expenses, the higher initial purchase price is a deterrent for many prospective buyers (Krishna, 2021). Government incentives, tax rebates, and subsidies have been instrumental in mitigating this barrier, but the sustainability of these incentives is a matter of policy and economic debate.

Social Influences and Norms

Social factors, including peer influence, societal norms, and cultural attitudes, significantly affect EV adoption. In regions where EVs are more prevalent, there is a social reinforcement effect, where seeing individuals adopt EVs encourages others to consider them. In contrast, in regions where EVs are less prevalent, unfamiliarity, and perceived social acceptance issues can serve as barriers (Rezvani et al., 2015).

Charging Infrastructure

The availability and convenience of charging infrastructure are paramount in consumer decision-making. Inadequate public charging infrastructure, especially in rural and less developed areas, exacerbates range anxiety and poses a significant barrier to EV adoption. Home charging is a solution for some, but it is not feasible for all, particularly those living in multi-unit dwellings or without dedicated parking.

Market Diversity and Vehicle Options

The variety and availability of EV models affect consumer choice. Initially, the EV market was limited in terms of model diversity, catering primarily to a niche segment. However, with an increasing number of manufacturers venturing into the EV realm and providing a broader spectrum of models encompassing SUVs, trucks, and budget-friendly options, the market is becoming more enticing to a wider array of consumers (Adnan et al., 2017).

Information and Misconceptions

A significant barrier to EV adoption is the lack of accurate information and prevalence of misconceptions. Many consumers lack comprehensive information about the capabilities, advantages, and operations of EVs. These persistent misinformation and myths, especially those related to battery life and charging times, continue to shape perceptions (Haddadian et al., 2015). Addressing these through education and awareness campaigns is crucial for changing public attitude toward EVs.

Regulatory Environment and Policy Support

The regulatory environment and policy support play a significant role in shaping consumers' perception and adoption of EV. Policies that favor EVs, such as low-emission zones, preferential parking, and usage benefits (like access to carpool lanes), can make EVs more attractive. Conversely, a lack of supportive policies or uncertainty about future regulations can be a barrier to adoption.

In summary, consumers' perception and adoption of EV and the barriers to EV adoption are influenced by a combination of environmental, technological, economic, social, infrastructural, and regulatory factors. Each of these aspects plays a critical role in how consumers view and decide on EVs. Addressing these multifaceted challenges requires a comprehensive approach that involves technological innovation, economic incentives, infrastructure development, societal engagement, and policy support. If these issues are addressed, consumer perceptions are likely to shift toward favoring EV adoption, paving the way for a more sustainable transportation future.

In sum, a set of elements ranging from environmental, social, and economic factors act as barriers to consumer adoption of EV, as shown in Fig. 2.1.

2.4 Policy and Regulatory Framework for Promoting Electric Mobility

The policy and regulatory framework for promoting electric mobility is a tapestry of initiatives and regulations, which vary widely across different regions and countries. These policies are critical in shaping the pace and

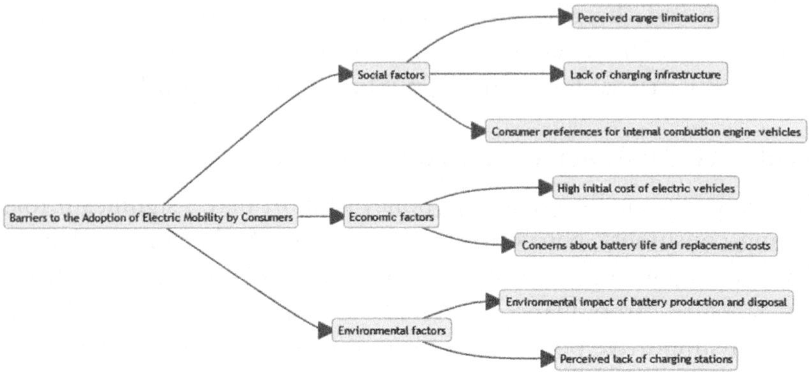

Fig. 2.1 Factors acting as barriers for consumer adoption of EM (personal elaboration)

nature of EV adoption, but their effectiveness and comprehensiveness are subjects of ongoing debate.

Incentives and Subsidies

Many governments have introduced financial incentives, including tax credits, rebates, and grants, to lower the cost barrier for EVs. While these incentives have been effective in stimulating initial market growth, they raise concerns about long-term sustainability and market distortion (Clinton & Steinberg, 2019). Critics argue that such subsidies often disproportionately benefit higher-income individuals who can afford EVs, rather than broadening access to all segments of the population.

Investment in Infrastructure

Investment in charging infrastructure is the cornerstone of many EV policies. Governments are funding the expansion of public charging networks, aiming to alleviate range anxiety and make EVs more viable for the average consumer. However, the uneven geographical distribution of these charging stations, favoring urban areas over rural ones, raises concerns about equity and accessibility.

Emission Standards and Zero-Emission Vehicle Mandates

Stricter emission standards and zero-emission vehicle (ZEV) mandates are pushing manufacturers toward electrification (Ashfaq et al., 2021). These regulations are instrumental in reducing transport emissions but can be challenging for the automotive industry, requiring significant investment in new technologies and sometimes eliciting resistance from manufacturers.

End-of-Life Vehicle Regulations

Some regions have introduced policies regarding the recycling and disposal of EV batteries, addressing environmental concerns. However, the effectiveness of these policies is often limited by the nascent state of recycling technologies and the complexity of battery compositions.

In conclusion, the policy and regulatory landscape for electric mobility is marked by approaches aimed at fostering EV adoption. Although these policies have spurred considerable growth in the EV sector, they have also encountered criticism regarding potential market distortion and equity concerns, and questions about the readiness of supporting infrastructure and technology have been raised (Wang et al., 2019). A balanced approach that addresses these criticisms while promoting sustainable growth in electric mobility is crucial for the long-term success of these policies.

Analyzing the effectiveness of policy measures in promoting electric mobility involves taking a critical look at how these policies translate into real-world impacts, with a focus on market adoption, technology advancement, and addressing environmental concerns.

Financial Incentives

Financial incentives like tax credits, rebates, and subsidies have been effective in reducing the high upfront cost barrier of EVs, thus encouraging consumer adoption. Norway, for instance, has seen significant

EV uptake due, in part, to substantial incentives. However, the effectiveness of these incentives could diminish over time as the market matures (Virmani et al., 2022). Furthermore, critics argue that such incentives often benefit wealthier segments who can afford EVs even without subsidies, questioning the equity of these measures.

Charging Infrastructure Development

Policies focusing on the expansion of charging infrastructure, including public investment and mandates for private sector involvement, have been crucial in addressing range anxiety and making EVs more practical for daily use. However, the effectiveness of these policies is contingent on the strategic placement of charging stations, ensuring accessibility across various regions, including underserved areas.

Emission Standards and ZEV Mandates

Stricter emission standards and ZEV mandates have compelled automakers to shift their focus toward EV production. California's ZEV program, for example, has been instrumental in increasing the availability of EVs (McConnell & Leard, 2021). However, these mandates can put significant pressure on the automotive industry, potentially leading to higher vehicle costs and requiring substantial investment in new technologies.

Education and Awareness Programs

Policies aimed at educating consumers about the benefits and practicalities of EVs are crucial for addressing misconceptions and resistance to change. Although often overshadowed by financial incentives, these programs are essential for long-term market transformation.

In conclusion, effective policy measures for promoting electric mobility are those that strike a balance between incentivizing EV adoption, ensuring equitable access, fostering technological innovation, and raising public awareness. The challenge lies in designing and implementing policies that address these multifaceted goals in a sustainable, equitable, and economically viable manner.

To bolster the effectiveness of policies advocating for electric mobility, a comprehensive set of targeted recommendations can be formulated, leveraging critical analysis and research insights. These recommendations should strive to bridge current gaps and promote a more sustainable, equitable, and resilient transition to EVs (Abduljabbar, 2021). Some of them are given below.

i) Gradual Phase-Out of Subsidies with a Shift to Broader Support Mechanisms: While subsidies have been effective in promoting EV adoption, they should be gradually phased out as the market matures. Instead, policies should focus on broader support mechanisms, such as investing in charging infrastructure and research and development. This shift ensures long-term sustainability and avoids market distortion.
ii) Equitable Distribution of Charging Infrastructure: Policies should mandate the equitable distribution of charging stations, ensuring access in rural and underserved areas. This approach will reduce disparities in EV adoption between urban and rural regions and support a more inclusive transition to electric mobility.
iii) Strengthening Battery Recycling and Lifecycle Management Policies: Given the environmental impact of battery production and disposal, policies must enforce and support the efficient recycling and lifecycle management of EV batteries (Mossali et al., 2020). Incentives for developing sustainable battery technologies and recycling processes can mitigate environmental concerns and resource scarcity.
iv) Integrating EV Policies with Broader Environmental and Energy Strategies: EV policies should be part of a larger environmental and energy strategy. This integration includes linking EV charging infrastructure with renewable energy sources and considering the impact of EV adoption on the electricity grid.
v) Incentivizing Innovation in Affordable EV Technology: Policies should encourage the development of more affordable EV models to broaden market access. This approach involves supporting research in cost-effective battery technologies and offering incentives to manufacturers who produce affordable EVs (Reinhardt et al., 2019).

vi) Public Awareness and Educational Campaigns: Governments should invest in public awareness campaigns to educate consumers about the benefits and practicalities of EVs. These campaigns can address common misconceptions and range anxiety, fostering a more informed and receptive consumer base.

Thus, in promoting electric mobility, policy improvements should focus on long-term sustainability, equitable access, environmental considerations, and the integration of EVs into broader energy strategies. These recommendations aim to create a conducive environment for a robust and inclusive transition to electric mobility.

The policy and regulatory framework for promoting electric mobility is a critical driver in the transition toward a more sustainable transportation ecosystem. Effective policies can accelerate the adoption of EVs, foster technological innovation, and ensure an equitable transition for all stakeholders. This framework expands beyond mere incentives, to encompass a holistic approach that considers infrastructure, technology, equity, environmental impacts, and economic factors (Bonges III & Lusk, 2016).

i) Integrated Urban Planning and Infrastructure Development: One of the key aspects of policymaking is integrating EV infrastructure into urban planning. Cities and municipalities play a crucial role in providing public charging stations and designated parking spaces for EVs and incorporating EV considerations into new construction projects. Therefore, this approach necessitates collaboration between various stakeholders, including city planners, utility companies, and EV manufacturers, to ensure a cohesive and accessible charging network.

ii) Standardization of Charging Infrastructure: The standardization of charging systems and connectors is essential for a user-friendly EV ecosystem. Policymakers should advocate for uniform charging standards to ease the user experience and encourage EV adoption (Martins et al., 2021). This includes standardizing the connectors, voltage requirements, and communication protocols between the vehicle and the charging station.

iii) Encouraging Private Sector Investment: While public investment is vital, leveraging private sector resources is equally important. Policies should incentivize private businesses to install EV charging stations and integrate EVs into their fleets. This can be achieved through tax breaks, subsidies, and mandates requiring a certain percentage of EVs in corporate fleets.

iv) Electrification of Public Transportation: Policies should also focus on the electrification of public transportation systems. Buses, taxis, and other public transport vehicles significantly contribute to urban emissions. Offering subsidies for the shift toward electric buses and taxis can yield significant results such as improved air quality and reduced carbon emissions (Rietmann & Lieven, 2019).

iv) Education and Workforce Training: As the EV industry grows, there is a need for skilled workers in EV manufacturing, maintenance, and infrastructure development. Policies supporting education and training programs in these areas can facilitate a smoother transition and create job opportunities.

v) Research and Development Support: Government support for research and development in EV technology is crucial. This includes funding for research on battery technology, alternative fuel sources, and new EV models. Such support can spur innovation and help overcome current technological barriers.

vi) Lifecycle Assessment and Environmental Regulations: Policies mandating lifecycle assessments for EVs should be enacted to ensure that environmental impact is minimized across the entire lifespan of the vehicle. This includes regulations on battery production, use, and recycling, as well as assessing the carbon footprint of EV manufacturing processes (Etxandi-Santolaya et al., 2023).

vii) Grid Management and Renewable Integration: As EV adoption increases, so does the load on the electrical grid. Policies should focus on grid management solutions, including smart grid technologies and the integration of renewable energy sources. This ensures that the environmental benefits of EVs are maximized by powering them with clean energy.

ix) Equity and Accessibility Measures: Ensuring equitable access to EV technology is vital. Policies should address the needs of lower-income communities, which are often left behind in technological transitions. This could include providing subsidies for affordable EV models, access to charging infrastructure in underserved areas, and programs that reduce the total cost of ownership for low-income consumers.

x) International Collaboration and Policy Harmonization: Electric mobility is a global issue, and international collaboration is key. Sharing best practices, harmonizing policies across borders, and making collaborative research and development efforts can accelerate the global transition to electric mobility.

In conclusion, a comprehensive and multifaceted policy and regulatory framework is essential for promoting electric mobility. Such a framework should tackle not just the immediate obstacles to EV adoption but also the broader implications on urban planning, the environment, the economy, and society as a whole (Smith & Hensher, 2020). By implementing integrated, forward-thinking policies, governments can foster a sustainable and equitable transition to electric mobility.

2.5 The Role of Lithium Batteries and Other Innovative Aspects

The importance of lithium batteries in electric mobility cannot be overstated, as they are pivotal in the functioning and advancement of EVs. However, this critical role comes with its own set of challenges and implications.

High Energy Density and Efficiency

Lithium batteries are favored in EVs due to their high energy density, which allows them to store more energy per unit of weight than other types of batteries. This characteristic is crucial for EVs, as it directly impacts their range and performance (Bican et al., 2023). Additionally, lithium batteries have a high-efficiency rate, meaning they can effectively convert stored energy into power, further enhancing the vehicles' performance.

Rapid Advancements and Cost Reduction

The technology behind lithium batteries has seen rapid advancements, which have led to significant improvements in their capacity, longevity, and safety. These advancements have also contributed to a decrease in battery costs, which, historically, have been a major component of the overall cost of EVs. As battery costs continue to decline, EVs become more financially accessible to a broader range of consumers, driving wider adoption.

Environmental Considerations

While lithium batteries have environmental advantages over fossil fuel-powered vehicles, such as reduced greenhouse gas emissions during operation, they also pose significant environmental challenges. The extraction of lithium and other minerals (like cobalt and nickel) used in manufacturing these batteries often involves environmentally harmful practices. Furthermore, the lifecycle management of lithium batteries, including their recycling and disposal, is a cause of growing concern, given the increasing volume of batteries that will reach the end of their life in the coming years (Rosendahl & Rubiano, 2019).

Supply Chain and Geopolitical Issues

The production of lithium batteries is subject to supply chain complexities and geopolitical issues. The concentration of lithium and other critical minerals in just a few countries creates potential vulnerabilities in the supply chain. This concentration can lead to market volatility and has raised concerns over the long-term availability of these essential materials.

Innovations and Alternatives

Research on how to make lithium batteries more sustainable, efficient, and cost-effective continues, and innovations such as solid-state batteries, which promise higher energy densities and improved safety, are on the horizon (Yang et al., 2020). Additionally, there is a growing interest in finding alternative battery chemistries that rely less on scarce and geopolitically sensitive materials.

In conclusion, lithium batteries are a cornerstone of the current electric mobility revolution, offering unmatched energy density and efficiency critical for the operation of EVs. However, the environmental impact of their production, concerns around the sustainability of raw material sourcing, and the need for effective recycling and disposal methods are significant challenges that must be addressed. The sustainable progression of electric mobility heavily relies on future advancements in battery technology and the diversification of battery chemistry (Armand et al., 2020).

Lithium battery technology has undergone significant advancements, playing a central role in the propulsion of the EV revolution. These advancements have been critical in addressing some of the initial limitations of EVs, but they have also brought forth new challenges and areas for further development.

Increased Energy Density

One of the most notable advancements in lithium battery technology is the increase in energy density. Modern lithium batteries can store more energy per unit weight than earlier versions, allowing for longer driving ranges in EVs. This increase in energy density has been achieved through improvements in battery chemistry and cell design, yet there remains a physical limit to how much energy density can be increased, posing a challenge for future advancements.

Improved Battery Life and Durability

Advances in battery management systems and cell chemistry have led to longer battery life and improved durability. These, in turn, have reduced the frequency of battery replacements over the vehicle's lifespan, thereby reducing long-term costs and environmental impact. Yet, the durability of batteries in real-world conditions, particularly considering the diverse environmental and usage patterns, remains a subject requiring much research (Bai et al., 2020).

Faster Charging Times

Advancements in battery technology have also led to faster charging times, a critical factor in EV usability. Innovations such as high-voltage batteries and improved thermal management systems have enabled quicker charging rates without compromising battery health (Xu et al., 2019). However, the infrastructure for ultra-fast charging is still limited, and there are concerns about the long-term effects of fast charging on battery strength.

Sustainability and Recycling

While advancements have been made in the efficiency and performance of lithium batteries, sustainability concerns persist. The extraction of raw materials like lithium, cobalt, and nickel has significant environmental and social impacts. Although recycling technologies for lithium batteries are developing, they are not yet widespread, and the recycling process is complex and costly.

Alternative Chemistries and Technologies

Research into alternative chemistries, such as lithium-sulfur and solid-state batteries, offers the potential for higher energy densities, reduced costs, and enhanced safety. These technologies are still in the developmental stages and are facing challenges in terms of scalability, cost, and performance stability.

In summary, while advances in lithium battery technology have been instrumental in the growth of the EV market, they are accompanied by challenges in terms of sustainability, materials sourcing, infrastructure development, and the ongoing quest for improved energy density and battery life. Addressing these challenges requires continued research and innovation, alongside a broader approach that includes developing alternative chemistries and improving recycling processes.

The environmental and sustainability considerations of lithium batteries, particularly in the context of EVs, are multifaceted, and while they offer significant advantages over traditional combustion engines, like reducing greenhouse gas emissions, their production, usage, and disposal raise several environmental concerns.

Environmental Impact of Resource Extraction

The extraction of lithium and other metals like cobalt and nickel used in battery production has substantial environmental impacts. Mining practices can lead to land degradation, water pollution, and biodiversity loss (Kall et al., 2023). Moreover, the concentration of these mineral reserves in specific geographical regions raises concerns about resource depletion and the sustainability of the supply chain.

Carbon Footprint of Battery Production

The manufacturing process of lithium batteries is energy-intensive, contributing significantly to their overall carbon footprint. Majority of the carbon emissions associated with EVs come from this production phase, and although operational emissions in EVs are significantly lower than those in combustion engines, the substantial manufacturing emissions require an extended usage period for EVs to offset this carbon debt (Cheng et al., 2021).

Battery Life and Degradation

While advancements in lithium battery technology have improved their lifespan and efficiency, battery degradation over time remains an issue. Degradation adversely impacts the range and performance of EVs, necessitating battery replacement, which in turn contributes to waste generation (Neumann, 2022).

Recycling and End-of-Life Management

The recycling infrastructure for lithium batteries is currently limited and facing technical and economic challenges. Efficient recycling is crucial to recovering valuable materials and reducing environmental impact. Indeed, the intricate nature of battery chemistries and absence of standardized designs pose challenges to the recycling process. Moreover, the economic feasibility of recycling processes relies on the market value of the recovered materials (Thompson et al., 2020).

Alternative Battery Technologies and Sustainability Practices

Research into alternative battery chemistries and technologies aims to reduce reliance on scarce and environmentally impactful materials. Furthermore, embracing sustainable practices in mining and manufacturing, such as incorporating renewable energy sources and enforcing stricter environmental regulations, is crucial to alleviating the environmental impact of lithium battery production (Zhao & Guo, 2020).

In conclusion, while lithium batteries are a key enabler of the transition to electric mobility and offer clear benefits in terms of operational emissions, their environmental and sustainability impact across the lifecycle—from resource extraction to manufacturing, usage, and disposal—presents significant challenges. Addressing these challenges requires a concerted effort in developing more sustainable battery technologies, improving recycling processes, and adopting more eco-friendly practices in the production and supply chain.

The disposal and recycling of lithium batteries, a critical part of EV use, is a complex issue fraught with both challenges and opportunities. As the adoption of EVs increases, so does the importance of addressing the end-of-life management of these batteries.

Current State of Recycling

The current recycling rate for lithium batteries is relatively low compared to that of other types of batteries, like lead-acid batteries. This is partly due to the technical complexity and cost of recycling lithium batteries, which contain a mix of valuable and hazardous materials. The recycling process involves collecting, sorting, and safely handling spent batteries, followed by processes like pyrometallurgy and hydrometallurgy to recover materials. However, these processes are energy-intensive and not always cost-effective, especially when the market value of the recovered materials is low.

Environmental and Health Impacts

Improper disposal of lithium batteries poses significant environmental and health risks; batteries thrown into landfills can leak toxic substances into the soil and water. Incineration, another disposal method, releases harmful emissions into the atmosphere. Therefore, effective recycling is not just a matter of resource recovery but also a matter of environmental protection and public health.

Economic and Material Recovery Challenges

Recycling lithium batteries is economically challenging, and the fluctuating market value of recovered materials like lithium and cobalt influences the financial viability of recycling operations. Moreover, the recovery rate of these materials is often less than optimal, leading to a loss of valuable resources and continued reliance on mining for fresh materials.

Technological and Policy Advancements

There are ongoing technological advancements aimed at improving the efficiency and reducing the cost of lithium battery recycling. These include developing new methods for directly recovering cathode material and enhancing the purity of recovered materials. Policy measures can also play a crucial role in this regard. Implementing robust battery stewardship programs and mandating recycling can drive improvements in recycling rate and technology.

The Need for a Circular Economy Approach

To address these challenges, a shift toward a circular economy model for lithium batteries is essential (Voskoboynik & Andreucci, 2022). This involves designing batteries for easier disassembly and recycling, developing more efficient recycling technologies, and creating closed-loop systems where materials from spent batteries are directly reused in new battery production.

In summary, while the disposal and recycling of lithium batteries pose significant environmental, economic, and technological challenges, they also offer opportunities for innovation and sustainable resource management. The development of more efficient recycling technologies and policies, coupled with a holistic approach to battery lifecycle management, is vital for mitigating the environmental impact of the EV industry and ensuring its long-term sustainability.

A comprehensive analysis of the literature concerning electric mobility, spanning from market and consumer research to technological advancements, policy frameworks, and the role of lithium batteries, culminates in several key conclusions.

Market and Consumer Research Insights

The evolving consumer perceptions and market dynamics underscore the complexity of the transition to electric mobility. While environmental consciousness and technological fascination drive consumer interest, concerns such as range anxiety, cost, and lack of infrastructure pose significant barriers. Effective marketing strategies that address these concerns and highlight the benefits of EVs are crucial in accelerating adoption.

Technological Advancements

Technological progress, particularly in lithium battery technology, has been a cornerstone in advancing electric mobility. Improvements in energy density, battery life, and charging infrastructure are pivotal in making EVs more practical and appealing. However, these advancements have made sustainable material sourcing difficult and highlighted the need for continued innovation in battery technologies and alternative energy sources.

Policy and Regulatory Landscape

Policies and regulations play a critical role in shaping the electric mobility landscape. Financial incentives, infrastructure development, and emission standards have been effective in promoting EV adoption. However, a strategic shift toward more sustainable and equitable policies is needed, focusing on the long-term development of infrastructure, fostering technological innovation, and addressing environmental concerns.

Environmental and Sustainability Considerations

The environmental benefits of EVs, primarily in operational emissions, are counterbalanced by concerns about the production and disposal of lithium batteries. Sustainable practices in battery production, recycling, and lifecycle management are essential to mitigate these impacts.

Thus, the transition to electric mobility represents a multifaceted challenge involving consumer behavior, technological innovation, policy frameworks, and environmental considerations. Addressing these challenges requires a concerted effort by industry stakeholders, policymakers, and consumers. The path forward involves not only embracing technological advancements but also fostering sustainable practices, equitable policies, and a broader cultural shift toward environmentally conscious transportation choices.

The role of lithium batteries in electric mobility is a cornerstone topic, but delving deeper, there are other innovative aspects intertwined with this core element that merit exploration. These innovations not only complement lithium battery technology but also extend the scope of electric mobility to broader dimensions, encompassing advancements in energy systems, materials science, regulatory frameworks, consumer engagement, and integration with renewable energy sources.

Energy systems in electric mobility are in a transformative phase, where the focus is not just on the vehicles themselves but also on the entire energy ecosystem they interact with. This includes the development of smart grids capable of supporting the increased load from EVs while optimizing energy distribution and consumption. Smart grid technology, which involves real-time data analytics, IoT integration, and predictive algorithms, is crucial for balancing the load on the grid, especially with the intermittent nature of renewable energy sources. This integration is pivotal in ensuring that the environmental benefits of EVs are maximized by powering them with clean energy.

In the realm of materials science, research has moved beyond conventional lithium-ion battery technology to exploring alternative materials that offer improved performance, reduced costs, and a lower environmental footprint. Innovations like lithium-sulfur batteries, solid-state batteries, and graphene-based supercapacitors present possibilities for higher energy densities, faster charging times, and enhanced safety. These advancements not only promise to address the limitations of current battery technology but also open up new avenues for electric mobility applications, e.g., in heavier forms of transport like trucks and buses, and even aviation.

Regulatory frameworks are also evolving in response to the growth of electric mobility. Policies are increasingly focusing on not just incentivizing EV adoption but also ensuring that the entire lifecycle of these vehicles is sustainable. This includes setting up regulations around battery recycling, mandating the use of recycled materials in battery production, and establishing standards for environmentally friendly manufacturing processes. These regulatory shifts are driving the industry toward a more circular economy model, where resource efficiency and sustainability are key.

Consumer engagement and education are vital in accelerating the adoption of electric mobility. As technology advances, there is a growing need to bridge the knowledge gap among consumers. This involves marketing the benefits of EVs as well as providing transparent information about their operation, maintenance, and environmental impact. Interactive platforms, virtual reality experiences, and educational campaigns are being utilized to engage consumers, demystify electric mobility, and foster a culture of sustainable transportation.

Integration with renewable energy sources is another crucial aspect of the future of electric mobility. The development of solar-powered EVs and charging stations, as well as wind-powered charging infrastructure, and the integration of EVs with home solar panels are steps toward a more sustainable energy ecosystem (Shafique & Luo, 2022). These integrations not only reduce the reliance on the traditional electricity grid but also enhance the self-sufficiency of the electric mobility sector.

Additionally, the emergence of wireless charging technology for EVs is poised to revolutionize the charging experience. Wireless or inductive charging systems eliminate the need for physical connectors, enabling greater convenience and the potential for charging EVs on the move, such as through equipped roadways. This technology, still in its developmental stages, could significantly reduce range anxiety and make EVs more user-friendly.

The role of AI and machine learning in optimizing EV performance and battery management is another area of significant advancement. Many AI algorithms are being developed to predict battery life, optimize charging schedules, and improve the overall efficiency of EVs. These technologies not only enhance user experience but also contribute to extending the lifespan of the batteries, thereby reducing waste and environmental impact.

In conclusion, the role of lithium batteries in electric mobility is a critical area of focus; however, it is part of a larger tapestry of innovations shaping the future of transportation. Advancements in energy systems and materials science, evolving regulatory frameworks, consumer engagement strategies, and the integration of renewable energy all collectively contribute to a more sustainable, efficient, and accessible electric mobility landscape. As these innovations continue to evolve, they will play a pivotal role in overcoming the current limitations of electric mobility and unlocking its full potential as a cornerstone of sustainable transportation.

3

Industry Perspective

Abstract The emergence of electric mobility (EM) significantly influences and reshapes the business models of organizations across various industries. This chapter explores electric mobility from the perspective of industries, dealing with the economic and environmental benefits of its implementation. It examines the significant impacts electric mobility has on various industries, discussing innovative business models and strategies related to electric mobility. The chapter also addresses how industries communicate their commitment to EM and their advancements to the market both online and offline. The chapter then addresses the implications for traditional manufacturers and the oil industry, highlighting the transformative effects of EVs adoption on such contexts. In conclusion, the chapter delves into the revolutionary changes in supply chains within the automotive industry and for urban logistics, showcasing the broader industrial shifts prompted by electric mobility.

Keywords business model innovation · business strategies · environmental benefits · traditional manufacturers · oil industry · automotive industry · supply chain innovation · urban logistics

D. D'Acunto, *The Future of E-Mobility*,
https://doi.org/10.1007/978-3-031-65053-6_3

3.1 The Environmental Benefits of Electric Mobility Implementation

The advent of electric mobility (EM) heralds a significant shift in how we perceive and interact with transportation, bringing forth numerous environmental benefits. One of the most impactful advantages of EM is the reduction in greenhouse gas emissions (Fig. 3.1). Unlike traditional internal combustion engine (ICE) vehicles, electric vehicles (EVs) produce zero tailpipe emissions. This is crucial in the fight against climate change, as transportation is a significant contributor to global greenhouse gas emissions (Buckley & Ghauri, 2004). Therefore, the shift to EVs plays a direct and positive role in reducing the carbon footprint of transportation. This benefit is further enhanced when the electricity used to charge these vehicles is sourced from renewable energy like wind and solar power, making the entire lifecycle of EVs cleaner.

Another environmental benefit of EM is the improvement in air quality, particularly in urban areas. Cities around the world grapple with air pollution, much of which is attributed to vehicle emissions. EVs, with their zero tailpipe emissions, contribute to a significant reduction in air pollutants like nitrogen oxides (NOx) and particulate matter. This shift can lead to considerable improvements in public health, as these pollutants are linked to several respiratory and cardiovascular diseases (Rongen

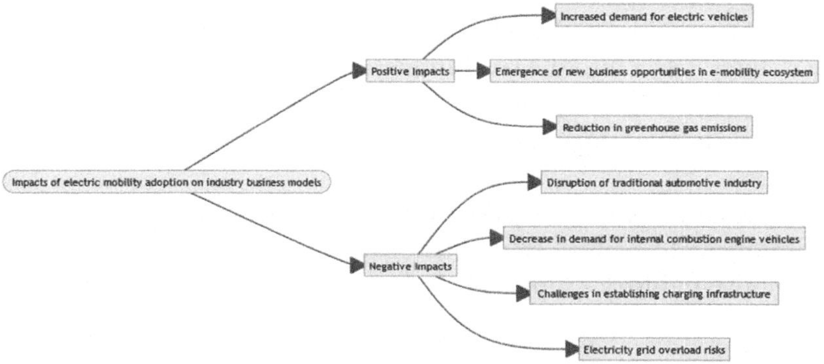

Fig. 3.1 The positive/negative effects of EM adoption on industry business models (personal elaboration)

et al., 2022). The quiet nature of EVs also contributes to noise pollution reduction, offering a more serene urban environment.

The environmental benefits of EM extend to the efficient use of resources. EVs are generally more efficient than traditional vehicles in converting energy into vehicle movement. This efficiency means that EVs use less energy to travel the same distance as their gasoline counterparts, which can lead to a decrease in the overall demand for energy in transportation (Mohd Yusof et al., 2014). Furthermore, the ongoing advancements in battery technology are leading to more efficient, longer-lasting batteries which make better use of resources. These advancements also include improving the sustainability of the battery lifecycle through initiatives like battery recycling, which mitigates the impact of battery production and disposal on the environment.

The EM revolution also spurs the development of sustainable energy infrastructure. As the demand for EVs grows, so does the need for renewable energy sources to power them. This can accelerate investments in renewable energy infrastructure, further reducing the reliance on fossil fuels and decreasing the carbon footprint of the energy sector. This synergy between EM and renewable energy creates a virtuous cycle that benefits the environment.

Moreover, the adoption of EVs has a knock-on effect on the automotive industry, prompting a shift toward more sustainable manufacturing practices. EV production increasingly incorporates environmentally friendly materials and processes, contributing to a more sustainable lifecycle for these vehicles (Rietmann & Lieven, 2019). The EV market also drives innovation in other environmental technologies such as regenerative braking systems that recover energy during braking, further enhancing the overall efficiency and environmental friendliness of these vehicles.

In addition to the direct environmental benefits, EM also offers broader ecological advantages. The integration of EVs with smart grid technologies can lead to more efficient energy use and distribution, reducing waste and further improving the environmental footprint of the energy sector (Böckin & Tillman, 2019). EVs can also play a role in energy storage, helping to balance supply and demand in the electricity grid, especially as the penetration of intermittent renewable energy sources like solar and wind increases.

The environmental benefits of EM are clear and multifaceted. From reducing greenhouse gas emissions and improving air quality to fostering sustainable resource use and energy efficiency, the shift to EVs represents a critical step in the journey toward a more sustainable and environmentally friendly future. As technology advances and the adoption of EM increases, these benefits are expected to grow, paving the way for a cleaner, healthier planet (Virshup et al., 2009). This transition not only helps in mitigating the adverse effects of climate change but also in creating a more sustainable and resilient transportation ecosystem for future generations. It is essential to delve deeper into the environmental implications of this shift, particularly regarding sustainable resource usage and the development of a green energy infrastructure.

The sustainable use of resources is a cornerstone in the environmental benefits brought about by EM. EVs, by design, offer a more efficient alternative to traditional combustion engines, and this efficiency is not limited to energy consumption but also extends to the lifetime management of vehicle components. For instance, EV batteries, a key component, have evolved significantly (Bengler et al., 2014). Modern EV batteries have a longer life and are also increasingly being made with sustainable materials. The emphasis on battery recycling further enhances the environmental credentials of EM. Battery recycling not only reduces the need for raw materials but also minimizes waste, ensuring that the components of used batteries are effectively reused. This circular approach in resource management is pivotal in reducing the ecological footprint of EM.

Moreover, the growing emphasis on sustainable energy sources in powering EVs is a critical aspect of their environmental benefit. The integration of EVs with renewable energy sources such as solar and wind power is a crucial step toward a zero-emission future. This integration not only ensures that the electricity used for powering EVs is clean but also drives the demand for renewable energy, accelerating the transition away from fossil fuels (Nikitas et al., 2021). The increase in renewable energy capacity is essential for a sustainable energy future, and EM is a significant catalyst in this transformation.

The EM revolution is not just about vehicles but also about the infrastructure that supports them. The development of EV charging infrastructure is an opportunity to implement environmentally friendly practices. For example, the installation of solar-powered charging stations reduces the reliance on grid electricity and maximizes the use of clean energy. Additionally, smart charging solutions that optimize charging times based on renewable energy availability can further reduce the carbon footprint of EVs.

Another environmental benefit of EM is the potential to improve urban planning and reduce the overall need for personal vehicle travel. With EVs, cities have the opportunity to redesign urban spaces, prioritizing public transport and reducing traffic congestion (Abduljabbar et al., 2021). The environmental impact of this shift can be profound, leading to lower emissions, reduced noise pollution, and an overall improvement in the quality of urban life.

The rise of EM also presents an opportunity for industries to innovate in eco-friendly technologies. For instance, the development of lighter and more efficient materials for EV production not only improves vehicle performance but also reduces energy consumption. Innovations in EV technology can also spill over into other sectors, fostering a culture of environmental responsibility and sustainable development across industries.

Furthermore, the environmental benefits of EM are tied to a broader societal shift toward sustainability. As consumers become more environmentally conscious, their preference for clean and sustainable modes of transportation grows (Rietmann & Lieven, 2019). This shift in consumer behavior is a powerful force driving the adoption of EVs and supporting the development of green technologies.

EM's contribution to environmental preservation extends beyond the immediate reductions in emissions and energy efficiency. It also plays a crucial role in promoting a larger cultural and industrial shift toward sustainability. This shift is critical in addressing the broader challenges posed by climate change and environmental degradation.

A significant aspect of this shift is the influence EVs have on consumer behavior and societal norms. As more people adopt EVs, it creates a ripple effect, encouraging others to consider the environmental impact of their transportation choices. This growing awareness and change in consumer preferences can lead to increased demand for sustainable products and services across various sectors, not just in transportation (Böckin & Tillman, 2019). Consequently, industries will be motivated to innovate and offer more environmentally friendly products, reinforcing a cycle of sustainability.

Furthermore, the rise of EM has a profound impact on urban development and planning. Cities worldwide are beginning to integrate EVs into their vision of a sustainable future. This includes not only the development of necessary infrastructure like charging stations but also the creation of EV-friendly policies such as low-emission zones, incentives for EV buyers, and investment in electric public transportation (Biresselioglu et al., 2018). Such initiatives can significantly reduce the carbon footprint of urban centers, making them more livable and sustainable.

The environmental impact of EM also extends to the conservation of natural resources. Traditional vehicles, reliant on fossil fuels, contribute to the depletion of non-renewable resources. In contrast, EVs, especially when paired with renewable energy sources, present a more sustainable alternative that reduces dependency on these dwindling resources. This is particularly important as the world grapples with the challenges of resource management and sustainability.

In conclusion, EM is much more than an alternative to conventional transportation. It is a catalyst for a broader environmental and societal transformation. By promoting the use of clean energy, encouraging sustainable urban development, and influencing consumer behavior, EM is at the forefront of the journey toward a more sustainable and eco-friendly world (Bohn & Braun, 2021). As technology evolves and adoption rates increase, the role of EM in shaping a sustainable future becomes increasingly significant, offering hope and direction in the global effort to combat environmental challenges. The environmental benefits of EM are extensive and multifaceted. From reducing greenhouse gas emissions and improving air quality to fostering sustainable resource use and energy efficiency, EM is a key player in the quest for a more sustainable and environmentally friendly future. As this technology continues to evolve and its adoption increases, these benefits are expected to expand, paving the way for a cleaner, healthier planet. The transition to EM is not just a technological shift but a fundamental change in how we view and interact with our environment, offering a path toward a more sustainable and resilient future.

3.2 Impact of Electric Mobility on Industries

The impact of EM on industries is profound and multifaceted, signifying a paradigm shift not just for the automotive sector but also for energy, infrastructure, and beyond. This transition to EVs is not merely a change in the type of vehicles produced and sold; it represents a significant transformation in industrial operations, supply chains, and market dynamics (Dou & Han, 2019).

In the automotive industry, the shift to EM necessitates a complete overhaul of manufacturing processes. Traditional combustion engine vehicles and EVs differ vastly in design and components, leading to the need for new production lines, supplier networks, and skills. The manufacturing of EVs requires fewer moving parts compared to traditional vehicles but introduces complex components like batteries and electric drive units (Dou & Han, 2019). This transition has a ripple effect on the entire automotive supply chain, from raw material suppliers to component manufacturers. Companies that previously specialized in engine components must pivot to new product lines or risk obsolescence. This shift is not just challenging but also an avenue for innovation and growth in areas like battery technology, electric powertrains, and advanced materials.

The energy industry is equally impacted by the rise of EM. The increasing adoption of EVs has significantly boosted the demand for electricity, presenting both a challenge and an opportunity for energy providers. On the one hand, this surge in demand requires upgrades to existing power grids to handle increased loads and ensure reliable and efficient energy distribution. On the other hand, it accelerates the transition to renewable energy sources. As consumers and policymakers demand greener electricity to power EVs, energy companies are motivated to invest more in renewable sources like solar, wind, and hydroelectric power (Llopis-Albert et al., 2021). This transition not only supports the environmental goals of EM but also helps in diversifying energy sources, enhancing energy security.

The infrastructure sector is also deeply influenced by the advent of EM. Widespread and accessible charging infrastructure is critical for EV adoption. This requirement spurs growth in sectors related to the construction and operation of charging stations. Companies specializing in electrical equipment, telecommunications, and network operations can find new opportunities in this emerging market (Requia et al., 2018). The development of charging infrastructure also involves innovations in technology, such as fast charging, wireless charging, and smart charging systems that integrate with the broader smart grid. This integration is key to efficiently and sustainably manage the increased energy demand.

Another industry that is significantly impacted is the oil and gas sector. As EVs become more prevalent, the demand for gasoline and diesel is expected to decline. This shift poses a substantial challenge to the oil industry, compelling it to diversify and explore new business models. Some oil companies are already investing in electric charging infrastructure and renewable energy projects, acknowledging the inevitable transition toward a low-carbon future.

The rise of EM also influences sectors like technology and telecommunications. The increasing sophistication of EVs, along with their need for advanced software, connectivity, and autonomous driving capabilities, opens new avenues for technology companies (Maggio et al., 2019). This interplay between automotive and technology sectors fosters collaborations and cross-industry innovations, blurring the lines between these traditionally distinct markets.

The impact of EM extends to the labor market and workforce skills. As industries adapt to the new demands of EM, there is a growing need for skills related to electric powertrain engineering, battery technology, and digital competencies like software development and data analysis. This shift in skill requirements presents a challenge for workforce development, necessitating targeted education and training programs.

Furthermore, environmental regulations and policies play a significant role in shaping the impact of EM on industries. Governments worldwide are implementing policies, such as subsidies, tax incentives, and emissions regulations, to encourage EV adoption (Sovacool et al., 2021). These policies not only accelerate the transition to EM but also influence how industries adapt and invest in this transition.

The impact of EM on industries is not limited to these direct effects. There are broader implications for global trade, urban planning, and consumer behavior. The move toward EM is reshaping industries in a way that aligns with global sustainability goals, prompting a reevaluation of business models, investment strategies, and corporate practices. Since the EM landscape continues to evolve, industries are compelled to innovate, collaborate, and adapt to remain competitive and relevant in this new era of transportation (Pichler et al., 2021). The comprehensive impact of EM extends well beyond the initial spheres of automotive, energy, and infrastructure industries, permeating into various facets of the global economy and industrial landscape.

Within the automotive industry, the transition to EM is not just about replacing combustion engines with electric motors but also about reimagining the entire vehicle ecosystem. This transition involves a significant shift in the value chain. For instance, the battery, the most critical component of an EV, represents a new battleground for innovation and competition (Abduljabbar, 2021). The development of more efficient, cost-effective, and sustainable batteries is a key focus area, leading to substantial investments in research and development. This has given rise to a new sector within the automotive industry that is centered around battery technology, which includes the mining of raw materials, battery manufacturing, and recycling. It also opens up new partnerships and alliances between automotive companies and battery technology firms, reshaping the industry's competitive landscape.

The energy industry, faced with the increasing uptake of EVs, is tasked with meeting higher electricity demands as well as ensuring that the energy mix becomes greener. This requirement accelerates the shift from fossil fuel-based power generation to renewable sources. It is not just about generating more electricity but also about transforming the entire energy generation and distribution infrastructure into a cleaner and more efficient one (Bengler, 2014). This shift to EM has significant implications for the global energy market, influencing everything from the geopolitics of energy to investments in renewable energy projects and grid modernization efforts.

Infrastructure development for EM goes beyond just installing charging stations to involve creating a comprehensive ecosystem that supports the seamless operation of EVs. This includes the development of smart grid technology to efficiently manage the increased load from EVs, the integration of renewable energy sources into the grid, and the deployment of advanced metering and billing systems (Böckin, 2019). The construction industry, telecommunications sector, and urban planners all have a role in creating this ecosystem. For example, new real estate developments are increasingly incorporating EV charging infrastructure into their designs, and cities are integrating EV considerations into their transportation and urban development plans.

The implications of EM for the oil and gas industry are profound. As the demand for petroleum products decreases with the rise of EVs, this sector is forced to diversify its portfolio and find new revenue streams (Jackson, 2023). Some oil companies are transitioning into energy companies, investing in renewable energy, battery technology, and even EV charging infrastructure. This shift is not just a business necessity but also part of a broader corporate responsibility strategy to align with global sustainability goals.

The technology and telecommunications industries are also deeply impacted by the EM revolution. The growth of EVs has spurred advancements in areas like Internet of Things (IoT) connectivity, AI, and data analytics. These technologies are critical in enhancing the functionality and user experience of EVs, from improving battery management systems to enabling autonomous driving features (Buckley, 2004). The data generated by EVs present vast opportunities for analysis and monetization, providing valuable insights into consumer behavior, vehicle performance, and energy usage.

The labor market dynamics are shifting in response to the EM transition. There is a growing demand for new skills and expertise, ranging from battery chemistry and electrical engineering to software development and data science. This shift presents both challenges and opportunities for workforce development. Educational institutions and training programs must adapt to provide the relevant skills, while industries must invest in retraining and upskilling their existing workforce. This transition also presents opportunities for job creation in new sectors and technologies associated with EM.

Environmental regulations and policies continue to play a critical role in shaping the industrial impact of EM. Governments worldwide are not only incentivizing the adoption of EVs but also setting ambitious targets for reducing carbon emissions (Mohd Yusof, 2014). These policies are a driving force behind the industrial shift toward EM, encouraging innovation and investments in sustainable technologies.

Moreover, the impact of EM extends to global trade and supply chains. The demand for raw materials like lithium, cobalt, and nickel, which are essential for battery production, is reshaping global mining and trading patterns. This has implications for international relations and trade policies, as countries and companies seek to secure stable and sustainable supply chains for these critical materials.

In conclusion, the transition to EM is a transformative force impacting several industries. It is reshaping the automotive and energy sectors, driving infrastructure development, influencing technology and telecommunications, and altering the global supply chain and labor market. This transition is not just about adopting a new type of vehicle but also about rethinking and reinventing entire industries and economies in alignment with a sustainable and electrified future. As this transition continues to unfold, its far-reaching impacts will become increasingly evident, paving the way for a more sustainable, efficient, and interconnected world (Nikitas, 2021). The transition to EM is a catalyst for widespread industrial transformation. From the automotive and energy sectors to infrastructure and technology, the ripple effect of this shift is vast and dynamic. Industries are not only adapting to the new realities of EM but are also actively shaping its evolution through innovation and strategic investments. As the world moves toward a more sustainable and environmentally conscious future, the role of industries in enabling and supporting this transition becomes increasingly vital. The impact of EM on industries is a testament to the transformative power of technological advancements and their ability to redefine markets and economies.

3.3 Adoption and Implementation of Electric Mobility by Industries

The adoption and implementation of EM by industries is a complex and multifaceted process, reflecting a significant shift in the global industrial landscape. This transition, driven by a combination of technological innovation, environmental concerns, and changing consumer preferences, has profound implications for numerous sectors, including the automotive, energy, infrastructure, and technology sectors.

In the automotive industry, the adoption of EM signifies a substantial transformation in product development, manufacturing processes, and supply chain management. Car manufacturers are reorienting their strategies toward EVs not just by designing new models but also by reconfiguring factories, retraining workforce, and establishing new supply chains. Traditional automotive giants are investing heavily in developing electric models, while new players specializing in EVs are emerging and challenging the existing market dynamics (Rietmann & Lieven, 2019). This shift necessitates a move toward more agile and adaptable production methods, as well as the integration of advanced technologies such as AI and robotics into manufacturing processes.

The technology sector is intrinsically linked with the adoption of EM, as the functionality of EVs relies heavily on advanced technologies, including battery technology, power electronics, and software. The development of more efficient and affordable batteries is particularly crucial since it directly impacts the range and cost of EVs. Tech companies are also playing a leading role in developing and implementing EV-related technologies such as vehicle-to-grid (V2G) systems, autonomous driving features, and enhanced connectivity solutions.

The adoption of EM has significant implications for the labor market. As industries pivot toward EM, there is a growing demand for new skills and expertise, including engineering and technical skills specific to EVs, such as battery technology and electrical engineering, as well as skills in software development and data analytics (Rongen, 2022). The transition to EM also creates opportunities for workforce development and job creation in new sectors related to EV production, charging infrastructure, and renewable energy.

Environmental regulations and policies are key drivers in the adoption of EM. Governments worldwide are implementing various policies to encourage the uptake of EVs. These include direct incentives such as tax rebates and grants for EV purchases, as well as indirect measures like setting ambitious emissions reduction targets and low-emission zones in urban areas. These policies not only accelerate the shift to EM but also provide a framework within which industries can plan and invest in this transition.

The adoption of EM also has broader implications for corporate strategy and business models. Industries are exploring new business models that are aligned with the principles of EM. For the automotive sector, this might mean a shift toward service-oriented models such as mobility-as-a-service (MaaS), which could redefine the relationship between consumers and vehicles (Virshup, 2009). For energy providers, it might involve becoming service providers for EV charging, offering a range of services from installation to maintenance of charging infrastructure.

Moreover, the transition to EM requires a collaborative approach across industries. This includes partnerships between automotive companies and technology firms, collaborations between energy providers and infrastructure developers, and cross-sector initiatives to standardize charging technologies and protocols. Such collaborations are essential to address the complex challenges of EM adoption and harness the synergies between different sectors (Virshup, 2009). The ongoing evolution and expansion of EM across various industries are not just reshaping existing practices but also paving the way for entirely new paradigms and opportunities. This transition, while challenging, offers a fertile ground for innovation, collaboration, and sustainable growth.

For the automotive industry, the shift to EM is not just about replacing combustion engines with electric motors but also about reimagining mobility for the future. This involves exploring new vehicle designs that leverage the unique capabilities of electric powertrains, such as increased cabin space due to the absence of a large engine block and the potential for modular vehicle platforms (Castellanos & Heutel, 2024). Furthermore, automotive manufacturers are exploring ways to integrate advanced technologies like autonomous driving and

IoT connectivity, which are more seamlessly compatible with EVs, into their processes. These innovations not only enhance the user experience but also promise to improve road safety and traffic efficiency.

The energy sector's role in supporting EM is becoming increasingly complex and integral. Beyond simply increasing electricity production to meet the growing demand by EVs, energy companies are actively involved in developing smart grid technologies, which enable more efficient energy distribution and use, including the integration of variable renewable energy sources like solar and wind (Pucihar et al., 2017). Additionally, the concept of V2G technology, where EVs can feed energy back into the grid during peak demand periods, is gaining traction. This not only provides a potential revenue stream for EV owners but also helps in stabilizing the grid, especially as renewable energy sources become more prevalent.

Infrastructure development for EM extends to urban and regional planning. Cities and municipalities are increasingly recognizing the need to integrate EV-friendly infrastructure into their long-term planning. This includes installing public charging stations as well as considering EVs in road design, parking facilities, and zoning laws (Kamran et al., 2021). The adoption of EM also encourages the development of more pedestrian-friendly and green urban spaces, as the reduction in vehicle emissions contributes to cleaner air and less noise pollution.

Technology companies are at the forefront of driving innovations in EM. The development of more efficient and compact batteries is a major area of focus, as it directly affects the range and affordability of EVs. Advances in solid-state batteries, for instance, promise to offer higher energy density, faster charging times, and enhanced safety compared to the current lithium-ion batteries. Moreover, technology firms are developing sophisticated software and AI algorithms for battery management systems, which optimize battery life and performance.

Collaboration across industries is crucial for the successful adoption of EM. Automotive companies are partnering with energy firms, technology providers, and infrastructure developers to create comprehensive mobility solutions (Tlili et al., 2019). These collaborations are essential for developing standardized technologies and practices, such as universal charging connectors and communication protocols between EVs and charging infrastructure.

The adoption and implementation of EM by industries represent a significant industrial and societal shift. It is driving innovation across the automotive, energy, technology, and infrastructure sectors, creating new opportunities and business models (Tlili et al., 2019). This transition also has profound implications for the labor market, urban development, and environmental policies. As industries continue to navigate and shape this transformation, the potential benefits—ranging from reduced environmental impact to enhanced urban livability and economic growth—are immense. The journey toward a fully electric future is complex and challenging but also full of possibilities for a more sustainable and efficient world.

In conclusion, the adoption and implementation of EM by industries is a dynamic and evolving process, encompassing several sectors and requiring coordinated efforts across the industrial spectrum. It involves not just the introduction of new products and technologies but also a fundamental rethinking of business models, infrastructure, and workforce skills. As industries navigate this transition, they are shaping the future of transportation and energy, contributing to a more sustainable and efficient world (Gruber, 2019). The challenges are significant, but so are the opportunities, promising a transformative impact on the global economy and environment.

3.4 Business Models and Strategies Related to Electric Mobility

The transition to EM has initiated a profound transformation in business models and strategies across multiple industries. This shift is not merely about adopting a new technology but also about redefining the very core of how businesses operate, innovate, and compete (De Rubens et al., 2020). In the realm of EM, traditional business models are being challenged and new strategies are emerging, reflecting the unique opportunities and challenges posed by this dynamic sector.

In the automotive industry, the move toward EM has compelled manufacturers to rethink their business models. Traditional revenue streams based on the sale of combustion engine vehicles and aftermarket services are being supplemented, and in some cases replaced, by new models tailored to EVs. One emerging model is the subscription-based service for EVs, where consumers pay a recurring fee for the use of a vehicle, often including additional services like maintenance, insurance, and even charging (Krommes & Schmidt, 2017). This model aligns well with the increasing consumer preference for access over ownership, a trend particularly pronounced among younger demographics.

Another significant shift in the automotive sector is the focus on MaaS. Companies are exploring models where transportation is offered as a service through a combination of vehicles, public transport, and other modes of mobility, all accessible through a single digital platform. This approach is particularly relevant in urban areas, where congestion and environmental concerns are driving the shift away from personal vehicle ownership.

The adoption of EM is also leading to strategic partnerships and collaborations, both within and across industries. Automotive companies are forming alliances with technology firms, energy providers, and infrastructure developers to create comprehensive EM solutions (Secinaro et al., 2020). These collaborations enable companies to leverage each other's strengths, share risks, and accelerate innovation. For instance, collaborations between car manufacturers and battery technology firms are crucial for advancing battery performance and reducing costs.

The energy sector is also adapting its business models to cater to the new demands of EM. Energy providers are developing specialized tariffs and services for EV charging, including home charging solutions and public charging networks. Some are venturing into the realm of smart energy management, offering systems that integrate EV charging with home energy usage, optimizing cost and efficiency (Biresselioglu, 2018). The concept of V2G technology, where EVs can supply energy back to the grid, opens up new business models for energy companies and EV owners alike.

Infrastructure development for EM is spawning new business models around the deployment and operation of charging stations. Companies are exploring various models for charging infrastructure, including pay-per-use, subscription models, and free charging subsidized by retail or commercial entities. The development of fast-charging networks along highways and in urban centers is particularly lucrative, as it caters to the needs of EV drivers on longer trips (Böckin, 2019). The technology sector has a pivotal role in shaping the business models related to EM. Tech companies are not only developing software and hardware solutions for EVs and charging infrastructure but are also at the forefront of data-driven services. The vast amounts of data generated by EVs and charging networks offer opportunities for value-added services, such as predictive maintenance, personalized insurance models, and even location-based advertising.

Retail and e-commerce sectors are also impacted by the rise of EM. The increasing popularity of EVs is leading to new retail models, such as online sales platforms for vehicles and charging equipment. Additionally, integrating EV charging stations into retail locations offers a unique value proposition, attracting customers, and potentially increasing dwell time and spending (Bohn, 2021). The transition to EM necessitates a strategic focus on sustainability and corporate social responsibility. Companies across various sectors are integrating broader sustainability goals into their EM initiatives because they recognize that environmental responsibility is not only a market imperative but also a key differentiator in the eyes of consumers and investors.

Financial models related to EM are evolving as well. Traditional financing and leasing models are being adapted for EVs, considering their unique value retention and total cost of ownership profiles (Dou, 2019). Moreover, the growing interest in green finance has led to new funding opportunities for EM projects, including green bonds and sustainable investment funds.

The advancement of EM is not only revolutionizing the automotive sector but also creating ripple effects across various industries, leading to the emergence of innovative business models and strategies.

The adoption of EM is catalyzing advancements in battery technology, leading to new business models around battery lifecycle management. Companies are investing in battery refurbishing and recycling processes because they recognize the value of the materials recovered from used

EV batteries (Llopis-Albert, 2021). This circular economy approach is not only environmentally sustainable but also economically viable as the demand for critical battery materials like lithium and cobalt increases.

Corporate fleet management is another sector undergoing transformation due to EM. Companies, driven by the desire to reduce operational costs and align with corporate sustainability goals, are increasingly adopting EVs for their corporate fleets (Maggio, 2019). Fleet management companies are responding by offering specialized EV fleet services, including charging solutions, telematics for tracking and optimizing energy usage, and tailored financing options.

The technology sector, particularly companies specializing in software and connectivity, is leveraging the potential of EM to develop new value propositions. The connectivity of EVs allows for the collection of vast amounts of data, which can be analyzed for insights into driving patterns, vehicle performance, and customer preferences. These data are valuable for a range of applications, from enhancing vehicle design to developing targeted marketing strategies (Pichler, 2021). Financial institutions and investors are also playing a key role in shaping the EM landscape. EV and charging infrastructure projects are increasingly being supported by green financing initiatives and environmental, social, and governance investment funds. Financial products tailored to unique aspects of EM, such as green auto loans and EV-related investment portfolios, are emerging in response to growing consumer and investor interest in sustainable finance.

The business models and strategies related to EM are multifaceted and evolving rapidly, touching on diverse aspects of industry and commerce. From changes in automotive sales and services to innovations in public transportation, energy, and technology, EM is driving significant transformations (Requia, 2018). These new business models and strategies are not only adapting to the unique characteristics and challenges of EVs but are also aligned with broader environmental and sustainability goals. As the adoption of EM continues to increase, these innovative business approaches will play a vital role in shaping a more sustainable and efficient future for mobility.

In conclusion, the business models and strategies related to EM are diverse and evolving. From subscription services and MaaS in the automotive industry to innovative energy services and data-driven business models in the tech sector, companies are exploring new ways to capitalize on the opportunities presented by EM (Rietmann, 2019). These models reflect a broader shift toward sustainability, collaboration, and customer-centricity, signaling a transformative period in the global business landscape. As the adoption of EM continues to increase, these business models and strategies will play a crucial role in shaping the future of transportation, energy, and the broader economy.

3.5 How Industries Communicate Electric Mobility (Online/Offline) to the Market

The communication of EM to the market by various industries is a multifaceted endeavor, encompassing various strategies, both online and offline. Since EM does not just represent a product but a significant shift in lifestyle and environmental consciousness, the messaging and communication channels used are as diverse as they are innovative (Sovacool, 2021). Online communication strategies have become central to EM marketing, with industries utilizing digital platforms to reach a broad audience with tailored messages. Social media platforms, such as Twitter, Facebook, Instagram, and LinkedIn, are used extensively to engage with both existing and potential customers. These platforms offer a dynamic space for sharing updates, educational content, and interactive materials. For example, automakers often use social media to showcase new EV models, share customer testimonials, and post multimedia content that highlights the features and benefits of their EVs. Social media campaigns are also used to drive awareness about environmental issues and the role of EM in addressing these challenges.

Websites and digital showrooms have become pivotal in the EM market, as they offer extensive information on EV models, including detailed specifications, pricing, comparisons with traditional vehicles, and environmental benefits. Interactive elements like virtual tours, three-dimensional models, and customization tools enhance user engagement

(Castellanos & Heutel, 2024). These digital platforms are also used to educate consumers about EV charging infrastructure, range, battery life, and maintenance, addressing common concerns and misconceptions about EM.

Email marketing is another tool being used effectively by industries to communicate with consumers about EM. Regular newsletters, promotional offers, and updates about new launches keep the audience informed and engaged. For instance, a company might send out a monthly newsletter highlighting the latest advancements in battery technology or the expansion of charging networks, keeping the brand and its products top-of-mind for consumers (De Rubens et al., 2020). Content marketing, through blogs and articles, is employed to educate and inform the public about EM. These pieces often cover topics like the benefits of EVs, comparisons with traditional vehicles, advancements in technology, and industry trends. By providing valuable and informative content, companies establish themselves as thought leaders in the EM space.

Video marketing, especially on platforms like YouTube, is a powerful medium for communicating the nuances of EM. Industries use videos for product launches, tutorials, customer testimonials, and behind-the-scenes looks at EV manufacturing. For example, a car manufacturer might release a video series documenting the development of its latest EV model, offering insights into the design and engineering process and thus creating a narrative that resonates with the audience.

Offline communication strategies also play a crucial role in the promotion of EM. Traditional advertising methods such as TV commercials, print ads, and billboards are used to reach a wider audience. These ads often focus on the environmental benefits of EVs, cost savings in terms of fuel and maintenance, and government incentives for EV buyers. By leveraging the mass appeal of traditional media, industries can effectively communicate the advantages of EM to a broader demographic (Gruber, 2019). From the exploration of how industries communicate EM to the market, it is evident that the strategies employed are as innovative as the technology itself, encompassing a blend of storytelling, education, and engagement to promote this transformative shift.

Regarding storytelling, many companies leverage narratives that highlight the journey from traditional gasoline-powered vehicles to electric ones. These stories often focus on the evolution of technology, the environmental impact, and the future of transportation. By crafting compelling narratives, companies are able to connect with their audience on an emotional level, fostering a deeper understanding and appreciation for EM. For example, an automaker might release a documentary-style video that follows the development of its first EV, showcasing the challenges and triumphs of this journey and thereby creating a more personal and relatable brand image.

Trade shows and professional conferences are additional platforms through which EM is prominently communicated to both industry stakeholders and the general public. These events provide an opportunity for companies to showcase their latest products, technologies, and innovations in EM. They also serve as a forum for discussions, presentations, and networking, facilitating the exchange of ideas and fostering collaborations across different sectors (Jackson, 2023). In addition to these strategies, industries are leveraging the power of influencers and brand ambassadors to communicate the message of EM. Influencers, with their substantial following on social media and other platforms, play a pivotal role in shaping public opinion and trends. By partnering with influencers who are passionate about sustainability and technology, companies can tap into new audiences and communicate their message in a relatable and authentic manner.

Offline, the role of experiential marketing is significant in communicating EM. Test drive events, pop-up stores, and interactive exhibits allow consumers to experience EVs firsthand. For example, a company might set up a temporary exhibit in a high-traffic urban area where people can explore different EV models, learn about the technology, and even take a test drive. Such experiences can be instrumental in changing the public's perception of EV and encouraging adoption (Kamran et al., 2021). Customer testimonials and case studies are also powerful tools of communication. Sharing stories of real people who have switched to EVs and the benefits they have experienced can be a persuasive method of communication. These testimonials can be featured in various formats, including video interviews, written articles, and social media posts, providing a human touch to the technology.

Print media, though traditional, still holds a significant place in the communication strategy for EM. Magazines, newspapers, and brochures are used to reach a segment of the public that prefers tangible, in-depth information. For instance, a special feature in a leading automotive magazine discussing the advancements in EV technology and the future of EM can attract a niche audience of automobile enthusiasts and industry professionals (Krommes & Schmidt, 2017). Communicating EM to the market is a dynamic and multidimensional endeavor, and industries employ a combination of online and offline strategies, from digital marketing and social media engagement to experiential marketing and community involvement, to convey the message of EM. These strategies are designed to not only inform and educate but also inspire and engage consumers, fostering a deeper understanding of and appreciation for EM. As the technology and market for EM continue to evolve, so too will the methods and approaches used for its communication, reflecting the ongoing journey toward a more sustainable and electrified future.

In conclusion, the communication of EM to the market involves a blend of online and offline strategies, each playing a crucial role in educating, engaging, and persuading the audience. From digital campaigns and social media engagement to traditional advertising and public events, industries employ diverse tactics to convey the benefits of EM and drive its adoption. These communication strategies are not just about selling a product but also about advocating for a shift toward a more sustainable and environmentally conscious mode of transportation. As EM continues to evolve, so too will the ways in which it is communicated to the market, reflecting the dynamic nature of this burgeoning industry.

3.6 Implications of Electric Mobility for Traditional Manufacturers and the Oil Industry

The rise of EM presents significant implications for traditional manufacturers and the oil industry, heralding a transformative era marked by challenges, opportunities, and a pressing need for adaptation (Pucihar et al., 2017). This shift toward EVs is not merely a change in consumer preference but a global movement driven by technological advancements, environmental concerns, and policy shifts.

For traditional automobile manufacturers, the advent of EM represents both a challenge and an opportunity. The challenge lies in the fundamental differences between the manufacturing processes of EVs and traditional ICE vehicles. EVs have simpler drivetrains but are more complex in terms of their electrical systems and battery technologies (Secinaro et al., 2020). This necessitates a retooling of manufacturing plants, a significant investment in new technologies, and a reconfiguration of supply chains. Traditional manufacturers need to develop or acquire expertise in areas such as battery chemistry, electrical engineering, and advanced software, areas that were not central to ICE vehicle production (Tlili et al., 2019). The transition to EV production also requires substantial capital investment. Manufacturers need to invest in new machinery, retrain their workforce, and establish partnerships with battery suppliers and other new entrants in the EV supply chain. This shift can be particularly challenging for smaller manufacturers and those in regions where the push for EM is less pronounced.

However, this transition also presents opportunities for traditional manufacturers. It opens the door to new markets and customer segments and allows these manufacturers to position themselves as leaders in the emerging field of sustainable transportation (Kraus et al., 2021). Some traditional automakers are leveraging their extensive experience in vehicle design and mass production to gain a competitive edge in the EV market. Others are exploring new business models, such as mobility services and energy storage solutions, utilizing the capabilities of EVs.

The implications of the transition to EM for the oil industry are profound since the shift toward EM represents a direct threat to the demand for petroleum products, which has been the cornerstone of the oil industry for over a century. As EV adoption grows, the demand for gasoline and diesel is expected to decline, potentially leading to overcapacity in the oil industry and a decrease in oil prices. This poses a significant challenge for oil companies, particularly those heavily invested in oil exploration and production.

In response to this threat, some oil companies have begun diversifying their portfolios to reduce their reliance on traditional petroleum products. This includes investing in renewable energy sources, such as wind and solar, and exploring new business ventures in the EM ecosystem, such as EV charging infrastructure (Alper & Orhan, 2017). By diversifying, these companies aim to mitigate the risk posed by the declining demand for oil and position themselves in the growing market for clean energy solutions.

The transition to EM also has broader implications for the global energy market. It is likely to affect geopolitical dynamics since countries that are heavily reliant on oil exports may see a decrease in their economic and political influence while countries with abundant renewable energy resources or strong EV manufacturing capabilities could see an increase in their global standing.

Furthermore, the rise of EVs is prompting a reevaluation of energy strategies and policies at both national and international levels, with governments increasingly recognizing the need to invest in renewable energy infrastructure and grid modernization to support the growing number of EVs. This shift toward cleaner energy sources is seen as critical for supporting EM as well as for achieving broader environmental and sustainability goals (Borras Jr et al., 2016). The implications for employment in both the automotive and oil industries are also significant. The transition to EV manufacturing may lead to job losses in traditional automobile production and the oil industry, particularly in roles specific to ICE vehicles and oil extraction. However, it could also create new job opportunities in the EV production, battery manufacturing, and renewable energy sectors. The nature of these jobs is likely to be more technologically oriented, requiring new skills and training.

In conclusion, the rise of EM has significant implications for both traditional manufacturers and the oil industry. For automakers, the transition to EVs presents a mix of challenges and opportunities, requiring substantial investments, new partnerships, and a rethinking of business models (Tekic & Koroteev, 2019). For the oil industry, the shift to EM poses a threat to traditional revenue streams, necessitating diversification and adaptation. Across both sectors, this transition is influencing global economic and geopolitical dynamics, energy policies, and labor markets. As the adoption of EM continues to increase, the ability of these industries to adapt and evolve will be critical to their future success and resilience.

3.7 Revolutionary Supply Chains in the Automotive Industry and Urban Logistics

The automotive industry is witnessing a paradigm shift in supply chain management, driven by the integration of EM (MacCarthy, 2016). Traditional supply chains are being reimagined to accommodate the rapid evolution of consumer demands and technological advancements. This transformation is particularly evident in urban logistics, where the need for efficiency, sustainability, and speed is paramount.

Revolutionary supply chains leverage EM to create responsive and adaptable networks which utilize data analytics and IoT devices to predict demand and optimize routes, reducing lead times and emissions (Mangan, 2016). EVs play a crucial role by offering cleaner transportation options that align with urban sustainability goals.

Automakers are adopting just-in-time delivery models to minimize inventory and reduce waste, and this approach is facilitated by EVs' ability to navigate urban environments more efficiently. Their reduced noise and pollution levels make them ideal for city logistics, allowing for off-peak deliveries without disrupting urban life.

The impact of these innovative supply chains is profound, as they contribute to decongesting cities, lowering transportation costs, and reducing the carbon footprint of the automotive industry. This is not just a theoretical proposition; case studies from leading automotive companies have showcased the tangible benefits (Zijm, 2016). For example, some companies have observed a significant decrease in delivery times and an improvement in supply chain visibility.

In the near future, the convergence of AI, machine learning, and EM will further revolutionize the automotive supply chain. Anticipatory shipping, powered by predictive analytics, will enable suppliers to dispatch goods even before an order is placed, based on consumer behavior patterns. This will be particularly transformative for urban logistics, where the fast-paced environment demands such preemptive measures (El Yadari, 2022). As the EV market grows, its synergy with a smarter supply chain will result in a more resilient and environmentally conscious automotive industry. This future-facing approach promises a leap in operational efficiency and customer satisfaction, heralding a new era for supply chain logistics.

Looking ahead, the potential for growth in this area is immense. As battery technology advances and charging infrastructure expands, the role of EVs in supply chains will only become more integral. There is a clear trajectory toward a more interconnected and electrically powered supply chain ecosystem, which promises to redefine urban logistics and set new standards for the automotive industry.

4

Consumer Perspective

Abstract This chapter delves into the consumer perspective on electric mobility, exploring and describing the key motivators and barriers affecting the adoption of electric vehicles (EVs). It analyzes consumer perceptions and experiences with EVs, shedding light on practical strategies currently used by EV manufacturers to meet market needs. Furthermore, it proposes solutions to overcome the existing barriers to consumer adoption, aiming to facilitate a smoother transition to electric mobility. The chapter then offers a specific focus on the next generation of consumers (e.g., Generation Z) exploring and discussing their unique attitudes and potential influence on the market. By examining these diverse facets, the chapter provides a thorough understanding of consumer behavior and the factors that drive or hinder the widespread acceptance of electric vehicles.

Keywords consumer adoption · consumer experience · functional-emotional-experiential aspects · market needs · EV manufacturers strategies · motivators · barriers · next-generation consumers · Generation Z

D. D'Acunto, *The Future of E-Mobility*,
https://doi.org/10.1007/978-3-031-65053-6_4

4.1 Motivators and Barriers to the Adoption of Electric Mobility by Consumers

According to Biresselioglu et al. (2018), understanding the consumer perspective on electric mobility (EM) is crucial in addressing the challenges and harnessing the opportunities it presents. The motivators and barriers to the adoption of EM by consumers encompass a range of factors from environmental concerns to practical considerations. One of the primary motivators for adopting EM is environmental consciousness. With the increasing awareness of climate change and its impacts, many consumers are turning to electric vehicles (EVs) as a way to reduce their carbon footprint. The zero tailpipe emissions of EVs appeal to those seeking to make a positive environmental impact. This is particularly pronounced in regions where there is a strong societal focus on sustainability and green living.

Another significant motivating factor is the economic benefits of EM. Consumers are becoming increasingly aware of the long-term cost savings associated with EV use. Although the upfront cost of an EV can be higher than that of a conventional vehicle, the lower operating costs, including reduced fuel and maintenance expenses, are appealing. Additionally, many governments are offering incentives, such as tax rebates, reduced registration fees, and other financial benefits, to EV buyers making EVs more economically attractive (Stockkamp et al., 2021). Technological fascination and the allure of new innovations also drive consumer interest in EVs. The integration of advanced technologies like regenerative braking, sophisticated battery systems, and autonomous driving features positions EVs as the vehicles of the future. Tech-savvy consumers are drawn to these innovations, viewing EVs than just as cars but as integrated mobility solutions with cutting-edge technology.

Despite these motivations, there are significant barriers to EM adoption among consumers. Range anxiety, i.e., the fear of running out of battery power before reaching a destination or charging point, remains one of the biggest concerns for consumers (Axsen, 2019). While battery technology has advanced significantly and now provides longer ranges than ever before, range anxiety persists, particularly in areas with inadequate charging infrastructure. The availability and convenience of charging infrastructure are another major barrier to EV adoption (Abbasi et al., 2021). Consumers accustomed to the widespread availability of gas stations may find the current level of EV charging infrastructure insufficient or inconvenient. This is particularly true for people living in apartments or urban areas without dedicated parking spaces. The perceived inconvenience of having to plan travel around charging stops and the time taken to charge an EV compared to simply refueling a gasoline vehicle can deter potential EV buyers.

The initial cost of EVs is also a significant hurdle. Despite the long-term savings, the higher upfront cost of EVs compared to internal combustion engine (ICE) vehicles can be prohibitive for many consumers. Additionally, there are concerns about the resale value of EVs, given the rapid pace of technological advancements in this field (Tarei et al., 2021). Consumer concerns about the longevity and replacement costs of EV batteries also play a role in their decision-making process regarding EVs. Batteries are a crucial and expensive component of EVs, and the potential need for replacement, along with concerns about battery performance degradation over time, can be deterrents to EV adoption.

The lack of variety and choice in the EV market has also been a barrier. Until recently, consumers had limited options when it came to choosing an EV, with most models being either small or medium-sized cars. However, this is rapidly changing with more manufacturers entering the market and offering a wider range of EVs, including SUVs and trucks. Misconceptions and lack of information about EVs further complicate the consumers' decision-making process (Adnan et al., 2017). Many potential buyers are not fully informed about the capabilities, maintenance, and operation of EVs, and this lack of information has led to uncertainty and reluctance to make the switch from a well-understood ICE vehicle to an EV.

The consumer decision-making process regarding EM is influenced by a complex interplay of motivators (Fig. 4.1) and barriers, each playing a critical role in shaping the future of transportation. Environmental concerns continue to be a major driving force behind the adoption of EM. Consumers are becoming increasingly aware of the urgent need to reduce carbon emissions and combat climate change; this environmental consciousness is particularly higher among younger generations, who are more likely to prioritize sustainability in their purchasing decisions. EVs, with their promise of reduced emissions and cleaner technology, resonate with these values, making them an attractive choice for environmentally minded individuals.

Economic considerations also play a significant role in consumer decisions. While the initial purchase price of EVs can be higher than that of their ICE counterparts, the total cost of ownership over time can be lower due to savings on fuel and maintenance. Electricity, per mile, is typically cheaper than gasoline, and EVs have fewer moving parts, reducing the likelihood of costly repairs. Governments and local authorities worldwide offer various incentives, such as tax credits, reduced registration fees, and exemptions from certain tolls and congestion charges, to make EVs more affordable. These incentives significantly lower the financial barrier to EV adoption (Vassileva & Campillo, 2017). The advancement in EV technology is a strong motivator as well. Modern EVs come equipped with cutting-edge features such as advanced driver assistance systems (ADAS), connectivity, and infotainment systems that are often superior to those in ICE vehicles. The rapid acceleration and smooth, quiet nature of EVs also appeal to consumers, offering a different and often more enjoyable driving experience.

However, significant barriers still impede the widespread adoption of EVs. For instance, range anxiety remains a primary concern. Despite the improvements in battery technology that have increased the range of EVs, the fear of running out of charge is still a deterrent for many potential buyers. This fear is compounded in regions where charging infrastructure is sparse or underdeveloped (Corradi et al., 2023). The availability and accessibility of charging infrastructure are critical factors in the adoption of EVs. Consumers living in urban areas without private garages or designated parking spaces find charging their vehicles challenging. The current public charging infrastructure, though improving, does not yet match the convenience of refueling ICE vehicles. Furthermore, the time required to charge an EV, even with fast chargers, is considerably longer than the time required to refuel a gasoline car, which can be inconvenient for users.

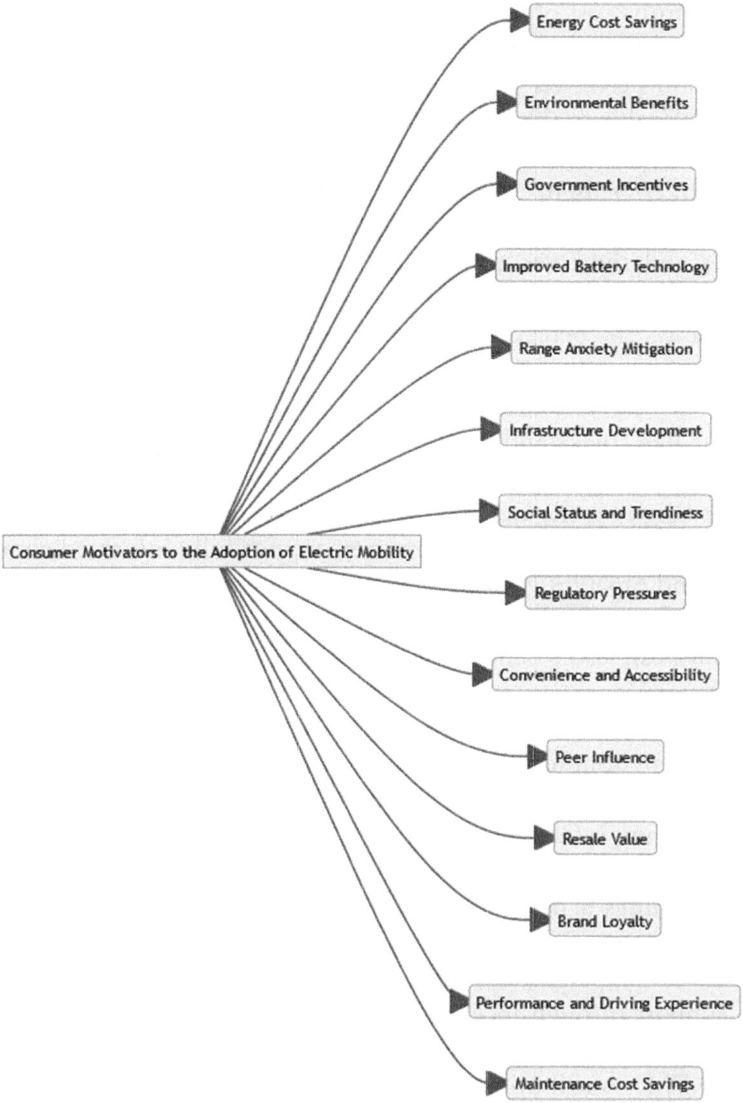

Fig. 4.1 Factors acting as consumer motivators toward the adoption of EM (personal elaboration)

The upfront cost of EVs, despite long-term savings, continues to be a barrier for many consumers, and although prices have been decreasing, EVs are still perceived as premium products. Concerns about the resale value of EVs due to the fast-paced nature of technological advancements and potential battery degradation also factor into consumer hesitancy (Haustein & Jensen, 2018). Battery life and replacement costs are other significant concerns. Consumers worry about the longevity of EV batteries and the costs associated with replacing them. While battery technology has advanced, leading to longer life spans and more robust performance, the perception of risk persists.

The variety and availability of EV models have been improving, but options are still limited compared to ICE vehicles, especially in certain segments like trucks and large SUVs. Therefore, consumers looking for specific types of vehicles may find their choices limited in the EV market. Another barrier is the lack of consumer awareness and understanding of EVs (Li et al., 2017). Many consumers are not fully informed about the benefits and capabilities of EVs. Misconceptions about EV performance, maintenance, and suitability for different lifestyles persist. This lack of knowledge can lead to uncertainty and reluctance to transition from ICE vehicles to EVs.

While there are compelling motivations for consumers to adopt EM, including environmental benefits, economic incentives, and advanced technology, significant barriers remain. These include concerns about range, charging infrastructure, upfront costs, battery life, vehicle variety, and general knowledge about EVs (Sovacool, 2017). Overcoming these barriers requires a multifaceted approach involving continued technological advancements, expanded and improved charging infrastructure, educational campaigns to inform potential buyers, and sustained government support through incentives and policies. As these efforts progress, it is likely that more consumers will overcome their hesitations and embrace EM, contributing to a more sustainable and eco-friendly transportation landscape.

The consumer landscape for EM is continually evolving, with increasing awareness and acceptance; however, it still faces hurdles that must be addressed to boost widespread adoption. One area that requires attention is consumer education and awareness. Many potential EV buyers lack accurate information about the capabilities and maintenance requirements of EVs (Zhang et al., 2018). Myths around EVs, such as their inability to perform well in extreme weather conditions and the notion that they are only suitable for short distances, persist. Educational initiatives by manufacturers, governments, and environmental organizations can play a pivotal role in dispelling these myths and providing factual information. For example, showcasing EVs in various real-world scenarios through test drives, experience centers, and interactive digital platforms can help demystify EV technology for the average consumer.

The development of a robust and user-friendly charging infrastructure is another critical area that needs addressing. Public charging stations need to be more widespread, faster, and easier to use. Innovations in charging technology, such as wireless charging pads and solar-powered charging stations, can significantly enhance the user experience (Priessner et al., 2018). The integration of charging infrastructure into existing networks, such as in shopping centers, office buildings, and public parking areas, can also help mitigate range anxiety and make the use of EVs more convenient.

Finally, the role of governments and policymakers is crucial in facilitating the shift to EM. Beyond financial incentives, governments can implement policies that create a more conducive environment for EVs. This might include mandating the installation of charging points in all new residential and commercial developments, setting stricter emissions standards for vehicles, and investing in renewable energy to ensure that the electricity used to power EVs is environmentally friendly. While consumer interest in EM is growing, driven by environmental concerns, economic benefits, and advancements in technology, challenges such as range anxiety, charging infrastructure, upfront costs, battery life concerns, and a lack of awareness still act as barriers (Higueras-Castillo et al., 2019). Addressing these challenges through education, infrastructure development, and supportive policies is essential for the widespread adoption of EM. As these barriers are progressively overcome, the path toward a sustainable, electrified transportation future becomes increasingly attainable.

In conclusion, while there are strong motivators driving consumer interest in EM, including environmental concerns, economic benefits, and technological allure, significant barriers remain, including range anxiety, charging infrastructure limitations, high initial costs, concerns about battery life, limited vehicle choices, and general misconceptions. Addressing these barriers requires concerted efforts by manufacturers, policymakers, and other stakeholders to provide adequate infrastructure, clear and accurate information, and economic incentives to make EVs a more viable and attractive option for a broader range of consumers. As these barriers are progressively overcome, the adoption of EM is likely to accelerate, contributing to a greener, more sustainable future.

4.2 Consumer Perceptions of Electric Vehicles

Understanding consumer perceptions of EVs is pivotal in assessing the potential growth of EM. These perceptions vary significantly across different regions and cultures, influenced by factors such as technological development, environmental consciousness, and government policies. A primary issue among potential EV consumers globally is range anxiety (Ghasri et al., 2019). This term describes the fear that an EV does not have sufficient battery range to reach a destination, leaving the driver stranded without a charging station. Although significant advancements in battery technology have considerably extended the driving ranges of new EV models, range anxiety remains a significant barrier to adoption (Kester et al., 2019). This anxiety is more pronounced in regions where long-distance driving is common or where charging infrastructure is not yet fully developed. For example, in the United States, where long road trips are a part of national culture, range anxiety is a notable concern. Conversely, in European countries like Norway, which leads the world in EV adoption, a robust network of charging stations and shorter average travel distances have helped alleviate this anxiety.

The availability and accessibility of charging infrastructure are other critical factors shaping consumer perceptions of EVs. In countries with well-developed EV charging networks, such as China and several European nations, the adoption of EVs has been rapid. Governments in these regions have invested heavily in charging infrastructure, making it more convenient for consumers to charge their EVs and thereby reducing the perceived inconvenience compared to traditional refueling (Sovacool et al., 2019). In contrast, concerns about the feasibility of owning an EV are more prominent in countries where such infrastructure is lacking or is in the early stages of development.

Cultural and economic factors also play a crucial role in shaping perceptions. In some countries, owning an EV is viewed as a status symbol, representing environmental consciousness and technological sophistication. In others, EVs are viewed more pragmatically, as vehicles that offer cost savings over time due to lower fuel and maintenance costs. These cost savings are particularly appealing in regions where fuel prices are high. However, the higher initial purchase price of EVs compared to ICE vehicles remains a barrier in many countries, especially developing economies, where the price sensitivity is higher (Sovacool et al., 2019). Consumer perceptions also vary depending on the availability of a diverse range of EV models. In markets where consumers have a wide selection of EVs across different vehicle segments, the adoption tends to be higher. For instance, the availability of electric SUVs and trucks in the United States is changing the perception that EVs are only small city cars. Similarly, in European markets, the introduction of luxury and high-performance EVs has attracted a demographic that traditionally purchased premium ICE vehicles.

The perception of EVs in terms of performance and convenience has been evolving positively. With technological advancements, modern EVs offer high performance, quick acceleration, and a smooth driving experience, which are becoming well-known and appreciated features (Brase, 2019). However, concerns about the longevity and performance of EV batteries over time continue to influence consumer decisions. Potential buyers often question the durability of batteries and the costs associated with replacing them. Environmental awareness and concerns about climate change significantly influence consumer perceptions of EVs. In regions where there is a strong emphasis on environmental conservation, EVs are more widely accepted and promoted (De Rubens, 2020). Consumers in these regions are more willing to overcome barriers such as range anxiety and the lack of charging infrastructure, motivated by the desire to reduce their carbon footprint.

Government policies and incentives also shape consumer perceptions and adoption of EVs. In countries with strong government support in the form of tax incentives, subsidies, and well-defined long-term policies favoring EM, consumers' perception of EV is generally more positive (Higueras-Castillo et al., 2020). For example, the Norwegian government's comprehensive incentives for EVs, including tax exemptions, free parking, and use of bus lanes, have resulted in Norway having the highest per capita number of all-electric cars in the world.

In contrast, in countries where such policies are non-existent or in their infancy, skepticism about EVs remains. Lack of awareness and understanding of EV technology contributes to this skepticism, with many consumers still not fully aware of the benefits and capabilities of EVs and often relying on outdated information and misconceptions. This lack of knowledge is a significant barrier that needs to be addressed through educational campaigns and hands-on experiences (Maghfiroh et al., 2021). Further, the diverse perceptions of EVs are shaped by cross-cultural differences and regional specificities, which influence consumer attitudes and behaviors toward EM. In countries like Japan and South Korea, known for their technological advancement, EVs are viewed as symbols of innovation and progress. These countries have a strong automotive industry that is actively involved in the development and promotion of EVs, which enhances consumer trust and interest. However, in these regions, the compact urban landscape and well-developed public transportation systems may impact the perceived necessity of owning any personal vehicle, including EVs.

In contrast, in countries with vast geographies like Australia and Canada, the concerns about range and the availability of charging infrastructure are more acute. In these countries, the perception of EVs is heavily influenced by their practicality for long-distance travel and the adequacy of charging networks along major travel routes (Abbasi, 2021). The perception of EVs in developing countries presents a different set of challenges and opportunities. In many of these regions, the lack of charging infrastructure and higher upfront costs of EVs are significant barriers; however, the potential long-term cost savings and reduced environmental impact are strong motivators. In countries like India and Brazil, there is a growing interest in EVs, particularly in urban areas where pollution and fuel costs are major concerns. However, the adoption is still in its nascent stages, largely due to economic constraints and infrastructure challenges. Cultural factors also play a role in shaping perceptions. In some cultures, there is a strong attachment to traditional ICE vehicles, either due to the heritage of automobile manufacturing or the perceived status associated with certain vehicle brands and types (Adnan, 2017). Transitioning to EVs in such cultures requires not only addressing practical concerns but also shifting deep-seated attitudes and preferences.

The role of policy and government incentives in shaping consumer perceptions cannot be overstated. In regions with aggressive environmental policies and substantial incentives for EV buyers, the adoption of EVs is significantly higher. These policies not only make EVs more financially accessible but also signal a commitment to sustainable practices, influencing public perception positively (Biresselioglu, 2018). For example, in European countries with strict emissions standards and substantial subsidies for EVs, there is a higher acceptance and interest in EM. However, in countries where fossil fuels are a significant part of the economy, there may be less governmental incentive to promote EVs. In such regions, the transition to EM may be slower, influenced mainly by economic interests and existing infrastructure heavily invested in supporting ICE vehicles.

The influence of social norms and peers also plays a crucial role in shaping consumer perceptions. In societies where there is a strong focus on sustainability and environmental responsibility, there is often a collective movement toward adopting greener practices, including EM. The sighting of EVs on roads, experiences shared by early adopters, and community initiatives can significantly influence consumer attitudes and accelerate the adoption of EVs (Corradi, 2023). The perception of EVs as a solution to urban pollution is another factor driving their adoption in many cities worldwide. In urban centers grappling with air quality issues, EVs are increasingly seen as a necessary step toward cleaner air. This is particularly relevant in densely populated cities in China and India, where pollution has become a major public health concern. The impact of global events and trends also shapes public perceptions of EVs. For instance, the increasing frequency of extreme weather events attributable to climate change has heightened awareness of environmental issues (Haustein, 2018), leading to a greater interest in sustainable practices, including EM, particularly among younger generations who are more environmentally conscious.

The perception of EVs is a complex interplay of technological, economic, cultural, and environmental factors that vary significantly across different regions and cultures. While range anxiety and charging infrastructure remain universal concerns, the extent to which they impact consumer decisions varies widely (Li, 2017). Economic considerations, cultural attitudes, government policies, and environmental awareness all play critical roles in shaping consumer perceptions of EVs. As the global landscape evolves with advancements in technology, expansion of infrastructure, and shifting cultural norms, the perceptions of EVs are likely to continue evolving, paving the way for increased adoption and integration of EM into everyday life.

In conclusion, consumer perceptions of EVs are influenced by a complex array of factors including range anxiety, charging infrastructure, cultural attitudes, economic considerations, vehicle choice and variety, performance and convenience, environmental awareness, and government policies (Sovacool, 2017). These perceptions vary widely across different countries and cultures, reflecting the diverse challenges and opportunities embedded in the global adoption of EM. Addressing these perceptions through improved technology, infrastructure development, educational initiatives, and supportive policies is crucial for enhancing the appeal of EVs and accelerating their adoption worldwide. As these efforts continue, it is likely that the positive aspects of EVs will become more widely recognized and accepted, leading to a significant shift in consumer attitudes and behaviors toward EM.

4.3 Consumer Experiences with Electric Vehicles

The consumer experience with EVs is pivotal in understanding their growing popularity and the challenges that still need to be addressed for wider adoption. This experience varies significantly across different regions and cultures, influenced by several factors, ranging from economic to technological and environmental (Stockkamp, 2021). One of the most talked-about aspects of the EV experience is the cost savings. Consumers who switch to EVs often report significant reductions in running costs, as EVs require less maintenance than ICE vehicles since they have fewer moving parts and do not need oil changes.

The cost of charging an EV is also typically lower than the cost of gasoline and diesel, resulting in considerable savings of money that would have been used for fuel. For example, studies in the United States have shown that EV owners can save thousands of dollars over the life of the vehicle compared to gasoline vehicles. However, these cost savings vary significantly by country, depending on the local cost of electricity and gasoline, as well as government incentives (Tarei, 2021). In countries like Norway and Denmark, where gasoline prices are high, the cost savings are even more pronounced. In contrast, in countries with lower gasoline prices and higher electricity costs, the economic advantage may be less evident.

The driving experience of EVs is another area that has garnered positive feedback from consumers. EVs are often praised for their quick acceleration and smooth, quiet ride. The instant torque provided by electric motors offers a different and more responsive driving experience compared to traditional ICE vehicles. Many consumers enjoy the quietness of EVs, which contributes to a more relaxed driving experience, particularly in urban settings (Vassileva, 2017). This aspect of the EV experience is relatively consistent across different cultures and countries, as it is a fundamental characteristic of electric propulsion.

However, the experience of charging an EV can vary widely and is a crucial factor in consumer satisfaction. In regions with well-developed charging infrastructure, such as many parts of Europe and China and specific areas in the United States, consumers find charging to be relatively convenient (Higueras-Castillo et al., 2020). The availability of fast-charging stations along highways and in public areas has significantly improved the experience, making long-distance travel more feasible. Conversely, in regions where the charging infrastructure is still developing, consumers often express frustration about the availability and speed of charging stations. This issue is particularly acute in rural areas and for consumers who do not have access to home charging.

The environmental impact of driving an EV is a significant part of the consumer experience, especially for those motivated by a desire to reduce their carbon footprint. In countries where the electricity grid is primarily powered by renewable sources, such as Iceland and Norway, the environmental benefits of driving an EV are substantial. However, in regions where the electricity grid is still heavily reliant on fossil fuels, the environmental advantage of EVs is less pronounced. This variation can influence consumer satisfaction and the perceived environmental benefits of owning an EV (Maghfiroh et al., 2021). Another aspect of the EV experience is the variety and availability of vehicle models. In markets like Europe and the United States, consumers have a wide range of EVs to choose from, including sedans, SUVs, and even luxury models. This variety allows consumers to find an EV that fits their lifestyle and needs. In contrast, in markets where the EV options are limited, consumers may feel constrained in their choices, impacting their overall satisfaction.

The impact of government policies on the EV experience cannot be overstated. In countries with strong support for EM, such as subsidies, tax breaks, and investments in charging infrastructure, consumers report a more positive experience. These policies not only make EVs more affordable but also signal a commitment to supporting EM, which can influence consumer attitudes and satisfaction. The resale value of EVs is an emerging concern for consumers (Varghese et al., 2021). Since the technology evolves rapidly, there is a perception that EVs may become outdated faster than ICE vehicles, potentially affecting their resale value. This concern varies by region and is influenced by factors such as the pace of technological advancement and availability of new models.

Cultural factors also play a role in shaping the EV experience. In some cultures, there is a strong tradition of car ownership and a deep-seated preference for certain types of vehicles, such as large SUVs and luxury cars. As the EV market expands to include more of these vehicle types, consumers in these cultures may find the transition to EVs more appealing (She et al., 2017). The experience of incentives and subsidies in different regions also varies significantly. In countries with generous incentives, consumers often report a high level of satisfaction with their decision to purchase an EV. However, in countries where such incentives are minimal or non-existent, the high upfront cost of EVs can be a deterrent, overshadowing the long-term savings and environmental benefits.

In regions where governments have prioritized the development of EV infrastructure, the experience is generally more positive. For instance, in China, which boasts the largest number of EV charging stations in the world, consumers enjoy a relatively hassle-free experience. This robust infrastructure has significantly contributed to China's position as one of the largest EV markets globally. Conversely, in countries where such development is lagging, the lack of sufficient charging options becomes a major inconvenience, dampening enthusiasm for EVs (Zhang et al., 2018). The experience of owning an EV is also shaped by cultural and societal factors. In countries with a strong automotive heritage, like Germany and Italy, there is often a deep-seated appreciation for driving performance and vehicle design. Therefore, EV manufacturers in these markets have focused on delivering high-performance and aesthetically pleasing electric models, aligning with these cultural preferences. This approach has helped in overcoming skepticism toward EVs, which were traditionally seen as lacking in performance compared to ICE vehicles.

Consumer experiences are also influenced by the reliability and longevity of EVs. Initial concerns about the durability of EV batteries have been largely allayed as more data show that modern EV batteries can last for several hundred thousand miles with minimal degradation. However, the long-term reliability of other EV components and overall vehicle lifespan are areas that continue to be monitored by consumers and industry experts alike (Lashari et al., 2021). Consumers' environmental consciousness plays a significant role in their adoption of and satisfaction with EVs. In regions with high levels of environmental awareness, such as Scandinavia, consumers are more likely to view EV ownership as a personal benefit as well as a contribution to a larger societal goal of sustainability. This collective ethos significantly boosts the appeal of EVs.

Cross-country differences in economic incentives also greatly influence consumer experience. In countries with high import duties or taxes on vehicles, the price difference between EVs and ICE vehicles can be substantial, making EVs a less attractive option despite their long-term savings benefit. Conversely, in countries with significant tax incentives, rebates, or subsidies for EV purchase, the financial barriers to EV adoption are reduced considerably, enhancing consumer experience and satisfaction (He et al., 2018). The resale value of EVs is a concern in some markets, particularly those in which technology is evolving rapidly. Consumers worry about their vehicle becoming outdated quickly, impacting its resale value. However, as the market matures and more data become available on the long-term performance of EVs, these concerns are likely to diminish.

The consumer experience with EVs is also affected by the pace of technological advancements. Continuous improvements in battery technology, charging speeds, and vehicle range have steadily enhanced the appeal of EVs. However, this rapid pace of development has also led to the perception that current models may soon become obsolete, which is a deterrent for some potential buyers (Ruan & Lv, 2023). The role of social influence in shaping consumers' experiences with and perceptions of EVs cannot be underestimated. Word-of-mouth recommendations, experiences shared by family and friends, and social media influence all play a significant role in shaping consumer attitudes toward EVs. Positive experiences shared within social networks can significantly boost consumer confidence and interest in EVs.

A consumer's experience with EVs is shaped by a complex interplay of factors including economic considerations, charging infrastructure, driving performance, environmental impact, cultural influences, government policies, and societal attitudes. These experiences vary significantly across different countries and cultures, reflecting the diverse challenges and opportunities present in the global adoption of EM (Santos & Davies, 2020). Addressing these varying consumer experiences through continued technological advancements, infrastructure development, educational initiatives, and supportive policies is key to enhancing the appeal of EVs and accelerating their adoption worldwide. As the market for EVs continues to evolve, it is expected that many of the current barriers will be overcome, leading to a more uniform and universally positive consumer experience with EVs (Brase, 2019).

The perceived lack of pleasure in driving EVs, especially in countries with a strong automotive heritage like Germany and Italy, is a challenge manufacturers like Tesla and Rimac are addressing using various strategies.

4.3.1 Practical Strategies Being Used

i) *Performance Enhancement*: Tesla has focused on enhancing the performance aspects of its EVs. The Tesla Model S Plaid, for instance, offers exhilarating acceleration (0–60 mph in less than 2 s), catering to the thrill-seeking segment of drivers (Santos & Davies, 2020).
ii) *Sound Experience*: Recognizing the importance of sound in the driving experience, companies are innovating with artificial sound systems. For instance, BMW's i4 offers a driving sound developed in collaboration with Hans Zimmer, delivering a unique auditory experience (Brase, 2019).
iii) *Driver Engagement*: Rimac focuses on driver engagement by offering customizable driving modes and advanced interfaces that allow drivers to determine their driving experience. The Rimac Nevera, with its intuitive controls and dynamic handling, exemplifies this approach (He et al., 2018).
iv) *Cultural Integration*: In Italy and Germany, manufacturers are integrating cultural elements into their EV designs (Lashari et al., 2021). For example, Fiat's electric 500 model incorporates classic Italian designs into modern EV technology, appealing to the consumers' sense of national pride and heritage.
v) *Community Building*: Tesla has been adept at creating a community around its brand, organizing events and forums where enthusiasts can share their experiences and passion for EVs. This fosters a sense of belonging and enjoyment among EV owners (She et al., 2017).

These strategies highlight how manufacturers are addressing the functional as well as emotional and experiential aspects of EM, which is crucial for wider acceptance, especially among discerning consumers in countries with a rich automotive heritage.

In conclusion, the consumer experience with EVs is multifaceted and varies across different regions and cultures. Factors such as cost savings, the driving experience, charging infrastructure, environmental impact, vehicle variety, government policies, resale value, and cultural attitudes all play a role in shaping this experience.

4.4 Focus on the Next Generation of Consumers

Understanding the perspectives and preferences of the next generation of consumers, particularly Gen Z and Gen Alpha, is critical in shaping the future of EM (Liao et al., 2017). These generations, more environmentally and technologically conscious than their predecessors, are poised to significantly influence the automotive market, including the demand for EVs.

Gen Z, typically defined as those born from the mid-1990s to the early 2010s, is coming of age in a world where issues like climate change, sustainability, and technological innovation are at the forefront. This generation has been exposed to environmental education from a young age and is more likely to prioritize sustainability in their lifestyle choices, including transportation. Huang et al. (2021) found that Gen Z consumers are more interested in purchasing products from brands that are environmentally responsible. This trend suggests a natural inclination toward EVs, which are perceived as a more eco-friendly alternative to traditional ICE vehicles.

Furthermore, Gen Z is a digital-native generation, having grown up with the internet, social media, and smartphones. This familiarity with technology translates into an openness toward technological innovations, including those in EVs. Features like ADAS, connectivity, and autonomous driving are likely to appeal to this tech-savvy generation (Tian et al., 2020). However, it is not just about the technology itself but about how these features integrate into their digital lifestyles, offering convenience, connectivity, and a personalized experience.

Gen Alpha, the cohort following Gen Z, born from the mid-2010s, is poised to take this integration of technology and sustainability even further. While still very young, Gen Alpha is expected to be the most technologically immersed generation yet (Abdellahi et al., 2017). For them, EVs and advanced mobility solutions will likely be the norm rather than the exception. Their perceptions of transportation will be fundamentally different from those of previous generations, with a focus on sustainable, connected, and potentially autonomous mobility solutions.

The values and preferences of these younger generations present both opportunities and challenges for the EV market. One of the key opportunities is the alignment of EVs with the strong environmental ethos of these generations. To capitalize on this, EV manufacturers and marketers need to emphasize not only the environmental benefits of EVs but also their role in a broader sustainable lifestyle. This involves integrating EVs into the narrative of a greener, more sustainable future, highlighting the use of sustainable materials in EVs, and showcasing the role of EVs in reducing urban pollution (Luca de Tena & Pregger, 2018). However, there are also challenges in catering to these younger consumers. Gen Z and Gen Alpha are likely to have different expectations around vehicle ownership than previous generations. The concept of owning a vehicle as a status symbol, prevalent in previous generations, may be less important to them. Instead, they might prioritize access over ownership, favoring models like car-sharing and subscription services, which provide flexibility and requires lesser financial commitment. The EV industry needs to anticipate and adapt to these changing attitudes, potentially shifting from a model of selling cars to providing mobility solutions.

Another challenge is the economic position of Gen Z, especially as they enter the workforce. The higher upfront cost of EVs compared to traditional vehicles could be a barrier for this generation. Innovative financing solutions, such as subscription models and long-term leases that include maintenance and charging, could be more appealing to these young consumers (Du et al., 2017). The role of digital marketing and social media is paramount in reaching these generations; traditional advertising methods may be less effective, as Gen Z and Gen Alpha are more likely to be influenced by social media, peer reviews, and influencers. A strong online presence, interactive digital marketing campaigns, and engagement through social media platforms are crucial strategies for attracting these younger consumers.

Additionally, the design and aesthetics of EVs will play a significant role in attracting these generations. A vehicle that not only incorporates advanced technology but also features a modern, appealing design is more likely to resonate with Gen Z and Alpha consumers. Further, customization options that allow them to personalize their vehicles to reflect their individual tastes and preferences could also be a significant draw. The next generations, particularly Gen Z and Alpha, are growing up in an era where environmental concerns and technological advancements are deeply intertwined, shaping their perceptions of and expectations about mobility (Gulzari et al., 2022). This context provides a fertile ground for the growth of EVs but also demands a nuanced understanding of these generations' values, aspirations, and concerns.

One of the defining characteristics of Gen Z is their commitment to environmental and social issues. This generation has been at the forefront of climate activism, pushing for sustainable practices across industries. Their preference for EVs stems not only from environmental concerns but also from a desire to support ethical and responsible businesses (Kumar & Alok, 2020). EV manufacturers and stakeholders in the EM ecosystem need to align their practices with these values, ensuring transparency and sustainability in their operations, from sourcing materials to manufacturing processes.

Gen Z's tech-savviness extends beyond a mere comfort with digital devices to encompass an expectation for seamless integration of technology in all aspects of life. For the EV industry, this means delivering vehicles that are environmentally friendly and equipped with the latest technological advancements. Features like AI-driven interfaces, advanced infotainment systems, and connectivity with other devices are likely to appeal to this demographic (de Kwant et al., 2021). Furthermore, this generation's familiarity with technology makes them more receptive to emerging concepts like autonomous driving, vehicle-to-grid (V2G) technologies, and smart charging solutions.

Gen Alpha, though still very young, is expected to take these trends even further. This generation is likely to view EVs as the norm rather than a novelty. For them, the integration of vehicles into a broader connected ecosystem, encompassing smart homes, cities, and various Internet of Things devices, will be a natural expectation. Therefore, the focus of the EV industry should be on developing vehicles that are sustainable and technologically advanced as well as seamlessly integrated into the fabric of a smart, connected world (Muniz & Belzowski, 2017). The changing concept of vehicle ownership is another critical aspect to consider. Younger generations are more inclined toward models that offer flexibility and convenience, such as car-sharing, ridesharing, and subscription services. The traditional model of car ownership is being challenged, and the EV industry must adapt to these changing paradigms. Offering EVs through flexible ownership and usage models can be an effective strategy to attract these younger consumers who may value access and experience over ownership.

However, the economic constraints faced by these younger generations cannot be overlooked. Gen Z, in particular, is entering adulthood in a complex economic environment, marked by concerns over job security and the rising cost of living. The higher upfront costs associated with EVs can be a significant barrier for this demographic (Kester et al., 2019). Financial solutions that make EVs more accessible, such as attractive financing options, leasing programs, and inclusive subscription models, will be crucial in making EVs a viable option for them.

Social influence and digital media play a pivotal role in shaping the perceptions and decisions of Gen Z and Gen Alpha. Traditional marketing methods are less likely to resonate with these digital natives. Instead, engaging with them through social media platforms, influencers they trust, and digital storytelling can be more effective (He, 2018). Interactive and immersive digital experiences, such as virtual reality test drives or augmented reality showrooms, can also be powerful tools in attracting these tech-savvy generations. Moreover, the role of education and awareness is paramount. Despite their inclination toward sustainability and technology, there may still be gaps in knowledge regarding the benefits and capabilities of EVs. Educational initiatives that provide clear, accurate information about EVs, addressing common misconceptions and highlighting their advantages, can be instrumental in fostering a positive attitude toward EM among these younger consumers.

Engaging with Gen Z and Gen Alpha consumers requires a multifaceted approach that goes beyond just selling a product. It involves understanding and aligning with their values, leveraging technology to meet their expectations, adapting to changing concepts of ownership, offering economic solutions that cater to their financial realities, and engaging with them on the digital platforms where they spend their time. As these generations become the dominant consumer force, their preferences and behaviors will increasingly shape the automotive market and the future of mobility (Higueras-Castillo, 2020). For the EV industry, tapping into the potential of these generations by addressing their unique needs and aspirations is essential for driving the transition toward a more sustainable, technologically advanced, and connected future in transportation.

The attitudes of Gen Z and Millennials toward EM, a rapidly evolving trend in Asia and globally, differ in several notable ways (Higueras-Castillo, 2020). To provide context, Generation Z (born between 1997 and 2012) and Millennials (born between 1981 and 1996) are the most environmentally conscious generations to date, with a strong inclination toward sustainability and innovation.

i) *Adoption Rates*: Millennials are currently leading in the adoption of EVs, with a study showing that approximately 40% of them are considering an EV for their next vehicle purchase. In contrast, Gen Z, being younger and mostly at the early stages of their careers, show a slightly lower adoption rate at around 30% (He, 2018).
ii) *Environmental Concerns*: Both generations exhibit a high level of environmental awareness, but Gen Z tends to prioritize this more heavily in their purchasing decisions. A report indicated that over 50% of Gen Z respondents listed environmental impact as a key motivator for their consideration of EVs; this is in comparison with 45% of Millennials (Kester et al., 2019).
iii) *Technology Adoption*: Gen Z, having grown up in a digital era, shows greater enthusiasm for technology integration in EVs. They are more interested in advanced features like autonomous driving and connected services (Muniz & Belzowski, 2017).

iv) *Brand Preferences*: Millennials are more likely to be brand loyal, with a preference for established players like Tesla. In contrast, Gen Z is more open to new and emerging brands, reflecting their desire for innovation and uniqueness (de Kwant et al., 2021).

v) *Price Sensitivity*: Gen Z is more price-sensitive, likely due to their lower-income levels. Affordable and compact EV models are more appealing to them, whereas Millennials, with higher disposable income, may opt for more premium models (Santos & Davies, 2020).

In conclusion, Gen Z and Alpha represent a paradigm shift in the consumer market for EVs. Their preferences for sustainability, advanced technology, and new forms of vehicle ownership present unique opportunities and challenges for the EV industry. Understanding and catering to these preferences through environmentally friendly practices, innovative technology, flexible ownership models, effective digital marketing, and appealing design are key to engaging these future consumers. As these generations come of age and gain purchasing power, their influence on the direction of EM and the automotive market as a whole will become increasingly significant, shaping the future of transportation.

4.5 Possible Solution to Overcome Barriers to Consumer Adoption of Electric Vehicles

The transition to EM is facing several barriers; however, there are numerous strategies that governments, policymakers, and the industry can employ to incentivize customers and accelerate adoption. A holistic approach involving innovative solutions, policy interventions, and industry-led initiatives is essential to effectively address these challenges (Lashari, 2021). One significant barrier is the high upfront cost of EVs. To address this, governments can implement a range of financial incentives to reduce the purchase price and total cost of ownership for consumers. These incentives can include direct subsidies or rebates on the purchase of EVs, tax exemptions, reduced registration fees, and lower road taxes for EV owners. For example, countries like Norway and Canada offer substantial rebates on the purchase of new EVs, significantly lowering the cost barrier for consumers.

Another effective strategy is the implementation of a battery-leasing model. The high cost of EVs is largely due to the battery; by decoupling the cost of the battery from the vehicle, consumers can purchase EVs at a price comparable to ICE vehicles. The battery-leasing model allows consumers to rent the battery, the most expensive component of the EV, instead of buying it with the car. This not only reduces the initial purchase price but also alleviates concerns about battery degradation and replacement costs. Renault's approach with the Zoe in Europe is a prime example of this model in action (Liao, 2017). Improving and expanding the charging infrastructure is critical in addressing range anxiety and the perceived inconvenience of charging EVs. Governments and local authorities can invest in public charging networks, ensuring the availability of charging options in urban and rural areas, along highways, and at workplaces and residential buildings. Public–private partnerships (PPPs) can be instrumental in this regard, leveraging private investment and expertise to build and operate charging stations. The success of countries like China in rapidly expanding their charging infrastructure demonstrates the effectiveness of such initiatives.

Policy interventions can also play a pivotal role in incentivizing EM adoption. Implementing low-emission zones in urban centers, where only electric and low-emission vehicles are allowed, can encourage consumers to switch to EVs. Governments can also set ambitious targets for phasing out ICE vehicles, providing clarity and certainty for consumers and manufacturers alike (Maghfiroh, 2021). The United Kingdom's plan to ban the sale of new petrol and diesel cars by 2030 is an example of a bold policy initiative that sets a clear direction for the market.

The automotive industry can contribute by focusing on research and development to enhance EV technology, particularly in improving battery efficiency, reducing charging times, and extending vehicle range. Industry-led initiatives can also include developing more affordable EV models to cater to a broader market and offering a wider range of vehicle types, such as SUVs and trucks, which are popular in certain markets (Ruan, 2023). Collaboration between car manufacturers and technology companies can lead to innovative solutions in battery technology and charging infrastructure. Furthermore, partnerships with energy providers to offer integrated home charging solutions, green energy plans, and smart charging options can also enhance the EV value proposition for consumers.

Education and awareness campaigns are essential in changing perceptions and increasing knowledge about EVs among consumers. Governments, industry players, and environmental groups can collaborate on educational initiatives to educate consumers about the benefits of EVs, debunk myths, and showcase the advancements in EV technology. Test drive events, EV experience centers, and interactive digital platforms can be effective tools in these campaigns (Santos, 2020). To address concerns regarding resale value, the industry can develop certified pre-owned programs for EVs, providing warranties and guarantees to boost consumers' confidence in the quality and longevity of used EVs. This can help establish a robust market for second-hand EVs, making them a more accessible option for a wider range of consumers.

Incentivizing corporate and fleet buyers to switch to EVs can also have a significant impact. Businesses and government fleets can play a leading role in the adoption of EM by transitioning their vehicle fleets to EVs. Incentives for corporate buyers, such as tax breaks, grants, and lower benefit-in-kind rates for company car drivers choosing EVs, can encourage this shift. Finally, integrating EVs into broader urban and transportation planning is crucial (She, 2017). This includes planning for EV charging infrastructure in new residential and commercial developments, integrating EM into public transportation strategies, and considering EVs in future mobility planning, such as car-sharing and autonomous vehicle services. While exploring solutions that will help overcome barriers to EM, it has become evident that a multifaceted approach is needed, involving direct incentives as well as broader systemic changes and educational efforts.

The development of a secondary market for EVs is another critical area. A thriving second-hand market can significantly lower the entry barrier for potential EV buyers who are unable or unwilling to pay the premium for a new vehicle. Governments and industry players can encourage this market by ensuring the longevity and reliability of EV batteries and offering battery certification programs (Varghese, 2021). This could include offering extended warranties or guaranteeing a minimum battery life, which would give consumers confidence in the quality and durability of used EVs.

Furthermore, innovative financing models beyond traditional car loans and leases can be explored to make EVs more accessible. For example, flexible financing options that link payments to the savings made on fuel and maintenance could make EVs more attractive to consumers. Subscription models, where consumers pay a monthly fee that covers the use of the vehicle as well as services like insurance, maintenance, and even charging, could appeal to younger consumers who prefer access over ownership (Zhang, 2018). The energy sector also has a crucial role in advancing EM. Energy providers can offer special tariffs for EV charging (making it more affordable) and bundle home energy and EV charging plans. Collaborations between the automotive and energy sectors could lead to innovative solutions like V2G systems, where EVs can feed energy back into the grid during peak times, potentially generating income for EV owners and stabilizing the grid.

Corporate responsibility and environmental stewardship can also be powerful motivators for businesses to adopt EVs. Governments can incentivize businesses to switch to electric fleets by offering tax deductions, grants, and other benefits. Businesses adopting EVs not only contribute to reducing emissions but also set a positive example, influencing their employees and customers (Abdellahi et al., 2017). Education and outreach are fundamental in shifting public perception and increasing EV adoption. Comprehensive education campaigns can demystify EV technology and showcase the benefits of electric driving. These campaigns can be conducted through various channels, including traditional media, social media, schools, community events, and dealerships. Educational efforts should also focus on addressing specific concerns, such as range anxiety and charging infrastructure availability, by providing clear and factual information.

Infrastructure development is another area where both government and private sector involvement is crucial. Governments can facilitate the expansion of charging infrastructure by providing funding, streamlining the permitting process for charging station installation, and setting targets for infrastructure development. Private companies can invest in charging infrastructure as either a part of their corporate social responsibility initiatives or as a business opportunity (de Kwant et al., 2021). Urban planning and policy can greatly influence the adoption of EVs. Additionally, integrating EV-friendly policies into urban development plans, such as mandating that new buildings have EV charging stations and dedicating parking spaces to EVs, can make owning an EV more convenient. Policies that prioritize EVs in urban areas, such as offering free parking, access to carpool lanes, and exemptions from congestion charges, can also be strong incentives.

Integrating EVs into the broader mobility ecosystem should also be considered. This includes supporting the role of EVs in car-sharing fleets, integrating them into public transportation strategies, and considering them in the development of autonomous vehicle technologies. Such integration not only promotes the use of EVs but also contributes to the overall efficiency and sustainability of the transportation system (Du et al., 2017). PPPs can be instrumental in advancing EM, and governments can collaborate with private companies to fund research and development in EV technology, build charging infrastructure, and run educational campaigns. These partnerships can leverage the strengths and resources of both sectors to accelerate the transition to EM.

Finally, international collaboration and sharing of best practices can play a significant role in overcoming the barriers to EM. Countries leading in EM adoption can share their experiences, strategies, and policies with those still in the early stages of adoption; this global exchange of knowledge and resources can help address common challenges and accelerate the adoption of EVs globally (Gulzari et al., 2022). Overcoming the barriers to EM requires a comprehensive and collaborative approach involving governments, the automotive industry, the energy sector, businesses, and consumers. From financial incentives and innovative financing models to infrastructure development, educational campaigns, and policy interventions, various strategies are needed to promote EV adoption. By addressing these barriers through concerted efforts, EM can be accelerated, contributing to a more sustainable and environmentally friendly transportation future.

To overcome the barriers to EM adoption, it is evident that a comprehensive approach is required, involving concerted efforts from various stakeholders, including governments, the automotive industry, energy providers, and consumers. Government policy plays a crucial role in shaping the EV landscape. By setting ambitious targets for EV adoption and emissions reduction, governments can provide a clear direction for the industry and consumers alike (Huang et al., 2021). Policies can range from mandating a certain percentage of new car sales to be electric by a specific date to implementing stricter emissions standards for vehicles. These policies not only drive the market toward cleaner options but also boost consumers' confidence that their investment in an EV is future-proof.

Financial incentives remain a key driver in encouraging consumers to switch to EVs. Beyond purchase rebates and tax exemptions, creative approaches such as reduced tolls for EVs, free parking in city centers, and access to carpool lanes can make EV ownership more attractive. In regions where EV adoption is still low, these incentives can be particularly effective in kick-starting the market (Kester et al., 2019). The development of infrastructure is another critical area. The establishment of widespread and accessible charging networks is essential in alleviating range anxiety. Governments can provide funding, streamline the permitting process for charging station installation, and offer incentives to private companies for building charging infrastructure. In urban areas, integrating charging stations into existing structures like parking lots, shopping centers, and office buildings can provide convenient charging options for EV users.

For the automotive industry, continued innovation is key. Manufacturers must focus on improving battery technology to increase range and reduce charging times. Additionally, offering a wider range of EV models to suit various consumer needs and preferences can attract a broader customer base. The industry should also explore partnerships with technology companies to integrate advanced features, such as enhanced connectivity and autonomous driving capabilities (which are particularly appealing to younger consumers), into EVs (Kumar &

Alok, 2020). Another significant factor that can accelerate EV adoption is consumer education and awareness. Misconceptions and lack of knowledge about EVs often deter potential buyers. Therefore, comprehensive education campaigns that provide clear and accurate information about the benefits, capabilities, and operation of EVs are necessary. These campaigns can include interactive experiences like test drives, EV experience days, and educational content shared through social media and online platforms.

Furthermore, fostering a second-hand market for EVs is crucial in making them accessible to a wider range of consumers. Ensuring the longevity and reliability of EV batteries can boost consumers' confidence in the used car market (Lew, 2020); programs like battery certification and extended warranties may be instrumental in this regard. Energy providers have a role to play in facilitating the shift to EM. They could offer special tariffs for EV charging during off-peak hours to make EV charging more affordable (Luca de Tena & Pregger, 2018). Additionally, investing in renewable energy sources to power EV charging stations could enhance the environmental benefits of EVs and appeal to eco-conscious consumers. Corporate fleets represent a significant opportunity in the transition to EVs. Businesses can lead by example by converting their fleets of ICE vehicles to EVs, lowering fuel and maintenance costs. Government incentives for corporate EV adoption, such as tax breaks and grants, can accelerate this transition.

The integration of EVs into broader urban planning and public transportation strategies is also crucial. Policies that support the use of EVs in car-sharing and ride-hailing services and the inclusion of EVs in public transportation fleets can increase the visibility and normalcy of EVs. PPPs can be effective in pooling resources and expertise to advance EV adoption. These partnerships can focus on areas such as infrastructure development, research and innovation in EV technology, and public awareness campaigns (Muniz & Belzowski, 2017). International collaboration and sharing of best practices can greatly benefit the global transition to EM, and learning from the experiences of countries that have successfully implemented EV policies and infrastructure can provide other regions with valuable insights and strategies.

Overcoming the barriers to EM requires a multifaceted and collaborative approach. Through strategic government policies and incentives, continued innovation from the automotive industry, infrastructure development, consumer education, second-hand market fostering, involvement of energy providers, corporate adoption, urban planning, PPPs, and international cooperation, the adoption of EVs can be significantly accelerated. This concerted effort will not only facilitate the transition to sustainable transportation but also contribute to broader environmental and economic goals.

In conclusion, overcoming the barriers to EM requires a concerted effort from governments, policymakers, and the automotive industry. Through financial incentives, innovative business models like battery leasing, investments in charging infrastructure, policy interventions, industry-led initiatives, educational campaigns, and integrated urban planning, the transition to EM can be accelerated. These efforts will facilitate the adoption of EVs and also contribute to the broader goal of creating a sustainable, efficient, and environmentally friendly transportation system for the future.

5
Empirical Evidence

Abstract The empirical evidence presented in this chapter offers significant insights into the factors that impact consumers' attitudes and intentions to buy electric vehicles. A sample of 153 Italian consumers has been surveyed to investigate their electro-compatibility profile and their general attitudes and knowledge towards EVs. The results underscore the crucial roles of transparent information dissemination and infrastructure development in speeding up the adoption of electric mobility in Italy. The findings also suggest the need for additional research to understand diverse perceptions beyond the Italian context, especially as circumstances evolve. These insights offer valuable data-driven perspectives on consumer behavior and market trends, contributing to a deeper understanding of the factors influencing electric vehicle adoption.

Keywords survey · mobility habit · consumer attitude toward EVs · electro-compatibility profile · intention to adopt EVs · Italian context

D. D'Acunto, *The Future of E-Mobility*,
https://doi.org/10.1007/978-3-031-65053-6_5

5.1 Background

Extant research on electric mobility has been attempting to give rational answers to questions such as, "what factors influence Italian consumers' intention to purchase EVs?" (Augurio et al., 2022). Most of these studies adopted surveys covering the following main areas of investigation (Table 5.1):

i) Sociodemographic characteristics of respondents;
ii) Mobility habits, i.e., how potential consumers use cars as a mode of transportation;
iii) Psychological variables, aiming at studying potential consumers' intentions to purchase EVs and relating it to beliefs, moral values, attitudes, and opinions about electric mobility; and
iv) Knowledge of EVs, i.e., how much respondents know about the main characteristics of EVs

Some studies have attempted to segment potential EV consumers. An interesting study by Jaiswal et al. (2022) identified three distinct groups of consumers, namely the i) "conservative,"ii) "indifferent,"and "enthusiastic." The authors argue that young and well-educated adults belonging to the Millennials generational cohort could be considered potential EV buyers.

The Conservatives

This segment shows an extremely unfavorable attitude toward EV adoption. These individuals have very low knowledge about EVs and their advantages and attributes. Conservatives are those who have shown a strong unwillingness to adopt or purchase EVs in the near future. In addition, these customers have a negative belief about the usefulness of EVs and their ease of use and affordability.

The Indifferent

The key characteristic of this group is the reluctance to consider EVs in their future choice. In addition, social influences such as positive feedbacks from friends and family do not help in persuading them to adopt EVs.

Table 5.1 Main dimensions of drivers in EV purchase decisions

Drivers of EV purchase decisions	Dimension	Source
Economic and technological attributes: (e.g., price, operational cost, acceleration, driving range, charging time, and carbon dioxide emissions)	Knowledge of EV	Giansoldati et al. (2018)
Attitude, behavioral control, and moral and subjective norms	Psychological	Mohamed et al. (2016)
Environmental concern	Psychological	Mohamed et al. (2016)
Age, educational level, and employment status	Sociodemographic	Mohamed et al. (2016)
Concerns about range, vehicle maintenance, and battery performance	Mobility habits	Mohamed et al. (2016)
Availability of a garage	Knowledge of EV	Mohamed et al. (2016)
Belief that EVs can contribute to the fight against climate change	Psychological	Bansal et al. (2021)
Trust in EV technology		Bansal et al. (2021)
High levels of attitude, perceived behavioral control, and subjective norms	Psychological	Ye et al. (2021)
Perceived usefulness	Psychological	Jaiswal et al. (2021)
Perceived ease of use	Psychological	Jaiswal et al. (2021)
Perceived risk	Psychological	Jaiswal et al. (2021)
High price, low range, and inadequate charging infrastructure	Knowledge of EV	Augurio et al. (2022)
Lower environmental impact of vehicles, lower operating cost of vehicles, and potential future savings	Psychological	Augurio et al. (2022)
Youth and high level of education	Sociodemographic	Augurio et al. (2022)
Attachment to traditional driving habits	Mobility habits	Augurio et al. (2022)

(continued)

Table 5.1 (continued)

Drivers of EV purchase decisions	Dimension	Source
Knowledge of EVs (e.g., awareness of their unresolved problems, high purchase cost, limited range, and poor infrastructure)	Knowledge of EV	Augurio et al. (2022)
Perception of an EV as one that can improve the quality of life		Augurio et al. (2022)

Note EV, electric vehicle

The Enthusiasts

This segment emerged as the largest distinctive group, holding positive and favorable beliefs toward all the variables examined for possible EV adoption. This group of individuals considers EV adoption to be a certain and imminent choice. Enthusiasts exhibit a positive attitude toward EV preference. The key characteristics of this segment are awareness and a high degree of information and specific knowledge about EVs. Consumers in this segment express positive beliefs about the performance and usefulness of EVs, as well as about their ease of use and driving comfort (Jaiswal et al., 2022).

Another attempt at EV adopters segmentation was made in a study by Mohamed et al. (2016). The authors' goal was to identify the recurring characteristics of early adopters of EVs. The findings showed the presence of three distinct segments—"typical early adopters," "emerging early adopters," and "interested retirees."

Typical Early Adopters

This segment comprised young and middle-aged, well-educated individuals with a career and a growing family. Typical early adopters have the financial capability to purchase an EV, having a high annual income. This group also preferred larger family car fleet sizes, suggesting that they are interested in EVs as an additional vehicle rather than a replacement vehicle within the next two years. The availability of a garage or shared area at their place was another key characteristic of this segment.

Emerging Early Adopters

This cluster mainly consists of small, highly educated families. Emerging adopters appear to be more city-oriented, living in apartments with associated garage/condominium parking available. Despite their lower annual income compared to typical early adopters, emerging early adopters are also interested in EVs as a future purchase; however, they expect to buy it over the next five years rather than the two-year time range of typical early adopters. For emerging early adopters, an EV could be adopted as either an additional vehicle, a replacement vehicle, or the first family vehicle.

Interested Retirees

This small target segment is characterized by elderly and retired households. Unlike the previous segments, interested retirees comprise small households interested in a replacement vehicle. Compared to the other segments, their average annual distance covered by car is lower, suggesting that the current EV technology would likely meet their travel needs (Mohamed et al., 2016).

Another interesting study by Bennet et al. (2016) focused on marketing and communication elements that can actually improve EV adoption. The study aimed at understanding how marketing can contribute to developing environmentally sustainable behavior in EVs' mass market. Specifically, the study analyzed the attractiveness of marketing and communication messages on potential EV buyers. The results showed that the most relevant terms affecting advertising effectiveness are "pleasure," "fuel," "price," "performance," "technology," "environment," and "energy."

Furthermore, the three semantic areas dominating promotional materials for EV manufacturers were found to be "drive experience," "economical," and "environment preservation."

Drive Experience

EVs offer an excellent driving experience, where "excellent driving experience" is a culmination of EV's driving pleasure, excellent performance, and the application of advanced technologies.

Economical

EVs are economical, where "economical" is characterized by the lack of need to fuel the car (buying fuel), the decreasing level of purchasing prices over time, and the availability of government incentives.

Environment Preservation

EVs help to preserve the environment, and the concept of "preserving the environment" is based on words related to cleaning up the environment and saving the country's energy resources.

Interestingly, reassurances about range anxiety (e.g., distances between recharges, battery charge duration, etc.) did not significantly recur within the data analyzed by the authors, suggesting that EV manufacturers tend to give less space for such topics in their communication strategies.

5.2 Research Methodology

This section presents the methodology used to analyze the variables that mostly influence the choice of adopting an EV. Having such information is key for EV manufacturers to develop effective digital and Customer Relationship Management (CRM) marketing tools that can actually increase potential consumers' adoption of EVs.

Data were collected in Italy between January 2023 and February 2023. The research methodology adopted involved the use of a survey for data collection, and this survey was administered online through social media (e.g., LinkedIn, Facebook, Instagram, and WhatsApp) and Google Form. To ensure data integrity, Internet Protocol (IP) addresses have been monitored to confirm unique responses and excluded questionnaires completed in less than 2 min. Confidentiality in the handling of the respondents' data was strictly guaranteed. This approach yielded 153 valid online responses.

The survey comprised thematic sub-categories investigating the different exploratory macro-objectives of the research.

For this study, the inclusion criteria were as follows:

i) The respondents' age should fall between 18 and 70 years. Respondents within this range are potential consumers of the broader automotive sector because they have a driver's license. In addition, respondents without a valid driver's license were not included in this study.

ii) The respondents should have sufficient purchasing power to potentially buy an EV. If they are still unable to independently purchase an EV, they should refer to the purchasing power of their household.
iii) The respondents should not already be owners of EVs, so that they can be identifiable as "non-users" of EVs.

The survey was divided into three macro-sections. The first part investigated the sociodemographic characteristics of the sample and comprised typical questions on gender, age, profession, educational background, area or residence, and purchasing power. Through these questions, it was possible to segment the respondents into sub-categories. The aim of this section was to collect data and understand whether the respondent's personal and professional backgrounds were associated with their decision to purchase an EV.

The second part of the survey included questions pertaining to the electro-compatibility profile of the sample. Questions in this section focused on daily behaviors, personal attitudes, and lifestyle. Other questions revolved around respondents' place of dwelling and the presence/absence of a parking space, an estimate of the weekly distance covered by car, reasons for traveling and the most frequented areas, as well as the individuals' attitude toward sustainability and technological innovation. This section aimed to gather information and identify the electro-friendly target segment, who, with the right features and attitudes available, could be considered potential EV consumers"

The third part of the survey investigated the more technical topics in the world of EV. Questions in this section revolved around respondents' environmental attitude; propensity and intention to purchase an EV; perceived usefulness, ease, and risks of adopting an EV; purchase aversion; level of industry knowledge; and perceived level of information regarding EV in the media. The purpose of this section was to evaluate the respondents' level of knowledge about the electric mobility world, including the current need to consider electric mobility and its related perceived barriers and, for those with a low level of awareness, the propensity to get information about the EV industry. This section allowed us to identify where the respondents were positioned in the conversion funnel, in order to provide the most appropriate suggestions for digital and CRM marketing strategies.

The sections of the questionnaire were developed by the author and the measures are validated by the existing literature. The items used in the survey are presented in Table 5.2, along with the most relevant sources used for scale adoption. The table is organized according to the three sections of the survey described above: i) sociodemographic analysis, ii) electro-compatibility analysis, and iii) personal knowledge assessment.

The author recognizes the relatively small sample size and the single nationality of the respondents (Italian) among the limitations of the data collection methods. Thus, further analysis should extend data collection to different countries and seek to improve the pool of respondents to enhance comparability of the results. The database is made available upon request for the sake of transparency.

5.3 Main Results

5.3.1 Descriptive Statistics of the Sample

The final sample consisted of 153 respondents who completed the online survey on electric mobility. The results of the first exploration of the sample's sociodemographic characteristics and descriptive statistics are provided below.

Regarding the sociodemographic profile of the respondents, majority (38.6%) belonged to the 25–39 age cohort, followed by the 18–24 (29.4%), 40–54 (15.7%), and 55–69 (15.0%) age cohorts. The data showed that 57.5% of the respondents were women, and 42.5% were men. Only 4% of the respondents said they did not have a driver's license, and only one respondent owns an e-mobility car.

Furthermore, 52.9% of the respondents were currently employed; 18.3% were student-workers, and 17.6% were students. The remaining respondents were either unemployed (7.2%) or retired (3.9%). Regarding education level, 36.6% of the respondents hold a bachelor's degree; 33.3% have a high school diploma, and 19.6% have a master's degree.

Table 5.2 Structure of Survey on E-mobility Adoption

Question and answer	Source
Section 1: Socio-demographic analysis	
Age (in years): •<18 •18–24 •25–39 •40–54 •55–69 •> 69	Augurio et al. (2022)
Do you have a valid driver's license? • Yes • No	Personal elaboration
Gender • Male • Female • Other	Jaiswal et al. (2021)
Current occupation: • Study • Work • Study and work • Unemployed	Personal elaboration
Education level • None • Primary school • High school • Bachelor's degree • Master's degree • Other	Personal elaboration
Field of work/study • Scientific • Social • Economic • Legal • Humanities • Medical • Design • Other	Personal elaboration
Number of family members • 1 • 2 • 3 • 4 • >4	Bansal et al. (2021)

(continued)

Table 5.2 (continued)

Question and answer	Source
Number of dependent children • 0 • 1 • 2 • 3 • >3	Bansal et al. (2021)
Personal/family annual income (in €): • 0–15.000 • 15.000–29.000 • 29.000–55.000 • 55.000–100.000 • 100.000–300.000 • > 300.000 • I prefer not to answer	Personal elaboration
Section 2: Electro-compatibility analysis	
Number of cars owned by the household: • 0 • 1 • 2 • >2	Ye et al. (2021)
Car power: Type of your car fleet (multiple answers can be selected): • Petrol • Diesel • Compressed natural gas (CNG) • Liquid petroleum gas (LPG) • Electric • Hybrid	Personal elaboration
Area of residence: • Urban area/city center • Suburban area	Giansoldati et al. (2018)
Parking availability: Where do you usually park your car? • Personal garage • Condominium area/parking slot • Occasional parking in the area nearby the dwelling	Giansoldati et al. (2018)
Do you own a charging station in your garage or condominium area? • Yes • No	Personal elaboration

(continued)

Table 5.2 (continued)

Question and answer	Source
Average distance (in km) you usually drive your vehicle in each of your trips • < 10 • 11–50 • 51–100 • > 100	Giansoldati et al. (2018)
Average distance (in km) you usually drive in one year • < 1.000 • 1.000–5.000 • 5.000–10.000 • 10.000–20.000 • 20.000–50.000 • > 50.000	Bennet et al. (2016)
Reasons for traveling by car (multiple answers can be selected)? • Going to work • Traveling for work • Vacations • Moving for family reasons (e.g., taking children to school) • Shopping • Other	Personal elaboration
What are your most frequented areas by car? • Mainly urban areas • Urban and suburban areas • Mainly suburban areas	Augurio et al. (2022)
Do you consider yourself an environmentally and sustainability-conscious person? • Yes • No	Personal elaboration
Do you consider yourself as a person positively attracted by technological innovation? • Yes • No	Personal elaboration
Section 3. Assessment of personal attitudes toward electric mobility	
Likert scale (1–7): Strongly agree/Agree/Neutral/Disagree/ Strongly disagree	
3.1 Environmental concerns: a) I think people should change their behavior to reduce climate change and protect the environment b) I am concerned about human behavior and its influence on climate change and the environment c) I think climate change is a threat to me and my family	Mohamed et al. (2016)

(continued)

Table 5.2 (continued)

Question and answer	Source
3.2 Attitudes toward electric vehicle adoption: a) In the long run, I think buying an electric vehicle is more cost-effective than owning a conventional vehicle b) With an excellent battery warranty, I would not worry about buying an electric vehicle c) Electric vehicles are able to meet my travel needs even with limited range d) I am willing to spend more to purchase an EV e) I am ready to modify my travel habits somewhat to own an EV f) I am willing to tolerate some occasional inconveniences related to battery charging for the benefits of driving an electric vehicle	Mohamed et al. (2016)
Purchase intention: a) I plan to purchase an electric vehicle in the next two years b) If I replace my car, I will first consider an electric vehicle	Ye et al. (2021)
Perceived usefulness a) I believe that the use of electric vehicles can reduce carbon emissions and energy consumption b) I believe that the use of electric vehicles can reduce family expenses for transportation c) I believe that the use of electric vehicles can improve my commuting efficiency	Jaiswal et al. (2021)
Perceived ease of use a) I think it is easy to use electric vehicles b) I think it would be easy for me to drive electric vehicles c) My interaction with electric vehicles would be clear and understandable	Jaiswal et al. (2021)
Perceived risk a) I am afraid of suffering financial losses when using electric vehicles b) I would not feel completely safe when I drive an electric vehicle on the road c) I worry about whether electric vehicles will really have the same performance as conventional vehicles d) I worry about the drawbacks of using electric vehicles (e.g., limited range, charging infrastructure, and charging time)	Jaiswal et al. (2021)
Attitude toward the environment and owning an electric car a) People need to change their lifestyles to protect the environment b) When I drive, I often use my car for my leisure time c) I have changed my buying habits to help the environment	Bennett et al. (2016)

(continued)

Table 5.2 (continued)

Question and answer	Source
Purchase aversion a) I don't want to take the risk of buying an electric vehicle because I know little about it b) I do not trust EV technology c) EVs are not a proven technology and this discourages me from buying d) It is not a good idea to buy EV because of the limited charging infrastructure e) It is not a good idea to buy an EV because of the low resale value	Bansal et al. (2021)
Level of information a) It seems to me that EV publicity has increased dramatically in recent months b) I am increasingly reading articles, watching television broadcasts, or hearing positive comments about EVs c) People close to me have a positive opinion about the purchase of electric vehicles d) From what I read or hear, I believe that conventional cars will disappear or become very few in the short to medium term e) I know that European policy guidelines are pushing toward the green transition, and electric vehicles are included in these guidelines f) When I buy a new car, I read up on everything there is to know about the car models that are available on the market g) I am informed about the pros and cons of electric vehicles	Augurio et al. (2022)
Knowledge of electric mobility a) I know the performance of electric vehicles (e.g., charging time, acceleration, driving comfort, and range) b) I know the operating costs of electric vehicles c) I know the environmental advantages of electric vehicles over conventional vehicles	Jaiswal et al. (2022)

The data showed great heterogeneity regarding professional fields of work. Standing out from the rest were respondents employed in business (41.2%), humanities (16.3%), socials (9.8%), and science (7.2%). Other fields mentioned were the medical, design, sports, music, information technology, and public administration fields (about 26%).

Majority of the respondents (37.9%) reported living in a 4-person household, while 22.2% and 21.6% reported living in a 3- and 2-person household, respectively. Additionally, 13.1% of the respondents reported living in a household comprising more than four persons. Most (82.4%) of the respondents do not have children, while 11.1% have one dependent child. Only a minority (6.6%) reported having two or more dependent children.

Additionally, 145 respondents (34.0%) declared an annual income between 15,000 and 29,000 euros, while 29.4% declared an annual income of 29,000–55,000 euros. Further, 17% of the respondents declared an annual income of 0–15,000 euros (these are probably students), while 11.8% reported earning 55,000–100,000 euros annually. Only four respondents reported earning more than 100,000 euros annually.

Age					
		Frequency	Percent	Valid percent	Cumulative percent
Valid	< 18	1	0.7	0.7	99.3
	18–24	45	29.4	29.4	29.4
	25–39	59	38.6	38.6	68.0
	40–54	24	15.7	15.7	83.7
	55–69	23	15.0	15.0	98.7
	> 69	1	0.7	0.7	100.0
	Total	153	100.0	100.0	

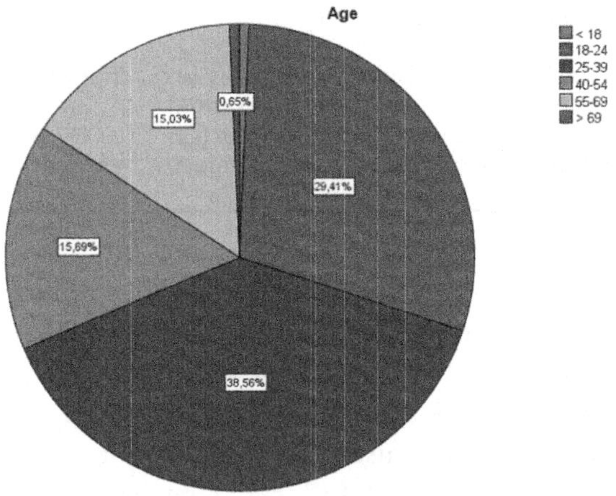

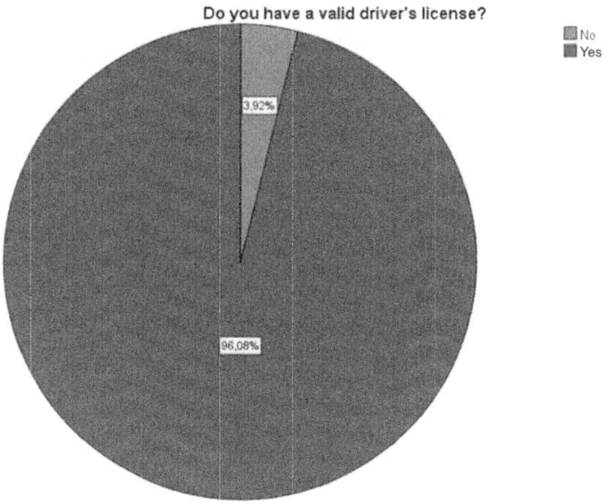
Do you have a valid driver's license?
No
Yes
3,92%
96,08%

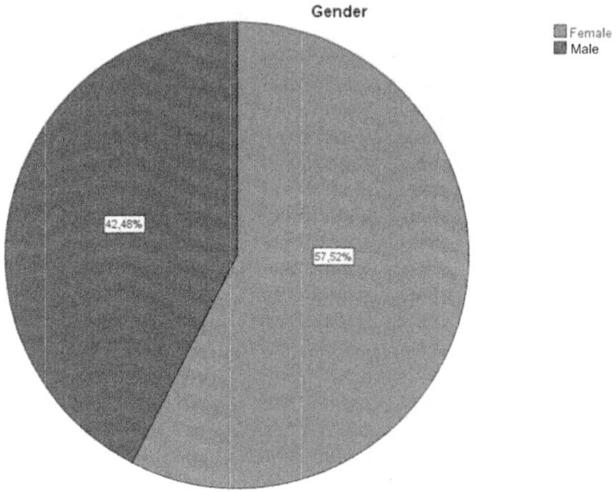
Gender
Female
Male
42,48%
57,52%

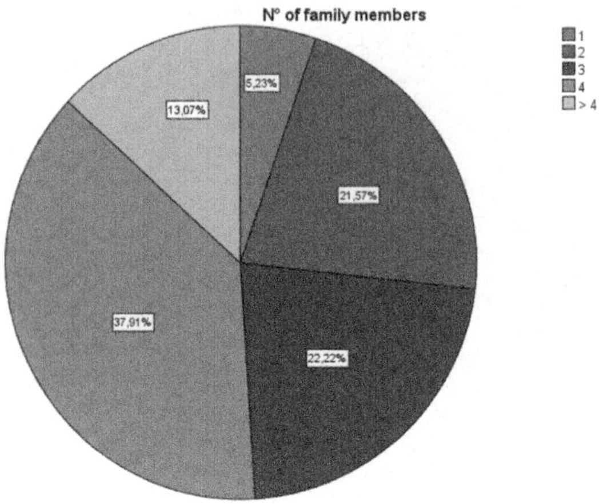
N° of family members
1
2
3
4
> 4
5,23%
21,57%
22,22%
37,91%
13,07%

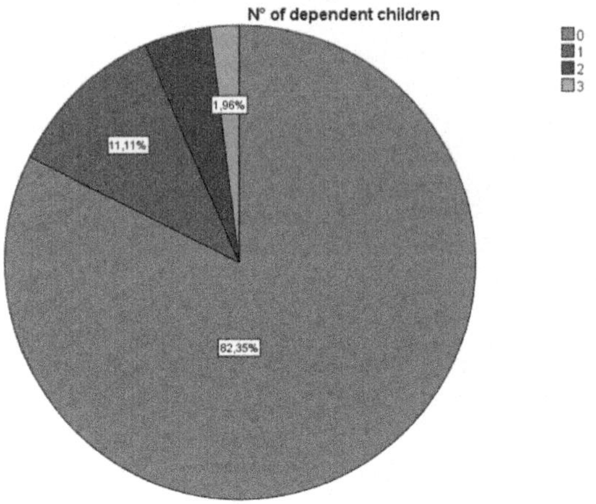
N° of dependent children
0
1
2
3
1,96%
11,11%
82,35%

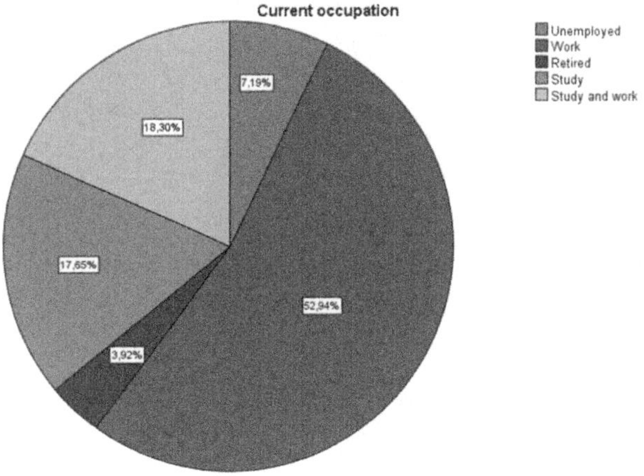
Current occupation
Unemployed
Work
Retired
Study
Study and work
7,19%
52,94%
3,92%
17,65%
18,30%

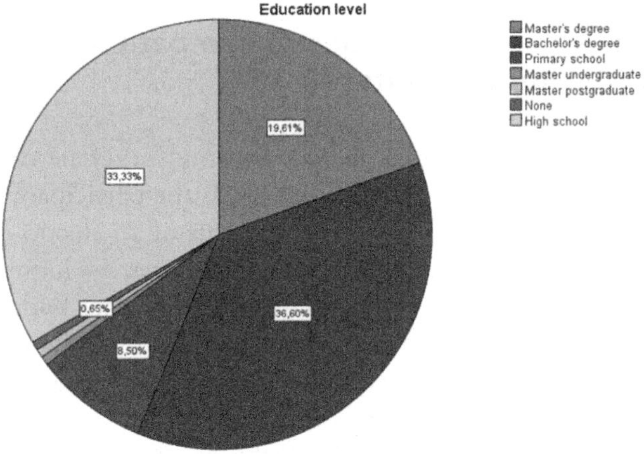
Education level
Master's degree
Bachelor's degree
Primary school
Master undergraduate
Master postgraduate
None
High school
19,61%
36,60%
8,50%
0,65%
33,33%

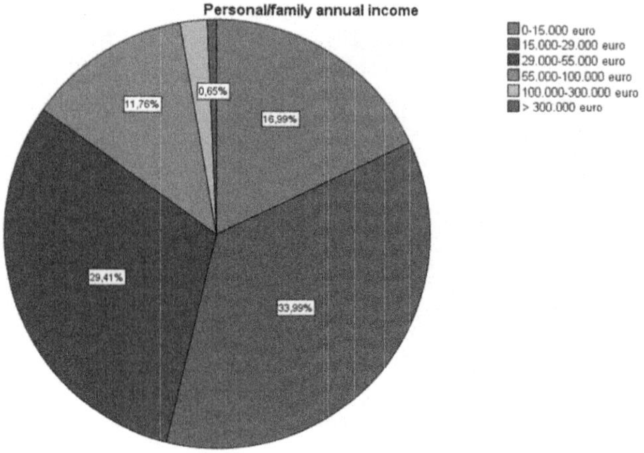

5.3.2 Assessment of the Electro-compatibility Profile of the Respondents

The second order of questions included in the survey pertained to the dimensions of electro-compatibility, as well as the participant's degree of affinity to the world of EVs. The key elements of an electro-compatible user can be summarized in a few simple attributes, including having a residence in the city, a personal or shared parking space with a charging station, an average to low amount of miles driven by car, a greater inclination to drive in urban areas, and environmental and technological awareness.

Considering the answers reported in this section of the survey, it was possible to analyze the respondents' degree of electro-compatibility.

First, majority of the respondents (42.5%) reported that they own two cars, while 37.3% owned more than two cars in their fleet. In contrast, 19.6% owned only one car in their fleet. Regarding car power types, majority of the respondents owned either a petrol car (71.2% of the total car fleet) or a diesel car (60.1% of the total car fleet); the rest owned either a liquid petroleum gas (LPG) (21.6%) or a compressed natural gas (CNG) (9.2%).

Number of cars owned by the household

		Frequency	Percent	Valid percent	Cumulative percent
Valid	0	1	.7	.7	.7
	1	30	19.6	19.6	20.3
	2	65	42.5	42.5	62.7
	> 2	57	37.3	37.3	100.0
	Total	153	100.0	100.0	

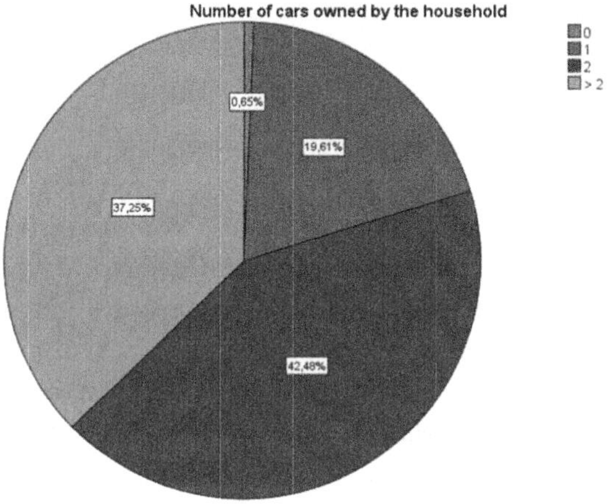

Regarding the area of residence, only 30.7% of respondents lived in an urban area; in the rest (69.3%) lived in suburban areas. This finding shows that the sample had a low degree of electro-compatibility.

Area of residence

		Frequency	Percent	Valid percent	Cumulative percent
Valid	Suburban area	106	69.3	69.3	69.3
	Urban area/ city center	47	30.7	30.7	100.0
	Total	153	100.0	100.0	

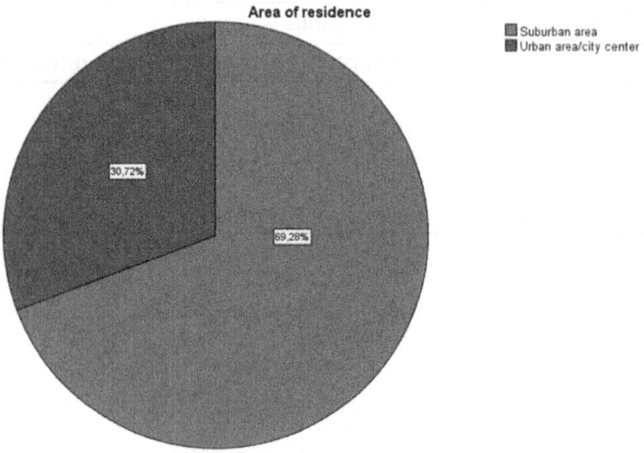

Conversely, a factor which positively affected the respondents' degree of electro-compatibility was the widespread availability of own parking; 66% of the respondents declared having a private garage, and 16.3% reported having a shared condominium parking. Only 17.0% reported a lack of parking space. Among those with parking, only 7.9% already have one with a charging station. This finding aligns with the number of respondents already owning an electric or hybrid vehicle (i.e., 12 out of 260 vehicles).

Parking availability: Where do you usually park your car?

		Frequency	Percent	Valid percent	Cumulative percent
Valid	Personal garage	101	66.0	66.0	66.0
	Condominium area/parking slot	25	16.3	16.3	82.4
	I have no car	1	.7	.7	83.0
	Occasional parking in the area nearby the dwelling	26	17.0	17.0	100.0
	Total	153	100.0	100.0	

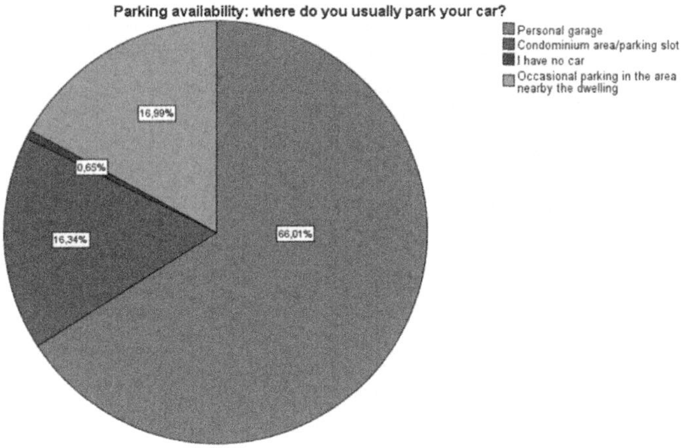

The survey also included a set of questions on the driving habits of the respondents. While estimating the distance traveled per trip, majority of the respondents (60.1%) reported that they travel between 11 and 55 km, followed by those who traveled a maximum of 10 km (27.5%). About 10% of the respondents travel about 50–100 km, while a few (2%) travel more than 100 km each trip.

Average distance (in km) you usually drive your vehicle in each of your trips

		Frequency	Percent	Valid percent	Cumulative percent
Valid	< 10 km	42	27.5	27.5	27.5
	11–50 km	92	60.1	60.1	89.5
	51–100 km	16	10.5	10.5	100.0
	> 100 km	3	2.0	2.0	29.4
	Total	153	100.0	100.0	

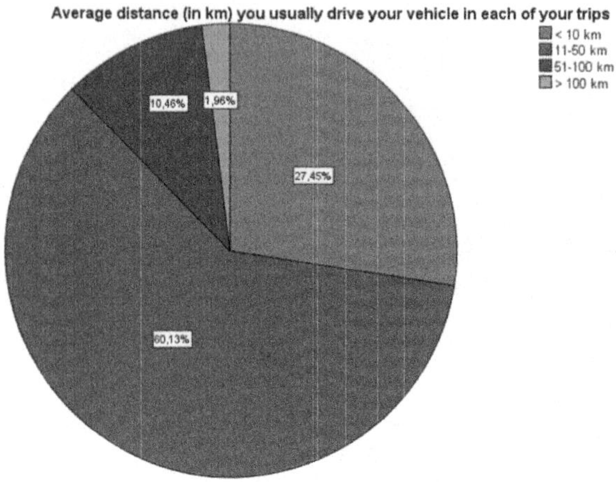

The data are consistent with the estimate of distances covered annually, with only four (2.6%) respondents declaring that they travel more than 50,000 km per year. The respondents declared an annual traveling distance of 10,000–20,000 km (31.4%) and 20,000–50,000 km (19.6%). However, most of the respondents (46.5%) reflected electro-compatibility, in that most of them declared driving no more than 10,000 km per year.

Average distance (in km) you usually drive in one year

		Frequency	Percent	Valid percent	Cumulative percent
Valid	< 1,000 km	14	9.2	9.2	97.4
	1,000–5,000 km	16	10.5	10.5	10.5
	5,000–10,000 km	41	26.8	26.8	88.2
	10,000–20,000 km	48	31.4	31.4	41.8
	20,000–50,000 km	30	19.6	19.6	61.4
	> 50,000 km	4	2.6	2.6	100.0
	Total	153	100.0	100.0	

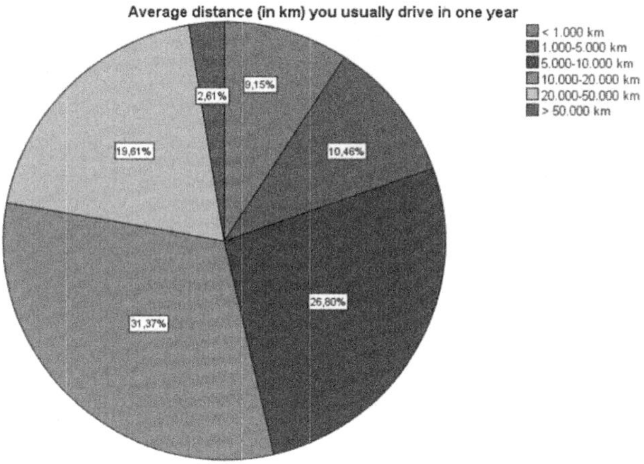

The most frequented areas by car were urban and suburban roads (68.0%), only urban roads (19%), and only suburban roads (11.8%). This finding reflects a high degree of EV compatibility among the sample that drives on both urban and suburban roads compared to those who only drive within suburban areas (e.g., highways and freeways).

What are your most frequented areas by car?

		Frequency	Percent	Valid percent	Cumulative percent
Valid	Urban and suburban areas	105	68.6	68.6	68.6
	Mainly suburban areas	18	11.8	11.8	81.0
	Mainly urban areas	29	19.0	19.0	100.0
	I have no car	1	.7	.7	69.3
	Total	153	100.0	100.0	

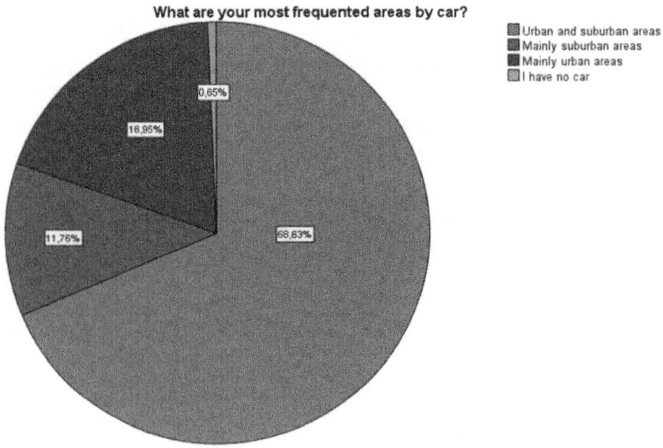

The respondents were also asked to give their reasons for traveling by car; this was aimed at analyzing the electro-compatibility of each trip. For instance, commuting by car to work or school and making short trips for errands or family reasons are considered to be "short trips" and therefore highly compatible with the use of an EV since they will not require recharging the car often. Contrarily, driving the car to work or for vacation reduces the respondents' level of electro-compatibility, given that it forces the driver to make frequent stops to recharge the car due to the limited range of batteries.

Finally, regarding the respondents' environmental consciousness and innovation attraction, the results showed that majority of the respondents exhibited some electro-friendly traits, with 81.7% of them declaring that they were concerned about sustainability and 84.3% declaring that they were attracted to technological innovation.

The third section of the survey investigated the respondents' personal attitudes toward electric mobility; the respondents were asked to rate, on a Likert scale ranging from 1 (strongly disagree) to 5 (strongly agree), their level of agreement/disagreement with several aspects of EV.

Cronbach's Alpha test was initially performed to test the reliability and verify internal consistency of the items adopted in each construct (Urbach & Ahlemann, 2010; Hinton et.al., 2004). All the items show a significant reliability as it satisfies the accepted rule of thumb of having more than 0.7 of Chronbach's Alpha coefficient values (Kline, 2005). The results of the reliability test are presented in Table 5.3.

Regarding environmental sustainability and related concerns (Section 3.1), majority of the respondents agreed with practices aimed at preserving the environment and stopping climate change, pollution also being seen as a health concern and risk factor. This finding reflects the eco-friendly behavior of most of the respondents.

One-sample statistics

	N	Mean	Std. deviation	Std. error mean
3.1.a. I think people should change their behavior to reduce climate change and protect the environment	153	4.50	.650	.053
3.1.b. I am concerned about human behavior and its influence on climate change and the environment	153	4.34	.771	.062
3.1.c. I think climate change is a threat to me and my family	153	4.20	.869	.070

(continued)

Table 5.3 Cronbach's alpha test of reliability results

Construct	N° of items	Cronbach's alpha
3.1 Environmental concerns	3	.794
3.2 Attitudes toward electric vehicle adoption	6	.876
3.3 Purchase intention	2	.800
3.4 Perceived usefulness	3	.785
3.5 Perceived ease of use	3	.853
3.6 Perceived risk	4	.745
3.7 Attitude toward the environment and owning an electric car	3	.824
3.8 Purchase aversion	5	.845
3.9 Level of information	7	.766
3.10 Knowledge of electric mobility	3	.839
Total	39	

(continued)

One-sample statistics

	N	Mean	Std. deviation	Std. error mean

One-sample test

	Test value = 0					
	t	df	Sig. (2-tailed)	Mean difference	95% Confidence interval of the difference	
					Lower	Upper
3.1.a. I think people should change their behavior to reduce climate change and protect the environment	85,553	152	.000	4.497	4.39	4.60
3.1.b. I am concerned about human behavior and its influence on climate change and the environment	69,636	152	.000	4.340	4.22	4.46
3.1.c. I think climate change is a threat to me and my family	59,837	152	.000	4.203	4.06	4.34

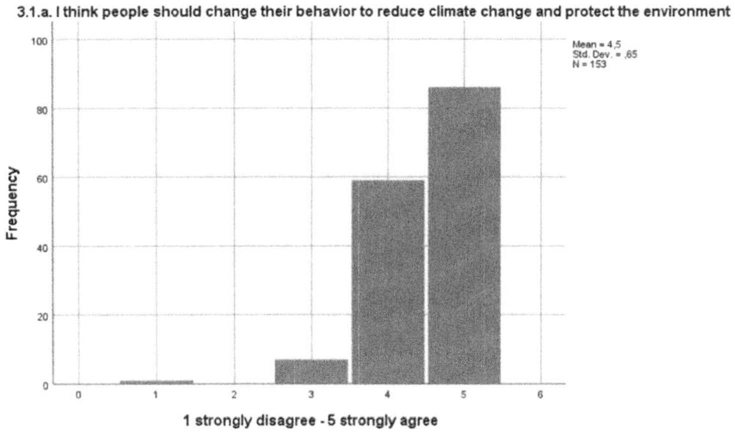
3.1.a. I think people should change their behavior to reduce climate change and protect the environment
Mean = 4,5
Std. Dev. = ,65
N = 153
Frequency
0
20
40
60
80
100
0
1
2
3
4
5
6
1 strongly disagree - 5 strongly agree

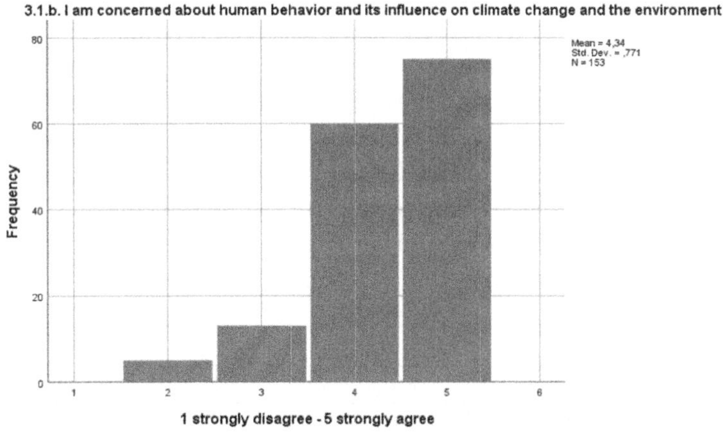
3.1.b. I am concerned about human behavior and its influence on climate change and the environment
Mean = 4,34
Std. Dev. = ,771
N = 153
Frequency
0
20
40
60
80
1
2
3
4
5
6
1 strongly disagree - 5 strongly agree

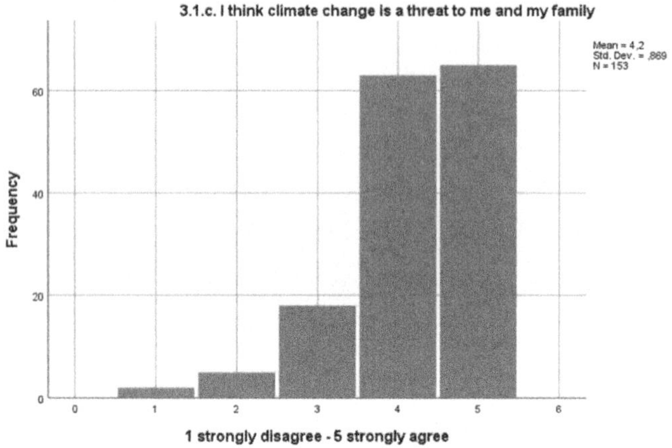

The respondents' attitudes toward potentially adopting an EV were rather interesting and deserved a closer analysis. First, it was found that having a battery life guarantee would encourage respondents to buy an EV (mean = 3.66), and respondents believed that purchasing an EV is economically profitable in the long run (mean = 3.63). Notably, their willingness to pay more for an EV still lagged behind (mean = 2.91), and they showed unwillingness to tolerate the inconveniences associated with limited range (mean = 2.94) or change their travel habits (mean = 3.02).

One-sample statistics

	N	Mean	Std. deviation	Std. error mean
3.2.a. In the long run, I think buying an electric vehicle is more cost-effective than owning a conventional vehicle	153	3.63	1.123	.091
3.2.b. With an excellent battery warranty, I would not worry about buying an electric vehicle.	153	3.66	1.187	.096
3.2.c. Electric vehicles are able to meet my travel needs even with limited range	153	3.28	1.206	.097

(continued)

(continued)

One-sample statistics				
	N	Mean	Std. deviation	Std. error mean
3.2.d. I am willing to spend more to purchase an EV	153	2.91	1.221	.099
3.2.e. I am ready to modify my travel habits somewhat to own an EV	153	3.02	1.195	.097
3.2.f. I am willing to tolerate some occasional inconveniences related to battery charging for the benefits of driving an electric vehicle	153	2.94	1.221	.099

One-sample test						
	Test value = 0					
	t	df	Sig. (2-tailed)	Mean difference	95% Confidence interval of the difference	
					Lower	Upper
3.2.a. In the long run, I think buying an electric vehicle is more cost-effective than owning a conventional vehicle	39,947	152	.000	3.627	3.45	3.81

(continued)

(continued)

One-sample test

	Test value = 0					
					95% Confidence interval of the difference	
	t	df	Sig. (2-tailed)	Mean difference	Lower	Upper
3.2.b. With an excellent battery warranty, I would not worry about buying an electric vehicle.	38,126	152	.000	3.660	3.47	3.85
3.2.c. Electric vehicles are able to meet my travel needs even with limited range	33,664	152	.000	3.281	3.09	3.47
3.2.d. I am willing to spend more to purchase an EV	29,457	152	.000	2.908	2.71	3.10
3.2.e. I am ready to modify my travel habits somewhat to own an EV	31,264	152	.000	3.020	2.83	3.21

(continued)

(continued)

One-sample test

	Test value = 0					
	t	df	Sig. (2-tailed)	Mean difference	95% Confidence interval of the difference	
					Lower	Upper
3.2.f. I am willing to tolerate some occasional inconveniences related to battery charging for the benefits of driving an electric vehicle	29,805	152	.000	2.941	2.75	3.14

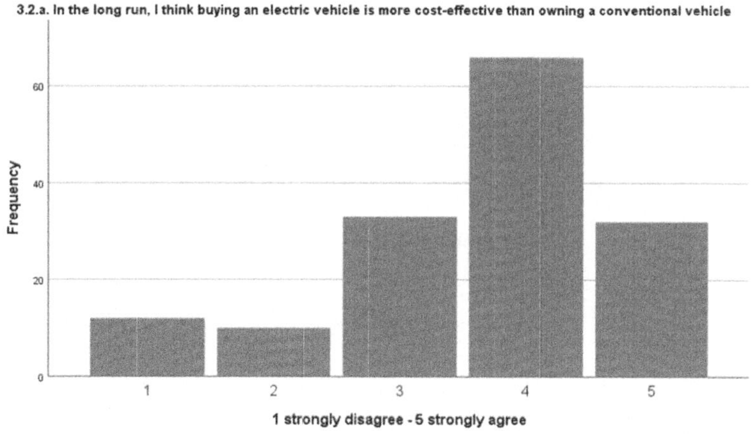

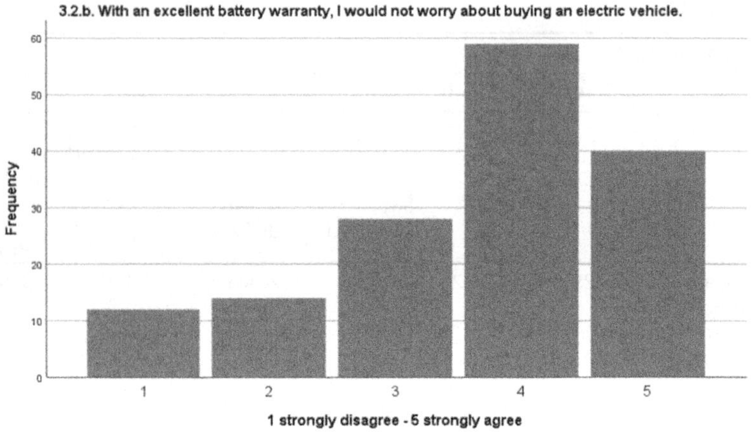
3.2.b. With an excellent battery warranty, I would not worry about buying an electric vehicle.
Frequency
0
10
20
30
40
50
60
1
2
3
4
5
1 strongly disagree - 5 strongly agree

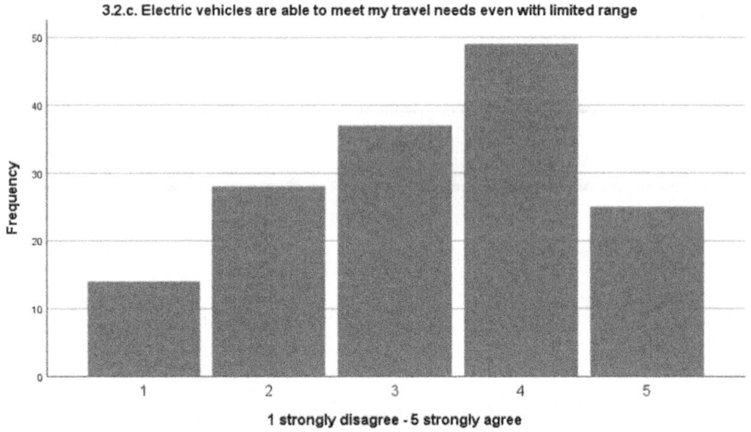
3.2.c. Electric vehicles are able to meet my travel needs even with limited range
Frequency
0
10
20
30
40
50
1
2
3
4
5
1 strongly disagree - 5 strongly agree

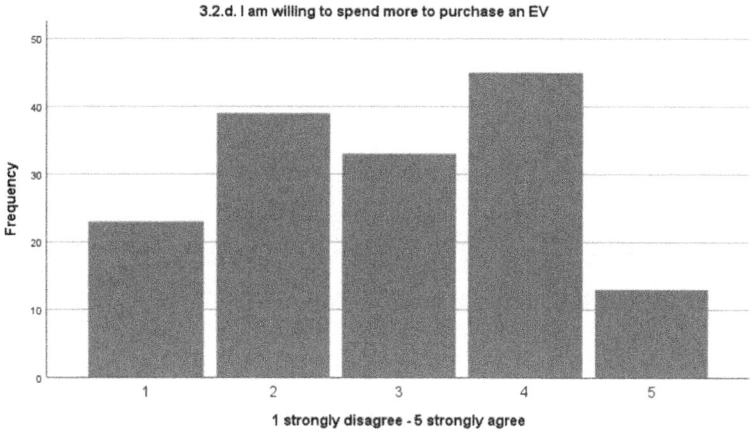
3.2.d. I am willing to spend more to purchase an EV
Frequency
0
10
20
30
40
50
1
2
3
4
5
1 strongly disagree - 5 strongly agree

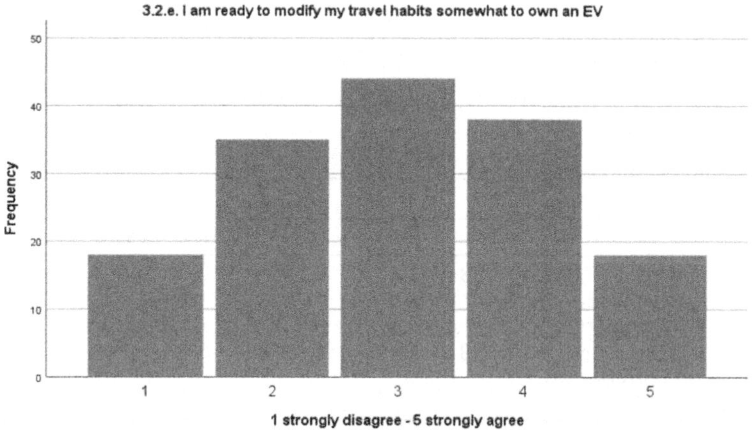
3.2.e. I am ready to modify my travel habits somewhat to own an EV
Frequency
0
10
20
30
40
50
1
2
3
4
5
1 strongly disagree - 5 strongly agree

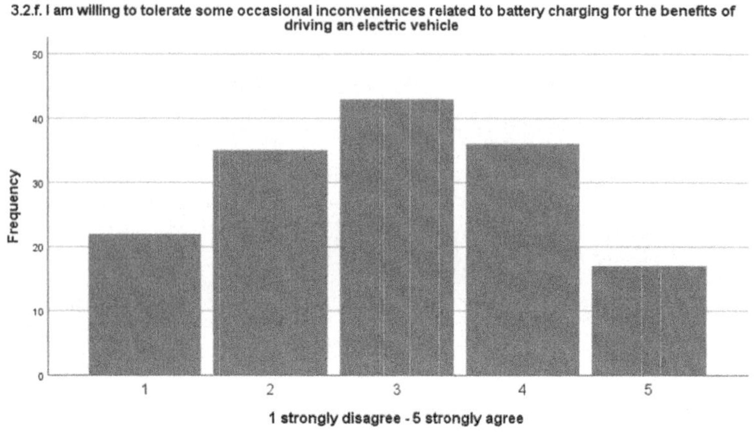

The sample's intention to purchase an EV (Section 3.3 of the survey) was still relatively low. The respondents' willingness to buy an EV in the next two years was low (mean = 2.67); however, they also declared that if they have to replace their car, they will first consider an EV (mean = 3.41).

One-sample statistics

	N	Mean	Std. deviation	Std. error mean
3.3.a. I plan to purchase an electric vehicle in the next two years	153	2.67	1.123	.091
3.3.b. If I replace my car, I will first consider an electric vehicle	153	3.41	1.189	.096

One-sample test

	Test value = 0					
	t	df	Sig. (2-tailed)	Mean difference	95% Confidence interval of the difference	
					Lower	Upper
3.3.a. I plan to purchase an electric vehicle in the next two years	29,446	152	.000	2.673	2.49	2.85
3.3.b. If I replace my car, I will first consider an electric vehicle	35,479	152	.000	3.412	3.22	3.60

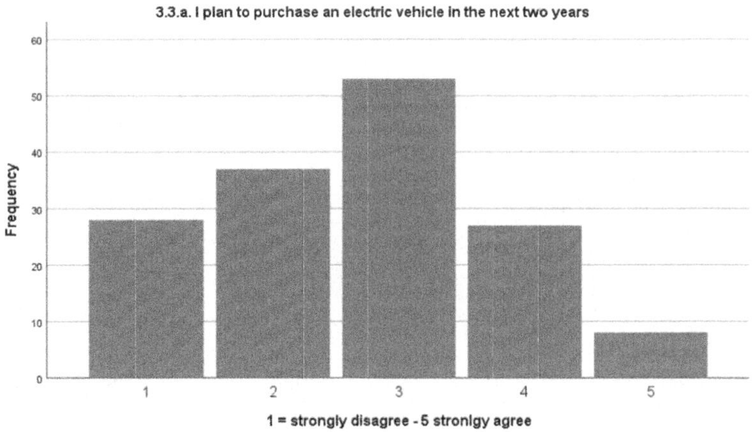

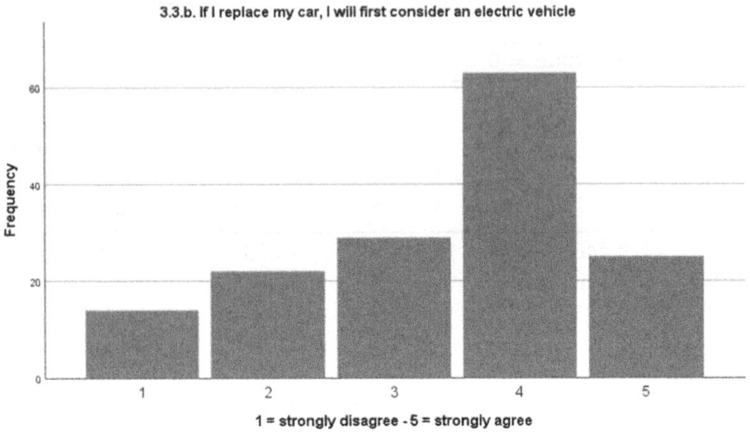

The perceived usefulness of EVs (Section 3.4 of the survey) showed some mixed results. While majority of the respondents acknowledged the sustainability-related advantages of EV use (e.g., decrease in emissions) as noteworthy (mean = 3.90), many remained neutral toward EV's ability to improve travel efficiency, such as by decreasing transportation-related expenses (mean = 3.46) and improving commuting efficiency (mean = 3.07).

One-sample statistics

	N	Mean	Std. deviation	Std. error mean
3.4.a. I believe that the use of electric vehicles can reduce carbon emissions and energy consumption	153	3.90	.994	.080
3.4.b. I believe that the use of electric vehicles can reduce family expenses for transportation	153	3.46	.994	.080
3.4.c. I believe that the use of electric vehicles can improve my commuting efficiency	153	3.07	1.064	.086

One-sample test

	Test value = 0					
	t	df	Sig. (2-tailed)	Mean difference	95% Confidence interval of the difference	
					Lower	Upper
3.4.a. I believe that the use of electric vehicles can reduce carbon emissions and energy consumption	48,451	152	.000	3.895	3.74	4.05
3.4.b. I believe that the use of electric vehicles can reduce family expenses for transportation	43,125	152	.000	3.464	3.31	3.62
3.4.c. I believe that the use of electric vehicles can improve my commuting efficiency	35,698	152	.000	3.072	2.90	3.24

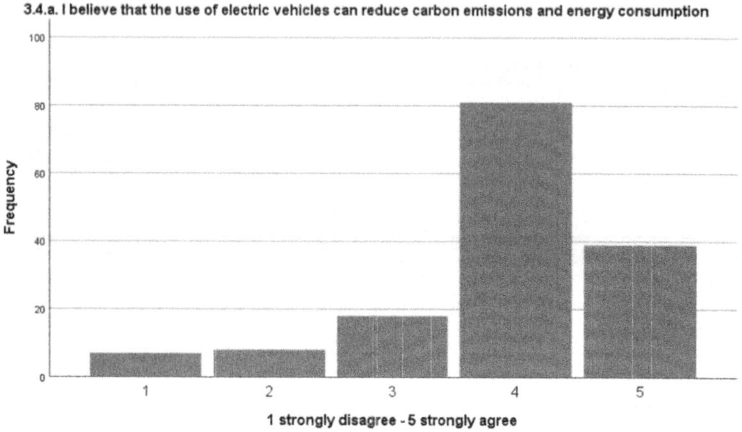
3.4.a. I believe that the use of electric vehicles can reduce carbon emissions and energy consumption
Frequency
100
80
60
40
20
0
1
2
3
4
5
1 strongly disagree - 5 strongly agree

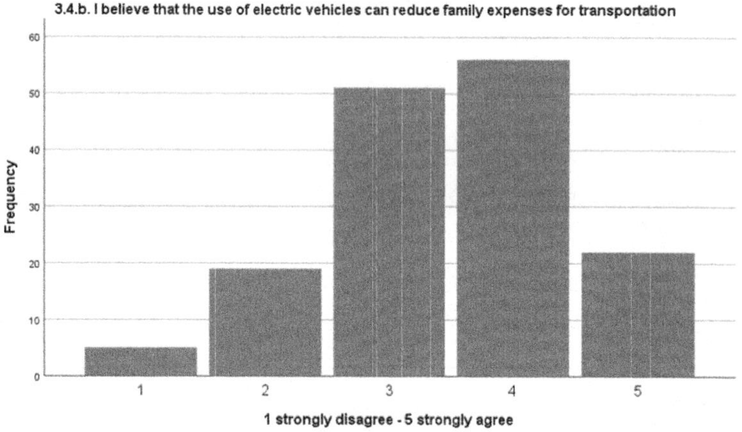
3.4.b. I believe that the use of electric vehicles can reduce family expenses for transportation
Frequency
60
50
40
30
20
10
0
1
2
3
4
5
1 strongly disagree - 5 strongly agree

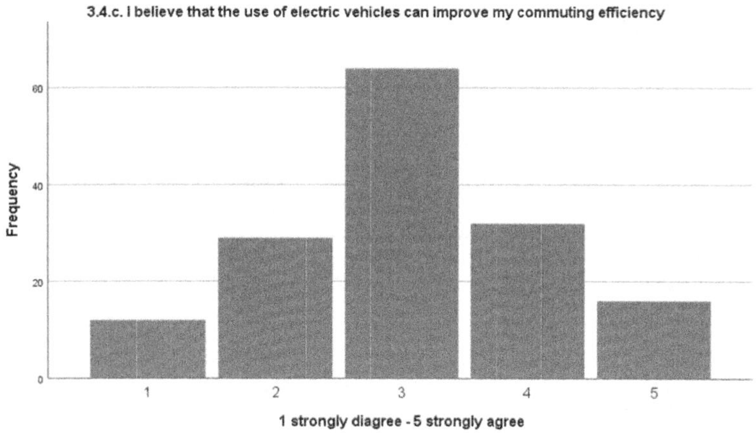

Regarding the perceived ease of use of EVs (Section 3.5 of the survey), the results show that majority of the respondents believe that it is easy (mean = 3.80) or would be easy (mean = 4.07) to drive an EV, and the interaction with it would be clear and understandable (mean = 3.91). Therefore, EVs' ease of use does not appear to be a barrier to purchase intentions.

One-sample statistics

	N	Mean	Std. deviation	Std. error mean
3.5.a. I think it is easy to use electric vehicles	153	3.80	.967	.078
3.5.b. I think it would be easy for me to drive electric vehicles	153	4.07	.804	.065
3.5.c. My interaction with electric vehicles would be clear and understandable.	153	3.91	.853	.069

One-sample test

	Test value = 0					
					95% Confidence interval of the difference	
	t	df	Sig. (2-tailed)	Mean difference	Lower	Upper
3.5.a. I think it is easy to use electric vehicles	48,660	152	.000	3.804	3.65	3.96
3.5.b. I think it would be easy for me to drive electric vehicles	62,660	152	.000	4.072	3.94	4.20
3.5.c. My interaction with electric vehicles would be clear and understand-able.	56,646	152	.000	3.908	3.77	4.04

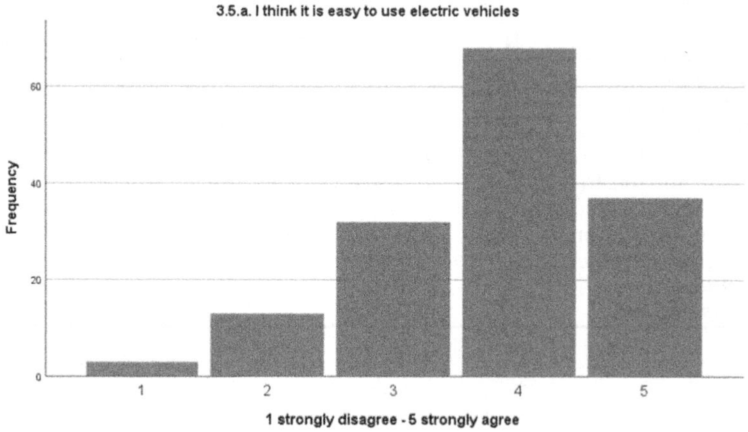

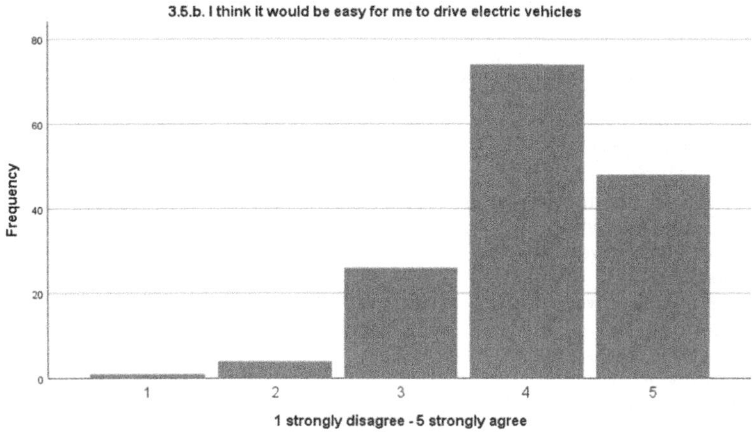

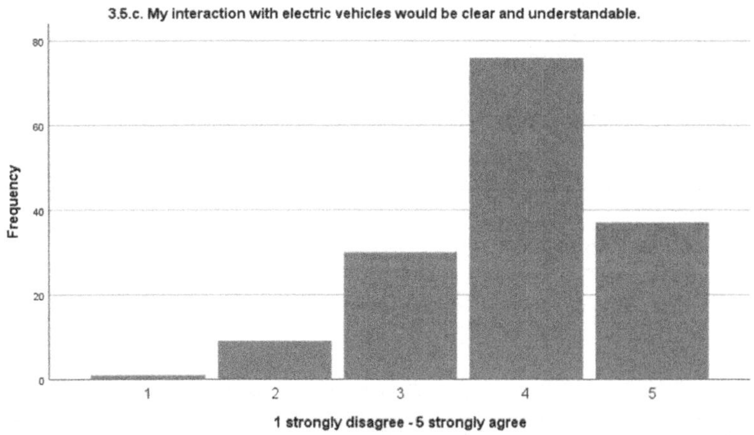

The data on perceived risk (Section 3.6 of the survey) showed rather mixed opinions. While majority of the respondents did not seem fazed by the risk of financial loss related to purchasing an EV (mean = 2.92) and did not believe that using an EV will affect their safety (mean = 2.52), their concerns regarding the performance of the vehicle (mean = 3.22), limited range, and insufficient charging infrastructure (mean = 3.75) were significantly higher.

One-sample statistics

	N	Mean	Std. deviation	Std. error mean
3.6.a. I am afraid of suffering financial losses when using electric vehicles	153	2.92	1.073	.087
3.6.b. I would not feel completely safe when I drive an electric vehicle on the road	153	2.52	1.113	.090
3.6.c. I worry about whether electric vehicles will really have the same performance as conventional vehicles	153	3.22	1.158	.094
3.6.d. I worry about the drawbacks of using electric vehicles (e.g., limited range, charging infrastructure, and charging time)	153	3.75	1.029	.083

One-sample test

	Test value = 0					
	t	df	Sig. (2-tailed)	Mean difference	95% Confidence interval of the difference	
					Lower	Upper
3.6.a. I am afraid of suffering financial losses when using electric vehicles	33,674	152	.000	2.922	2.75	3.09

(continued)

(continued)

One-sample test

	Test value = 0					
	t	df	Sig. (2-tailed)	Mean difference	95% Confidence interval of the difference	
					Lower	Upper
3.6.b. I would not feel completely safe when I drive an electric vehicle on the road	28,047	152	.000	2.523	2.35	2.70
3.6.c. I worry about whether electric vehicles will really have the same performance as conventional vehicles	34,344	152	.000	3.216	3.03	3.40
3.6.d. I worry about the drawbacks of using electric vehicles (e.g., limited range, charging infrastructure, and charging time)	45,003	152	.000	3.745	3.58	3.91

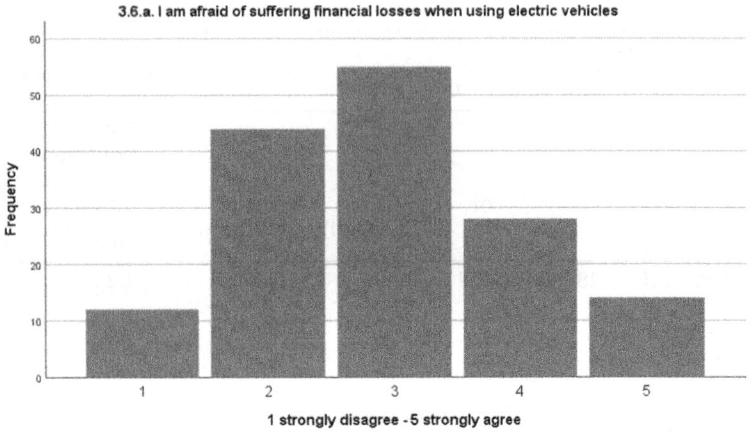
3.6.a. I am afraid of suffering financial losses when using electric vehicles
Frequency
0
10
20
30
40
50
60
1
2
3
4
5
1 strongly disagree - 5 strongly agree

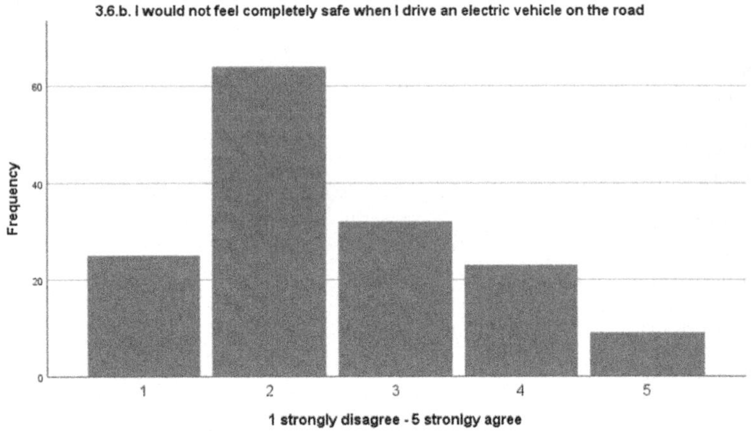
3.6.b. I would not feel completely safe when I drive an electric vehicle on the road
Frequency
0
20
40
60
1
2
3
4
5
1 strongly disagree - 5 stronigy agree

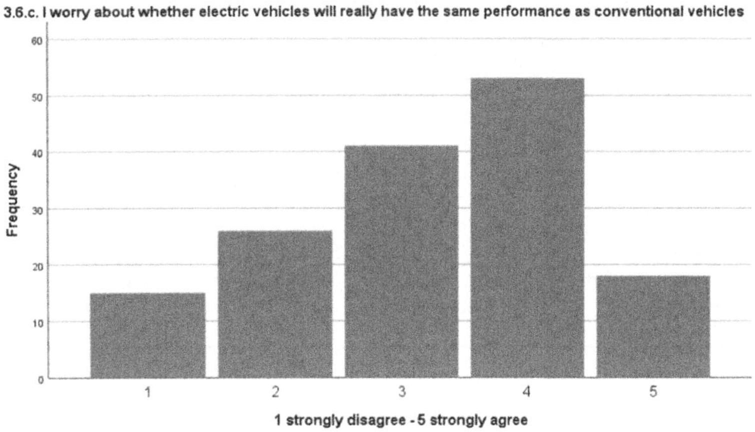

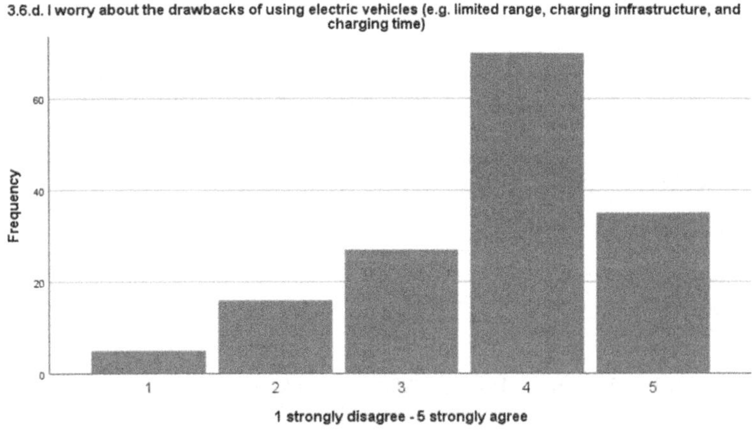

Section 3.7 of the survey investigated the respondents' attitude toward the environment and owning an EV. The results indicate that the respondents strongly agree that people need to change their lifestyle to protect the environment (mean = 4.24); they also declare that they have changed their buying habits to help the environment (mean = 3.42).

One-sample statistics

	N	Mean	Std. deviation	Std. error mean
3.7.a. People need to change their lifestyles to protect the environment	153	4.24	.803	.065
3.7.b. When I drive, I often use my car for my leisure time	153	3.64	.964	.078
3.7.c. I have changed my buying habits to help the environment	153	3.42	.958	.077

One-sample test

	Test value = 0					
	t	df	Sig. (2-tailed)	Mean difference	95% Confidence interval of the difference	
					Lower	Upper
3.7.a. People need to change their lifestyles to protect the environment	65,327	152	.000	4.242	4.11	4.37
3.7.b. When I drive, I often use my car for my leisure time	46,716	152	.000	3.641	3.49	3.79
3.7.c. I have changed my buying habits to help the environment	44,238	152	.000	3.425	3.27	3.58

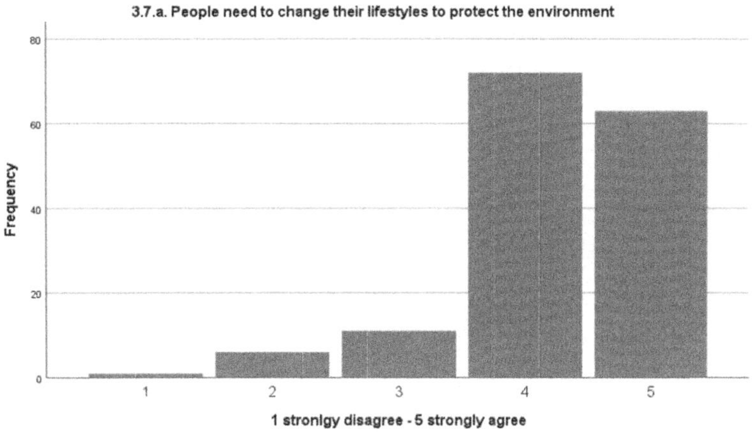
3.7.a. People need to change their lifestyles to protect the environment
Frequency
0
20
40
60
80
1
2
3
4
5
1 stronlgy disagree - 5 strongly agree

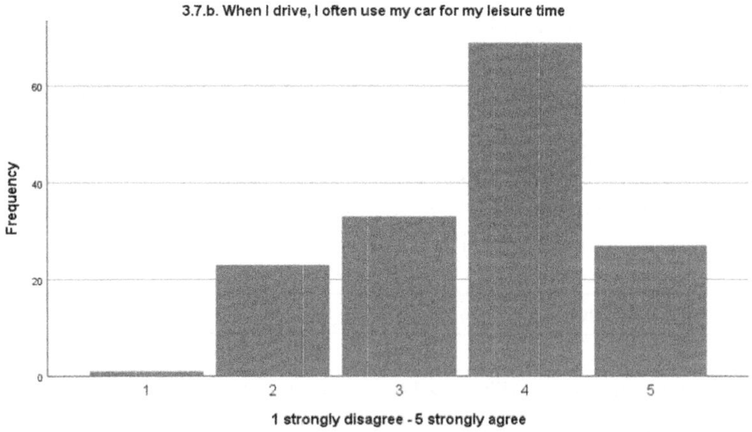
3.7.b. When I drive, I often use my car for my leisure time
Frequency
0
20
40
60
1
2
3
4
5
1 strongly disagree - 5 strongly agree

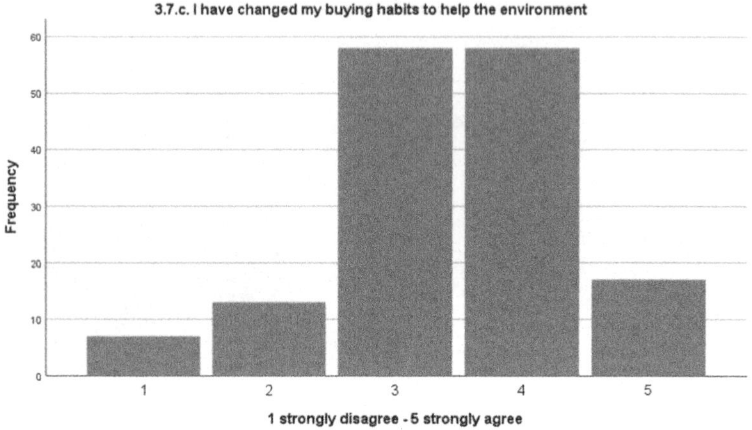

It is worth noting that overall, the respondents' level of purchase aversion (Section 3.8 of the survey) was rather neutral. Limited charging infrastructure was the main barrier to EV purchase (mean = 3.12). Another barrier toward EV purchase was found to be lack of knowledge about EV technology (mean = 2.90). However, the respondents did not consider EVs' low resale value (mean = 2.70), EVs' reliance on rather new technology (mean = 2.56), and the fact that they do not fully trust this technology (mean = 2.49) to be major barriers.

One-sample statistics

	N	Mean	Std. deviation	Std. error mean
3.8.a. I don't want to take the risk of buying an electric vehicle because I know little about it	153	2.90	1.044	.084
3.8.b. I do not trust EV technology	153	2.49	1.046	.085
3.8.c. EVs are not a proven technology and this discourages me from buying	153	2.56	1.099	.089
3.8.d. It is not a good idea to buy EV because of the limited charging infrastructure	153	3.12	1.120	.091

(continued)

(continued)

One-sample statistics				
	N	Mean	Std. deviation	Std. error mean
3.8.e. It is not a good idea to buy an EV because of the low resale value	153	2.70	1.039	.084

One-sample test						
	Test value = 0					
	t	df	Sig. (2-tailed)	Mean difference	95% Confidence interval of the difference	
					Lower	Upper
3.8.a. I don't want to take the risk of buying an electric vehicle because I know little about it	34,397	152	.000	2.902	2.74	3.07
3.8.b. I do not trust EV technology	29,454	152	.000	2.490	2.32	2.66
3.8.c. EVs are not a proven technology, and this discourages me from buying	28,831	152	.000	2.562	2.39	2.74
3.8.d. It is not a good idea to buy EV because of the limited charging infrastructure	34,506	152	.000	3.124	2.95	3.30

(continued)

(continued)

One-sample test

	Test value = 0					
	t	df	Sig. (2-tailed)	Mean difference	95% Confidence interval of the difference	
					Lower	Upper
3.8.e. It is not a good idea to buy an EV because of the low resale value	32,128	152	.000	2.699	2.53	2.87

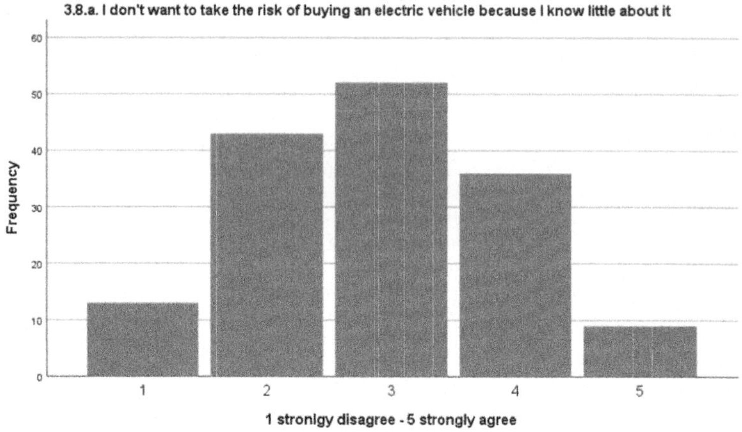

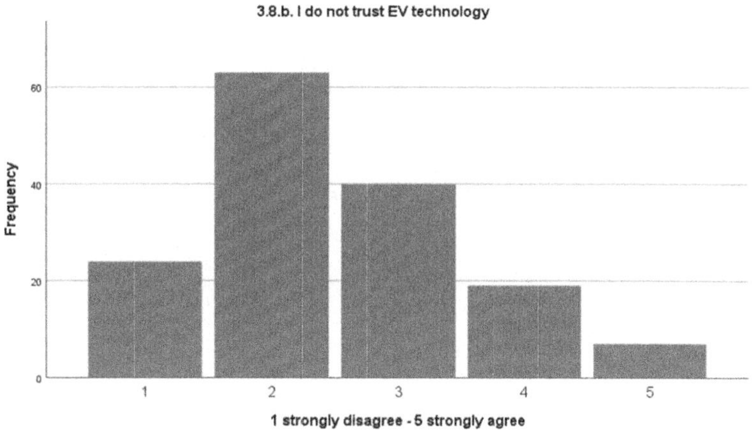
3.8.b. I do not trust EV technology
Frequency
0
20
40
60
1
2
3
4
5
1 strongly disagree - 5 strongly agree

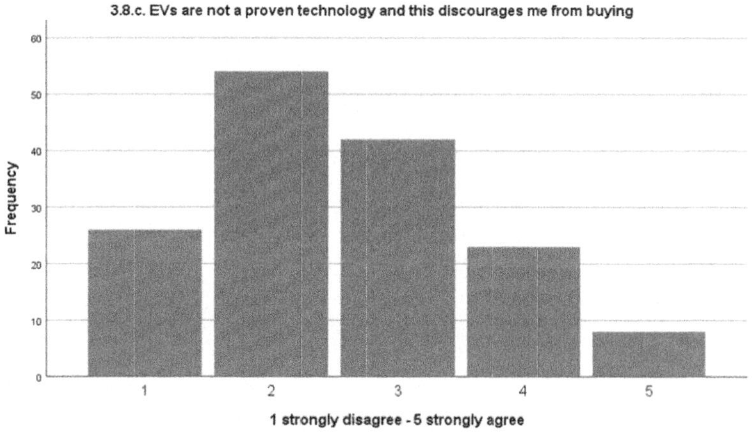
3.8.c. EVs are not a proven technology and this discourages me from buying
Frequency
0
10
20
30
40
50
60
1
2
3
4
5
1 strongly disagree - 5 strongly agree

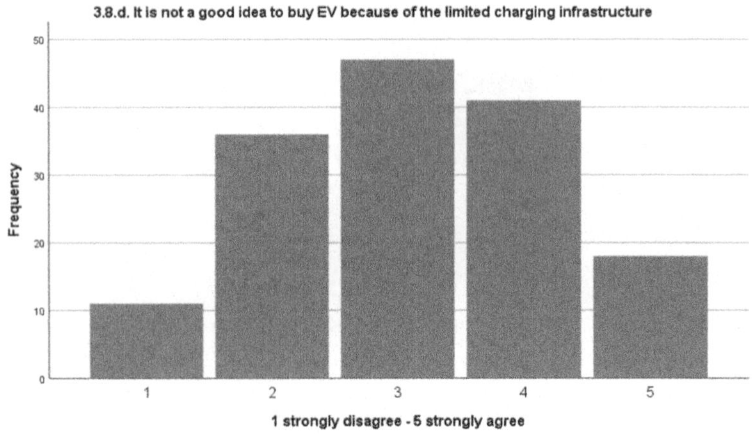

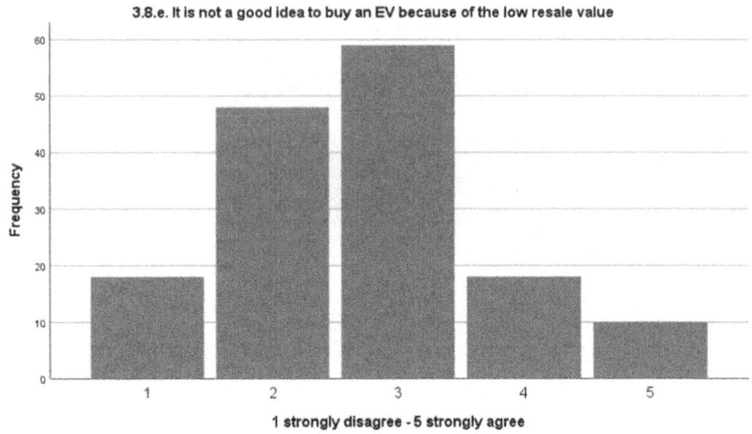

The "Level of Information" variable (Section 3.9 of the survey) showed that majority of the respondents are clearly aware of the increase level of advertising regarding EVs (mean = 4.07). In addition, the respondents showed a high degree of awareness about the European guidelines aimed at reducing emissions by 2030 through the European Green Deal and the Fit for 55 standards package (mean = 3.91). Furthermore, those in the process of buying a new car had a good level of information about the market and available models (mean = 3.85) and declared that they were increasingly reading articles, watching television broadcasts, and hearing positive comments about EVs (mean = 3.78).

One-sample statistics	N	Mean	Std. deviation	Std. error mean
3.9.a. It seems to me that EV publicity has increased dramatically in recent months	153	4.07	.762	.062
3.9.b. I am increasingly reading articles, watching television broadcasts, or hearing positive comments about EVs	153	3.78	.819	.066
3.9.c. People close to me have a positive opinion about the purchase of electric vehicles	153	3.27	.954	.077
3.9.d. From what I read or hear, I believe that conventional cars will disappear or become very few in the short to medium term	153	3.29	1.030	.083
3.9.e. I know that European policy guidelines are pushing toward the green transition, and electric vehicles are included in these guidelines	153	3.91	.853	.069
3.9.f. When I buy a new car, I read up on everything there is to know about the car models that are available on the market	153	3.85	.923	.075
3.9.g. I am informed about the pros and cons of electric vehicles.	153	3.52	1.077	.087

One-sample test

	Test value = 0					
	t	df	Sig. (2-tailed)	Mean difference	95% Confidence interval of the difference	
					Lower	Upper
3.9.a. It seems to me that EV publicity has increased dramatically in recent months	66,116	152	.000	4.072	3.95	4.19
3.9.b. I am increasingly reading articles, watching television broadcasts, or hearing positive comments about EVs	57,175	152	.000	3.784	3.65	3.92
3.9.c. People close to me have a positive opinion about the purchase of electric vehicles	42,436	152	.000	3.275	3.12	3.43

(continued)

(continued)

One-sample test						
	Test value = 0					
	t	df	Sig. (2-tailed)	Mean difference	95% Confidence interval of the difference	
					Lower	Upper
3.9.d. From what I read or hear, I believe that conventional cars will disappear or become very few in the short to medium term	39,470	152	.000	3.288	3.12	3.45
3.9.e. I know that European policy guidelines are pushing toward the green transition, and electric vehicles are included in these guidelines	56,646	152	.000	3.908	3.77	4.04
3.9.f. When I buy a new car, I read up on everything there is to know about the car models that are available on the market	51,580	152	.000	3.850	3.70	4.00

(continued)

(continued)

One-sample test						
	Test value = 0					
	t	df	Sig. (2-tailed)	Mean difference	95% Confidence interval of the difference	
					Lower	Upper
3.9.g. I am informed about the pros and cons of electric vehicles.	40,397	152	.000	3.516	3.34	3.69

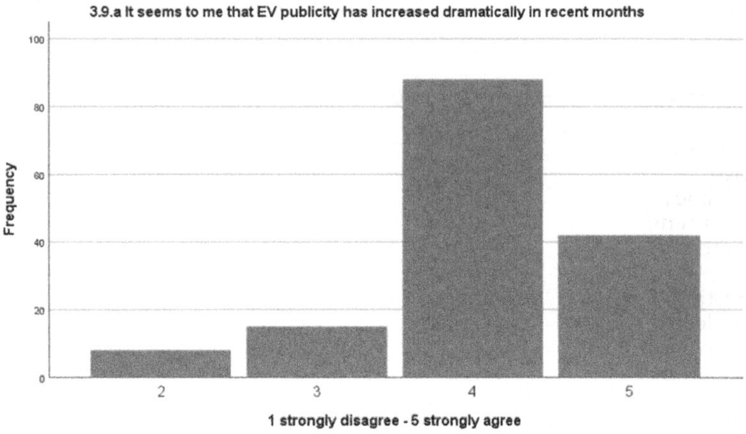

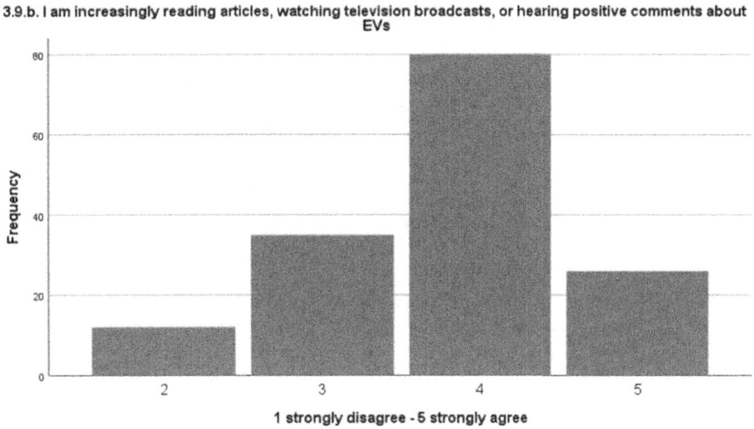
3.9.b. I am increasingly reading articles, watching television broadcasts, or hearing positive comments about EVs
Frequency
0
20
40
60
80
2
3
4
5
1 strongly disagree - 5 strongly agree

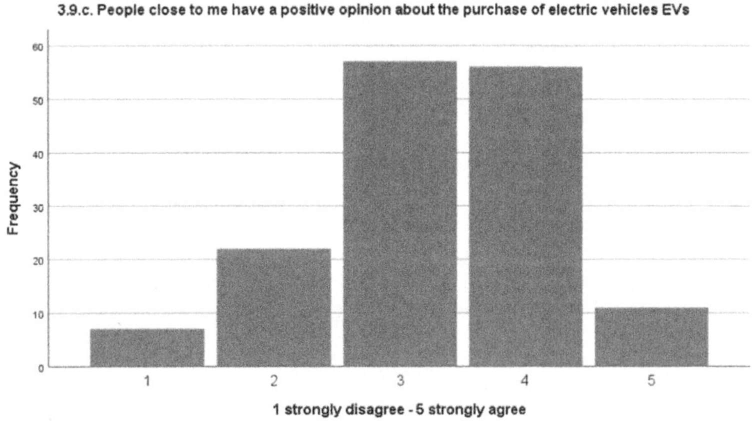
3.9.c. People close to me have a positive opinion about the purchase of electric vehicles EVs
Frequency
0
10
20
30
40
50
60
1
2
3
4
5
1 strongly disagree - 5 strongly agree

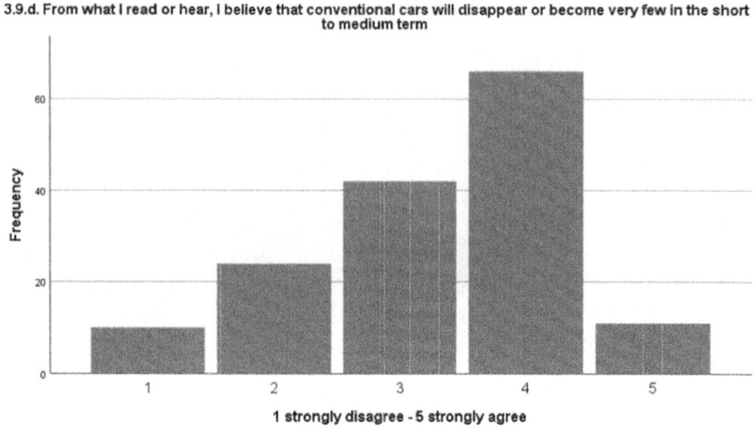
3.9.d. From what I read or hear, I believe that conventional cars will disappear or become very few in the short to medium term
Frequency
0
20
40
60
1
2
3
4
5
1 strongly disagree - 5 strongly agree

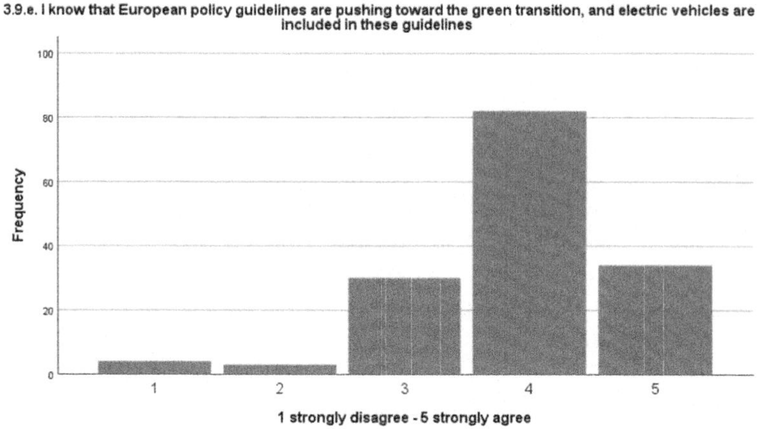
3.9.e. I know that European policy guidelines are pushing toward the green transition, and electric vehicles are included in these guidelines
Frequency
0
20
40
60
80
100
1
2
3
4
5
1 strongly disagree - 5 strongly agree

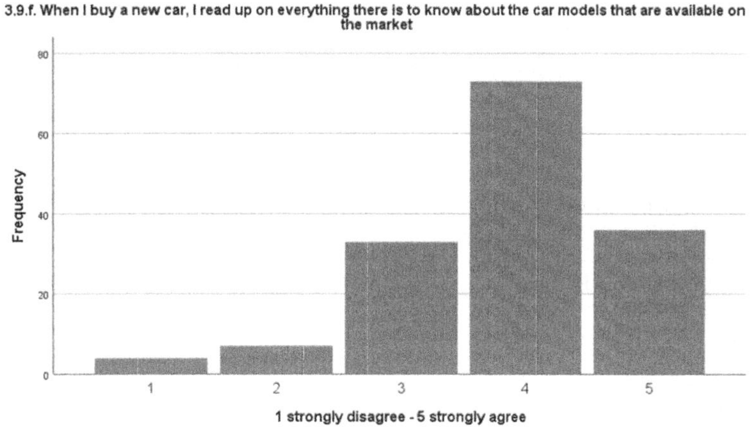

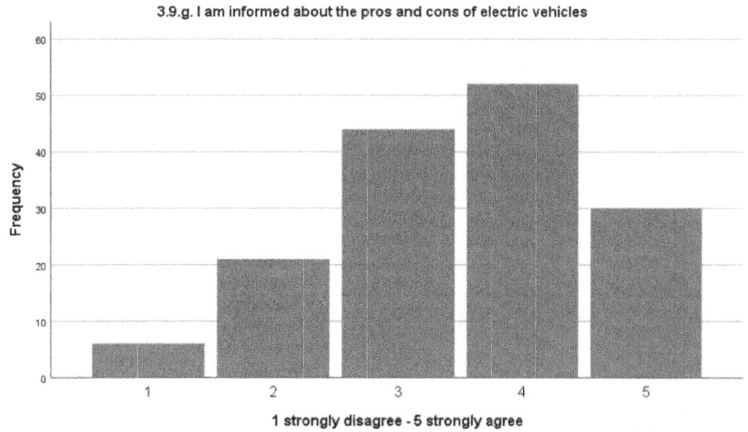

Finally, the "Knowledge of Electric Mobility" variable (Section 3.10 of the survey) showed the respondents' level of knowledge about the performance (mean = 3.29) and costs (mean = 3.20) of using EVs to be rather neutral. However, considering the environmental advantages of EVs over traditional vehicles, the respondents showed a higher degree of knowledge (mean = 3.70).

One-sample statistics				
	N	Mean	Std. deviation	Std. error mean
3.10.a. I know the performance of electric vehicles (e.g., charging time, acceleration, driving comfort, and range).	153	3.29	1.168	.094
3.10.b. I know the operating costs of electric vehicles	153	3.20	1.161	.094
3.10.c. I know the environmental advantages of electric vehicles over conventional vehicles.	153	3.70	.974	.079

One-sample test						
	Test value = 0					
	t	df	Sig. (2-tailed)	Mean difference	95% Confidence interval of the difference	
					Lower	Upper
3.10.a. I know the performance of electric vehicles (e.g., charging time, acceleration, driving comfort, and range).	34,817	152	.000	3.288	3.10	3.47
3.10.b. I know the operating costs of electric vehicles	34,134	152	.000	3.203	3.02	3.39

(continued)

(continued)

One-sample test

	Test value = 0					
	t	df	Sig. (2-tailed)	Mean difference	95% Confidence interval of the difference	
					Lower	Upper
3.10.c. I know the environmental advantages of electric vehicles over conventional vehicles.	46,985	152	.000	3.699	3.54	3.85

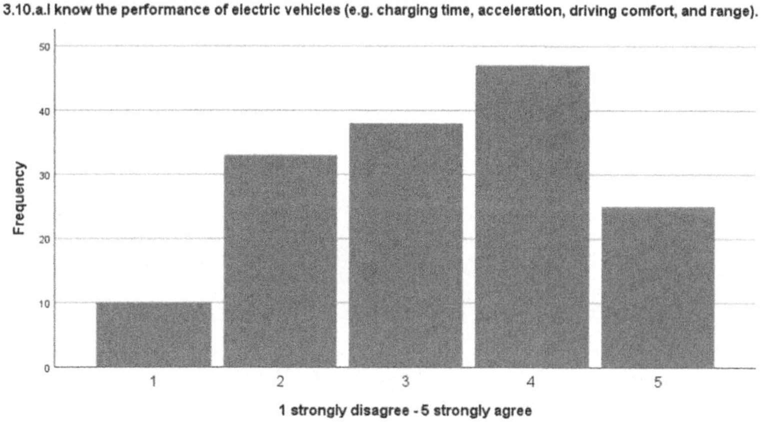

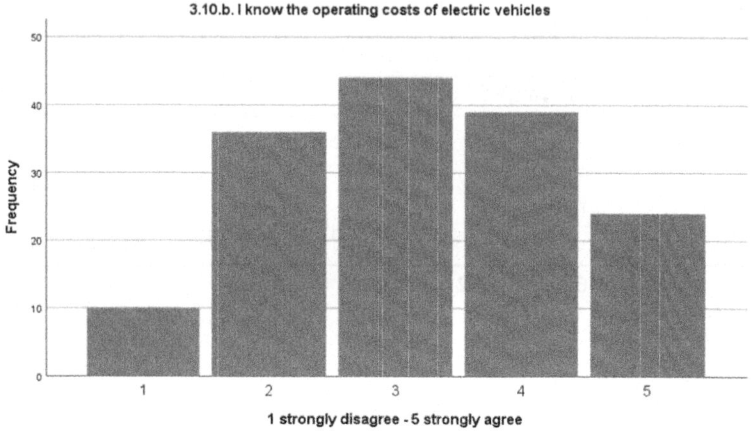
3.10.b. I know the operating costs of electric vehicles
Frequency
50
40
30
20
10
0
1
2
3
4
5
1 strongly disagree - 5 strongly agree

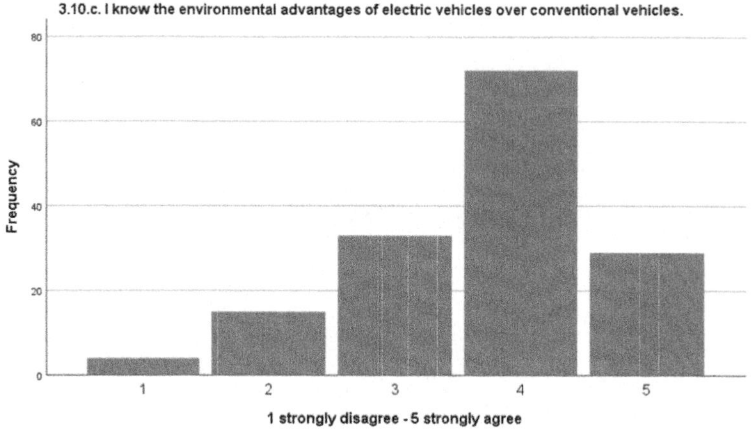
3.10.c. I know the environmental advantages of electric vehicles over conventional vehicles.
Frequency
80
60
40
20
0
1
2
3
4
5
1 strongly disagree - 5 strongly agree

6
Discussion

Abstract This final chapter provides a comprehensive discussion on electric mobility, summarizing the book contribution and highlighting key areas of intervention. It explores the integration of e-mobility with the United Nations Sustainable Development Goals (SDGs), specifically addressing how electric mobility contributes to Affordable and Clean Energy (Goal 7), Industry, Innovation, and Infrastructure (Goal 9), Sustainable Cities and Communities (Goal 11), Responsible Consumption and Production (Goal 12), and Climate Action (Goal 13). The chapter underscores the pivotal role of electric mobility in achieving these goals, providing key insights and contributions to the field. Recommendations are made for consumers, industries, and policymakers to further enhance the adoption and impact of electric mobility. Additionally, future research directions are proposed.

Keywords sustainable development goals · UN Agenda 2030 · e-mobility integration · policy recommendations · future research

As we conclude our exploration of the transformative potential of electric mobility (e-mobility) for consumers and industries, it becomes evident

D. D'Acunto, *The Future of E-Mobility*,
https://doi.org/10.1007/978-3-031-65053-6_6

that this innovation stands at the confluence of sustainability and technological advancement (Ajanovic et al., 2021). Through rigorous analysis and comprehensive discussion, this study has underscored the significant role e-mobility plays in addressing some of the most pressing environmental challenges of our time, while also paving the way for a more sustainable and resilient economic future.

E-mobility is not merely a technological innovation but also a catalyst for societal transformation. By aligning closely with the United Nations (UN) Sustainable Development Goals (SDGs), specifically Goals 7, 9, 11, 12, and 13, e-mobility initiatives promise to usher in a new era of affordable and clean energy, spur industry innovation and infrastructure resilience, promote sustainable cities and communities, encourage responsible consumption and production, and take decisive action against climate change (Ruggieri et al., 2021). This alignment is not coincidental but rather indicative of the intrinsic value e-mobility brings to the global sustainability agenda.

The findings of this study have illuminated the multifaceted benefits of e-mobility, from reducing greenhouse gas emissions and lowering dependency on fossil fuels to enhancing urban mobility and fostering economic growth through new job creation (Biresselioglu et al., 2018). For consumers, the transition to electric vehicles (EVs) offers a cleaner, more efficient, and increasingly affordable mode of transportation, thanks, in part, to ongoing advancements in battery technology and a growing network of charging infrastructure. For industries, the shift toward e-mobility represents both a challenge and an opportunity—a challenge to traditional automotive manufacturers and energy suppliers and an opportunity for new entrants and innovators to redefine market paradigms.

Our recommendations for consumers, industries, and policymakers are designed to accelerate the adoption of e-mobility and help it realize its full potential. For consumers, education on the benefits of EVs, coupled with financial incentives, can increase adoption. Industries must embrace change by investing in research and development and forging new partnerships to innovate and scale up e-mobility solutions (Laurischkat et al., 2016). Further, policymakers must play their role in creating a conducive environment for e-mobility through supportive policies, incentives, and infrastructure investments.

Looking ahead, the journey toward a fully electric future is fraught with challenges, including technological barriers, economic considerations, and the need for comprehensive policy frameworks (Skrúcaný et al., 2019). However, the opportunities far outweigh the challenges. Future research should focus on overcoming these barriers, exploring new technologies such as solid-state batteries, advancing smart charging infrastructure, and evaluating the socioeconomic impacts of e-mobility.

In conclusion, e-mobility stands as a beacon of hope and a testament to the ingenuity of humans in our collective quest for a sustainable future. By embracing e-mobility, we not only pave the way for cleaner, greener transportation options but also contribute to the broader goals of sustainable development and climate action (Rietmann & Lieven, 2019). This study's findings affirm the critical role of e-mobility in shaping the future of our planet and society. It is incumbent upon all stakeholders—consumers, industries, and policymakers—to work collaboratively toward realizing the vision of a sustainable, electrified world.

6.1 Summary of the Study and Key Areas of Intervention

This study was an in-depth investigation into the benefits of e-mobility for consumers and industries, against the backdrop of an urgent global need for sustainable transportation solutions. The advent of EVs and the infrastructure supporting them presents a promising pathway to mitigate climate change, reduce pollution, and enhance energy efficiency

(Hoarau & Perez, 2018). Our research methodology combined quantitative data analysis and comprehensive literature reviews to offer a holistic view of the current state and future potential of e-mobility.

Environmental Benefits

The environmental benefits of e-mobility extend beyond the reduction of greenhouse gas emissions. Our study identified that EVs contribute significantly to the reduction of noise pollution, an often overlooked advantage. Urban areas, in particular, stand to benefit from the widespread adoption of EVs, as this will create quieter and more serene city environments (Requia et al., 2018). Additionally, the shift toward e-mobility encourages the integration of renewable energy sources into the grid, further reducing the carbon footprint of transportation.

Economic Impact

The economic implications of e-mobility are vast and varied. Beyond job creation and operational savings for consumers, the study uncovered that the EV supply chain has the potential to bolster local economies. By incentivizing the production of EV components and batteries domestically, countries can reduce their reliance on imported oil, improve trade balances, and foster technological innovation (Carteni et al., 2020). Furthermore, the growth of e-mobility is stimulating investments in smart grid technologies, which are essential for managing the increased electrical load from EV charging and integrating renewable energy sources.

Consumer Adoption and Behavioral Insights

While initial studies highlighted the positive attitude of consumers toward EVs, further analyses revealed a nuanced picture of consumer behavior. The decision to purchase an EV is influenced by a complex interplay of factors, including environmental consciousness, perceived economic benefits, and social influences (Bubeck et al., 2016). The current study found that early adopters are typically more environmentally conscious and tech-savvy. However, to broaden the appeal of EVs, it is essential to address the practical concerns of mainstream consumers, such as charging convenience and vehicle range.

Industry Transformation Beyond Automotive

The transformative impact of e-mobility on industries extends beyond the automotive sector to reshape the energy, technology, and service industries. Energy providers are exploring new business models, such as vehicle-to-grid (V2G) services, which allow EV batteries to store and return electricity to the grid, thereby enhancing grid stability and integrating more renewable energy sources into the grid (Croce et al., 2019). In the technology sector, advancements in artificial intelligence and Internet of Things technologies are enabling smarter, more efficient charging solutions and enhanced vehicle connectivity. The service industry is also witnessing the emergence of new mobility services, such as electric car-sharing and ride-hailing platforms, which are redefining urban mobility.

Policy and Regulatory Environment: A Closer Look

The role of policy and regulation in facilitating the transition to e-mobility cannot be overstated. Our study's in-depth analysis revealed that successful e-mobility adoption is often preceded by strong government initiatives, including financial incentives for EV buyers (tax rebates, grants, and subsidies), investments in charging infrastructure, and stringent emissions standards (Ala et al., 2021). Additionally, urban planning policies that prioritize EV-friendly infrastructure, such as dedicated EV parking and charging stations, are critical for supporting the growth of e-mobility in urban areas.

The synthesis of our findings underscores the transformative potential of e-mobility as a cornerstone of sustainable development. However, realizing this potential requires a concerted effort across multiple fronts; consumers, industries, and policymakers must collaborate to overcome the remaining barriers and seize the opportunities presented by e-mobility (Longo et al., 2018). As we look to the future, it is clear that the journey toward a sustainable, electrified transportation system is well underway. Continued innovation, strategic investments, and inclusive policies will be key in accelerating this transition. The insights gained from this study not only contribute to the understanding of e-mobility's role in sustainable development but also serve as a guidepost for stakeholders navigating the path toward a cleaner, more sustainable future.

Implications for Sustainable Development

The findings of this study have profound implications for sustainable development, particularly in relation to the UN SDGs. E-mobility directly supports the achievement of the SDGs related to affordable and clean energy (Goal 7), industry innovation and infrastructure (Goal 9), sustainable cities and communities (Goal 11), responsible consumption and production (Goal 12), and climate action (Goal 13).

In conclusion, this study has provided comprehensive insights into the benefits of e-mobility for consumers and industries, highlighting its potential to drive environmental sustainability, economic growth, and social well-being (Afonso et al., 2020). The transition to e-mobility is not without its challenges, but the opportunities it presents for advancing sustainable development are unparalleled. Continued innovation, supportive policies, and collaborative efforts among all stakeholders are essential in realizing the full potential of e-mobility.

6.2 Integration of E-Mobility with the United Nations Sustainable Development Goals

The integration of e-mobility with the UN SDGs is a pivotal area of study that underscores the broader implications of this transformative technology on sustainable development. E-mobility's alignment with the SDGs, particularly Goals 7, 9, 11, 12, and 13, highlights its potential to contribute significantly to global efforts aimed at addressing some of the most pressing challenges of our time, including climate change, energy access, urban sustainability, innovation, and responsible consumption. Figure 6.1 shows the UN SDGs directly and indirectly involved by the adoption of electric mobility.

Fig. 6.1 The UN SDGs involved in the adoption of EM (personal elaboration)

6.2.1 Affordable and Clean Energy (Goal 7)

E -mobility stands at the forefront of the transition toward more sustainable energy systems, directly contributing to SDG 7, which aims to ensure access to affordable, reliable, sustainable, and modern energy for all. The shift from internal combustion engine (ICE) vehicles to EVs embodies a paradigm shift in how societies consume energy for transportation, steering away from fossil fuels toward cleaner, renewable sources of power (Plananska, 2020). This transition is pivotal for several reasons, each underscoring the critical role of e-mobility in achieving affordable and clean energy.

Firstly, EVs offer a more efficient alternative to traditional vehicles, with electric motors converting a higher percentage of electrical energy from the grid into power to drive the wheels. This efficiency translates into reduced energy consumption per kilometer traveled, lowering the overall demand for energy in the transportation sector, which is one of the largest consumers of fossil fuels globally (Bi et al., 2016). By decreasing the reliance on oil and other non-renewable energy sources, e-mobility contributes to energy diversification and security, reducing vulnerability to oil price fluctuations and supply disruptions.

Secondly, the integration of EVs with renewable energy sources further enhances the sustainability of the transportation sector. As the share of renewables in the global energy mix grows, charging EVs with green energy minimizes their carbon footprint, making them a cornerstone in the efforts to reduce greenhouse gas emissions (Calise et al., 2021). This synergy between e-mobility and renewable energy generation is vital for decarbonizing the energy sector, a critical step in combating climate change. Moreover, advancements in battery storage technology have not only improved the range and performance of EVs but have also offered the potential to store excess renewable energy, thus addressing one of the key challenges in the renewable energy sector—intermittency.

The role of e-mobility in promoting affordable and clean energy extends beyond environmental benefits; it also has significant economic implications. The operational costs of EVs are generally lower than those of traditional vehicles, owing to fewer moving parts requiring maintenance and the lower cost of electricity compared to gasoline and diesel. This affordability aspect is crucial for increasing the accessibility of clean transportation options for a broader segment of the population (Laurischkat et al., 2016). Furthermore, the global shift toward e-mobility is driving down the costs of EVs and batteries through economies of scale, making clean energy technologies more accessible and affordable.

Government policies and incentives play a pivotal role in accelerating the adoption of e-mobility and its integration with clean energy sources. Initiatives such as tax rebates for EV purchases, subsidies for charging infrastructure, and renewable energy targets encourage both consumers and industries to invest in clean energy technologies (Bergman et al., 2017). These policies promote the growth of the e-mobility sector and also stimulate innovation in renewable energy generation and storage solutions, reinforcing the positive feedback loop between clean transportation and sustainable energy systems.

The societal benefits of e-mobility in the context of SDG 7 are profound. By reducing air pollution, EVs contribute to improved public health outcomes, especially in urban areas where traffic emissions are a major source of air quality issues (Ajanovic, 2021). Additionally, the transition to e-mobility supports the development of modern, resilient, and sustainable energy infrastructure, facilitating the broader societal shift toward sustainability and resilience against the impacts of climate change.

In conclusion, e-mobility is an indispensable ally in the quest to achieve affordable and clean energy (SDG 7). Through its synergy with renewable energy, contribution to reducing greenhouse gas emissions, economic benefits, and support for resilient energy infrastructures, e-mobility encapsulates the essence of sustainable development (Biresselioglu, 2018). However, concerted efforts by governments, industries, and the society are required to maximize e-mobility's potential, overcome existing barriers, and embrace the opportunities it presents. Investments in charging infrastructure, continued innovation in battery technology, and supportive policy frameworks are essential to ensure that the benefits of e-mobility are realized on a global scale, paving the way for a sustainable, energy-secure future.

6.2.2 Industry, Innovation, and Infrastructure (Goal 9)

The integration of e-mobility into the fabric of modern society is a testament to its extraordinary capacity for industry innovation and the development of resilient infrastructure, aligning with the SDG 9, which emphasizes the need for building resilient infrastructure, promoting inclusive and sustainable industrialization, and fostering innovation (Bubeck et al., 2016). E-mobility represents a significant shift in the automotive industry and also catalyzes advancements across various sectors including the energy, technology, and urban development sectors. This multifaceted impact underscores the essential role of e-mobility in achieving SDG 9.

At the heart of the e-mobility revolution is the innovation in battery technology and EV design. The quest for longer range, shorter charging times, and more affordable EVs has spurred substantial research and development efforts. These innovations are not confined to the vehicles themselves but extend to the creation of advanced charging infrastructure, including fast-charging stations and smart charging networks that optimize energy usage and integrate renewable energy sources (Carteni, 2020). Such advancements are crucial for enhancing the efficiency and sustainability of the transportation sector, directly contributing to the industrial innovation aspect of SDG 9.

Moreover, the rise of e-mobility necessitates and drives the development of resilient and sustainable infrastructure. The deployment of extensive charging networks, the integration of V2G technologies, and the adaptation of power grids to accommodate the increasing demand for electricity due to EVs are examples of how e-mobility is reshaping infrastructure planning and development (Hoarau, 2018). These efforts ensure the reliability and sustainability of transportation systems and enhance the overall resilience of urban infrastructure against environmental pressures and the growing demands of urbanization.

The ripple effects of e-mobility extend beyond transportation and energy to foster innovation in digital technologies and services. For instance, the proliferation of connected and autonomous vehicles, enabled by advances in EV technology, is driving the evolution of smart mobility solutions (Laurischkat et al., 2016). These innovations promise to improve traffic management, reduce congestion on the roads, and enhance the safety and convenience of urban transportation. Furthermore, e-mobility is stimulating the growth of new business models, such as the mobility-as-a-service (MaaS) model, which integrates various forms of transport services into a single accessible platform (Requia, 2018). These developments exemplify the innovative spirit encapsulated in SDG 9 and also contribute to more efficient and sustainable urban ecosystems.

The transition to e-mobility also presents opportunities for sustainable industrialization. The manufacturing of EVs and its components, such as batteries and charging equipment, is becoming a growing sector within the global economy (Rietmann, 2019). This shift toward e-mobility can stimulate job creation, drive technological advancements, and promote the development of green industries. However, to fully leverage these opportunities, industries must prioritize sustainability and resilience throughout the supply chain, from raw material extraction to end-of-life recycling. Such an approach aligns with the goals of SDG 9 by ensuring that industrialization supports broader environmental and societal objectives.

Government policies and international cooperation are pivotal in catalyzing the innovation and infrastructure development necessary for the widespread adoption of e-mobility. Investments in research and development, incentives for clean technology adoption, and regulations that encourage the development of sustainable infrastructure are essential for propelling the e-mobility sector forward (Ruggieri, 2021). By fostering an enabling environment for innovation and investing in the infrastructure that supports e-mobility, governments and international organizations can significantly contribute to achieving SDG 9.

In conclusion, e-mobility embodies the principles of SDG 9 by driving industry innovation, promoting sustainable industrialization, and necessitating the development of resilient infrastructure. The transformative impact of e-mobility extends across sectors, catalyzing advancements in technology, energy, and urban development (Skrúcaný, 2019). To realize the full potential of e-mobility in contributing to SDG 9, a concerted effort by governments, industries, and communities is required. By embracing innovation, investing in sustainable infrastructure, and fostering an environment conducive for sustainable industrial growth, the global community can leverage the benefits of e-mobility to build a more resilient, sustainable, and prosperous future.

6.2.3 Sustainable Cities and Communities (Goal 11)

E-mobility is emerging as a cornerstone in the development of sustainable cities and communities, directly contributing to the SDG 11, which aims to make cities and human settlements inclusive, safe, resilient, and sustainable. The advent of EVs and the associated infrastructure is not only transforming urban mobility but also acting as a catalyst for broader societal shifts toward sustainability (Bubeck et al., 2016). This transition is critical for addressing the myriad challenges faced by urban areas, including air pollution, traffic congestion, and reliance on non-renewable energy sources.

The impact of e-mobility on urban regions is profound and multifaceted. By replacing ICE vehicles with EVs, cities can significantly reduce air pollution, one of the most pressing health hazards in urban areas (Croce et al., 2019); the resultant improvement in air quality can lead to better public health outcomes, reduced healthcare costs, and a more pleasant urban living environment. Furthermore, the quiet nature of EVs contributes to reducing noise pollution, enhancing the quality of life of city dwellers and creating more tranquil urban spaces.

E-mobility also plays a pivotal role in the decarbonization of urban transportation systems, aligning with global efforts to combat climate change. By integrating EVs with renewable energy sources, cities can move toward a more sustainable and resilient energy model, reducing their carbon footprint and helping to mitigate greenhouse gas emissions (Ala et al., 2021). This shift is essential for the long-term sustainability of urban areas, ensuring that they remain habitable and vibrant for future generations.

The adoption of e-mobility necessitates and encourages the development of smart, connected urban infrastructure. The deployment of EV charging stations, integration of smart grid technologies, and advancement of V2G systems are ways in which e-mobility can drive innovation in urban infrastructure. These technologies support the charging and operation of EVs and also enhance the overall efficiency and resilience of urban energy systems (Longo et al., 2018). Furthermore, smart mobility solutions, enabled by e-mobility, can improve traffic management, reduce congestion, and facilitate more efficient use of urban spaces.

E-mobility's contribution to sustainable urban development extends beyond environmental benefits to encompass social and economic dimensions. By promoting the use of EVs, cities can foster greater social inclusion and accessibility. Electric public transportation options, such as buses and taxis, can provide cleaner, more reliable, and affordable mobility solutions, especially for vulnerable populations and those living in underserved areas (Plananska, 2020). Moreover, the e-mobility sector offers new economic opportunities, from jobs in EV manufacturing and maintenance to roles in the development and operation of charging infrastructure and related services.

The transition to e-mobility in urban areas also underscores the importance of comprehensive planning and policymaking. To fully realize the benefits of e-mobility for sustainable cities and communities, governments, city planners, and stakeholders must collaborate to create supportive regulatory frameworks, invest in necessary infrastructure, and foster public–private partnerships (Bi et al., 2016). Policies that incentivize EV adoption, such as subsidies, tax breaks, and the provision of charging facilities in public spaces, are crucial for accelerating the shift toward cleaner urban mobility.

Furthermore, engaging communities in the transition to e-mobility is essential in ensuring that the shift is inclusive and meets the needs of all urban residents. Public awareness campaigns, educational programs, and community-based initiatives all play a significant role in promoting the acceptance and use of EVs, thereby fostering a culture of sustainability and innovation within cities.

In conclusion, e-mobility is a key enabler of sustainable urban development, offering a pathway to achieving SDG 11 by transforming urban mobility, reducing environmental impacts, and enhancing the livability of cities. Through the integration of EVs into urban transportation systems and the development of supportive infrastructure and policies, cities can become more inclusive, safe, resilient, and sustainable. The success of this transition requires a holistic approach which embraces technological innovation, strategic planning, and community engagement. As cities worldwide strive to meet the challenges of the twenty-first century, e-mobility stands as a beacon of sustainable urban development, guiding the way toward a cleaner, greener, and more equitable urban future.

6.2.4 Responsible Consumption and Production (Goal 12)

E-mobility has emerged as a transformative force in promoting responsible consumption and production, aligning directly with the UN SDG 12, which aims to ensure sustainable consumption and production patterns, a critical endeavor as the world grapples with the dual challenges of environmental degradation and resource depletion (Calise et al., 2021). The shift toward EVs and the broader adoption of e-mobility principles are pivotal strategies in redefining how societies produce, consume, and think about transportation.

Central to e-mobility's contribution to SDG 12 is the reduction of dependency on non-renewable energy sources and the minimization of the environmental impact of the transportation sector. Traditional vehicles powered by ICEs are significant contributors to global oil consumption and CO_2 emissions (Laurischkat et al., 2016). In contrast, EVs, especially when charged with electricity generated from renewable sources, present a cleaner, more sustainable alternative. This shift not only reduces emissions but also diminishes the environmental footprint of personal and public transport, marking a critical step toward more sustainable consumption patterns.

Furthermore, the lifecycle of EVs embodies the principles of responsible production. Advances in battery technology, materials science, and recycling processes are enhancing the efficiency, longevity, and sustainability of EVs. Moreover, from sourcing eco-friendly materials to implementing energy-efficient manufacturing processes, manufacturers are increasingly focusing on reducing the environmental impact of vehicle production (Bergman et al., 2017). The growing emphasis on the circular economy within the e-mobility sector, including battery recycling and repurposing, further exemplifies the commitment to responsible production practices. These efforts not only mitigate the environmental impact of EVs but also ensure that the benefits of e-mobility extend throughout the vehicles' entire lifecycle.

Responsible consumption is another dimension of SDG 12 that is greatly impacted by e-mobility. The adoption of EVs encourages consumers to rethink their transportation choices, steering them toward more sustainable options. Government policies and incentives, such as tax rebates, subsidies for EVs, and investments in charging infrastructure, play a crucial role in shaping consumer behavior (Rietmann & Lieven, 2019). By making e-mobility accessible and attractive, these initiatives promote a shift in societal norms and values toward greater environmental stewardship and sustainability.

Moreover, e-mobility fosters innovation in business models that support sustainable consumption. Car-sharing services, electric public transport solutions, and MaaS platforms are redefining access to transportation, moving away from vehicle ownership toward shared use (Pan et al., 2021). These models not only reduce the number of vehicles on the road but also maximize the utilization rates of EVs, further decreasing the per capita environmental impact of transportation. In doing so, e-mobility aligns with the broader goals of SDG 12 by encouraging more efficient use of resources and reducing waste.

The global transition to e-mobility also underscores the need for systemic changes in energy production and infrastructure development to support responsible consumption and production. The integration of EVs with smart grid technologies and renewable energy sources is essential for maximizing the environmental benefits of electric transportation (Musolino et al., 2019). This integration not only ensures that the increased demand for electricity does not lead to higher emissions but also contributes to the overall resilience and sustainability of the energy grid.

In conclusion, e-mobility stands as a pivotal contributor to achieving SDG 12 (Responsible Consumption and Production). By promoting the shift away from fossil fuels, enhancing the sustainability of vehicle production, and encouraging shifts in consumer behavior toward more sustainable transportation options, e-mobility embodies the essence of SDG 12. However, realizing its full potential requires concerted efforts across multiple sectors, including government, industry, and civil society (Calise et al., 2019). Policies that support EV adoption, investments in renewable energy, and initiatives that foster sustainable consumer behaviors are essential for ensuring that e-mobility contributes effectively to the global pursuit of sustainable consumption and production patterns. As the world moves toward a more sustainable future, e-mobility offers a clear pathway for reducing the environmental impact of transportation, fostering innovation in sustainable technologies, and promoting a more responsible and sustainable relationship with our planet.

6.2.5 Climate Action (Goal 13)

The advancement of e-mobility is a critical lever in the global effort to combat climate change, resonating deeply with the SDG 13, which calls for urgent action to combat climate change and its impacts. The transportation sector, a significant contributor to global greenhouse gas emissions due to its heavy reliance on fossil fuels, is at a pivotal juncture (Biresselioglu et al., 2018). The transition to EVs offers a tangible way to drastically reduce these emissions, underscoring the vital role of e-mobility in achieving climate action objectives.

E-mobility's contribution to climate action is multifaceted, encompassing both direct and indirect mechanisms of reducing carbon footprints and mitigating the effects of global warming. Directly, EVs, by virtue of their zero tailpipe emissions, significantly lower the amount of CO_2 released into the atmosphere, especially when compared to conventional vehicles powered by ICEs (Pavić et al., 2020). This direct reduction in greenhouse gas emissions is critical for urban areas, where traffic congestion exacerbates pollution and contributes to poor air quality, affecting millions of lives.

Indirectly, the shift toward e-mobility accelerates the transition toward renewable energy sources. As the demand for electricity to power EVs grows, there is a concurrent push to decarbonize the electricity grid by integrating more renewable energy sources such as wind, solar, and hydroelectric power (Franke et al., 2016). This transition ensures that the operation of EVs becomes increasingly cleaner over time and also fosters a broader shift in energy production patterns away from fossil fuels, contributing to global efforts to limit climate change.

Furthermore, e-mobility adoption promotes technological innovations and infrastructure development that are essential for climate resilience. For instance, innovations in battery storage and charging technology not only improve the efficiency and convenience of EVs but also enhance the storage capabilities for renewable energy, addressing one of the key challenges in the energy sector (Abd Alla et al., 2021). The development of smart grids and V2G technologies allows EV batteries to store excess renewable energy and feed it back into the grid during peak demand times, thereby stabilizing the grid and optimizing renewable energy use.

The global momentum toward e-mobility also stimulates international cooperation and policy alignment in climate action efforts. Governments worldwide are implementing policies and incentives, such as subsidies, tax incentives, and the development of EV charging infrastructure, to accelerate the adoption of EVs. These measures are complemented by international agreements and collaborations aimed at reducing global carbon emissions, an endeavor in which the promotion of e-mobility plays a key role (Kovačić et al., 2022). This collective action is crucial for achieving the ambitious targets set forth in international climate agreements, such as the Paris Agreement, which aims to limit global warming to well below 2 °C above pre-industrial levels.

However, realizing the full potential of e-mobility in contributing to climate action requires addressing several challenges. These include enhancing the sustainability of the EV supply chain, particularly in the extraction and processing of raw materials for batteries; ensuring equitable access to e-mobility solutions, especially in developing countries; and continually improving the energy efficiency of EVs and the renewable share of the electricity grid (Barisa et al., 2016). Addressing these challenges necessitates a holistic approach that integrates technological innovation, policy support, and international collaboration.

In conclusion, e-mobility emerges as a cornerstone in the quest for sustainable climate action under SDG 13. By significantly reducing greenhouse gas emissions, fostering the shift toward renewable energy, and driving technological innovation in support of climate resilience, e-mobility presents a compelling avenue for mitigating climate change. The path forward requires sustained commitment from all sectors of society—governments, industries, and individuals—to embrace e-mobility as part of a broader strategy to achieve the urgent and ambitious goals of climate action (Afonso, 2020). As the world grapples with the escalating challenges of global warming, the transition to EVs offers a beacon of hope, demonstrating the potential for innovative solutions to pave the way for a more sustainable and climate-resilient future.

6.3 The Comprehensive Role of Electric Mobility in Achieving the Sustainable Development Goals

The integration of e-mobility into the framework of the UN SDGs encapsulates a paradigm shift in global efforts toward sustainable development. This complex interplay is best visualized through a comprehensive framework that illustrates how e-mobility intersects with key SDGs, namely affordable and clean energy (Goal 7); industry, innovation, and infrastructure (Goal 9); sustainable cities and communities (Goal 11); responsible consumption and production (Goal 12); and climate action (Goal 13). This visualization not only highlights the multifaceted role of e-mobility in advancing these goals but also underscores the synergistic effects that can accelerate global progress toward sustainability (Fig. 6.2).

At the core of this framework is e-mobility's contribution to affordable and clean energy (Goal 7). EVs, powered by renewable energy sources, exemplify the transition to cleaner, more sustainable energy systems. This shift is represented visually by connections between EV charging infrastructure and renewable energy grids, symbolizing the direct link between e-mobility and the reduction of fossil fuel dependence (Ala, 2021). Furthermore, innovations in battery technology and energy storage are depicted as foundational supports, reinforcing the stability and efficiency of renewable energy sources and ensuring that clean energy remains accessible and affordable for all.

Regarding industry, innovation, and infrastructure (Goal 9), the framework illustrates e-mobility's role in catalyzing technological advancements and infrastructure development. This is visualized through the interconnectedness of EV manufacturing, smart grid technology, and charging infrastructure, highlighting the cross-sectoral innovation that e-mobility spurs (Bergman, 2017). The representation of advanced materials and manufacturing processes emphasizes the push toward more sustainable industrial practices, while the integration of digital technologies with transportation infrastructure showcases the role of e-mobility in building resilient and adaptable urban systems.

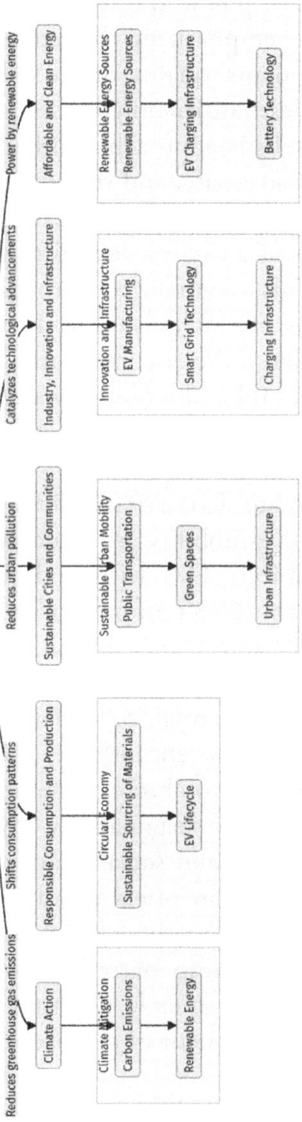

Fig. 6.2 Theoretical Framework (personal elaboration)

The visualization further explores the impact of e-mobility on sustainable cities and communities (Goal 11). Here, EVs are shown as central nodes within a network of public transportation options, green spaces, and urban infrastructure, emphasizing the reduction of urban pollution and enhancement of residents' quality of life (Bi, 2016). The depiction of charging stations, pedestrian-friendly spaces, and cycling lanes alongside EVs illustrates the holistic approach to urban mobility that supports the development of inclusive, safe, and sustainable urban environments.

For responsible consumption and production (Goal 12), the framework presents e-mobility as a catalyst for shifting consumption patterns toward sustainability. This is visualized through the lifecycle of EVs, from sustainable sourcing of materials to production, use, and recycling, highlighting the principles of the circular economy (Bubeck, 2016). The representation emphasizes the reduction of waste and pollution through efficient design and highlights consumer behavior shifts toward more sustainable mobility options.

Finally, regarding climate action (Goal 13), this framework underscores the critical role of e-mobility in reducing greenhouse gas emissions. The imagery connects EVs with a declining curve of carbon emissions, symbolizing the direct impact of e-mobility on mitigating climate change. The backdrop of this section features renewable energy sources and green landscapes, reinforcing the message that e-mobility, powered by clean energy, is essential for achieving a low-carbon future.

E-mobility's role in the SDGs encapsulates the interconnected nature of these global goals and the pivotal role of e-mobility in driving progress across multiple dimensions of sustainability. By weaving together the technological, environmental, and social strands of e-mobility's impact, this comprehensive visualization offers a holistic view of how electric transportation can contribute to the realization of the SDGs (Calise, 2021). It serves as a compelling narrative tool, illustrating that the transition to e-mobility is not merely a matter of technological adoption but a fundamental component of a broader strategy for sustainable development.

In conclusion, this framework demonstrates the transformative potential of e-mobility in aligning with and advancing the UN SDGs. It highlights the importance of cross-sectoral collaboration, innovation, and policy support in leveraging e-mobility for sustainable development. As the world moves toward a more sustainable future, the role of e-mobility in achieving the SDGs offers a roadmap for action, emphasizing the need for collective effort and integrated approaches to address the complex challenges of our time.

This framework succinctly captures the interconnected relationship between e-mobility and its role in advancing several key UN SDGs. The diagram illustrates how e-mobility contributes to and is influenced by five specific SDGs: climate action (Goal 13); responsible consumption and production (Goal 12); sustainable cities and communities (Goal 11); industry, innovation, and infrastructure (Goal 9); and affordable and clean energy (Goal 7).

At the top center, e-mobility is positioned as the driving force that influences and is influenced by the goals on either side. This central placement emphasizes e-mobility's pivotal role in sustainable development.

On the left, the relationship between e-mobility and climate action (Goal 13) is established through the reduction of greenhouse gas emissions. E-mobility, by facilitating a shift away from fossil fuel-dependent vehicles, directly mitigates carbon emissions, contributing to climate change mitigation. The flow from climate action leads down to renewable energy, representing the idea that the electrification of transportation should ideally be coupled with clean energy sources to maximize climate benefits.

Adjacent to this, responsible consumption and production (Goal 12) is linked with e-mobility through the promotion of circular economy principles. E-mobility encourages sustainable sourcing of materials and responsible end-of-life vehicle processing, contributing to a more sustainable EV lifecycle that minimizes waste and environmental impact (Croce, 2019).

At the center-right of the diagram, sustainable cities and communities (Goal 11) is shown to benefit from e-mobility through the reduction of urban pollution. The deployment of EVs is integral to sustainable urban mobility, improving public transportation and contributing to greener urban spaces (Laurischkat, 2016). The flow from Goal 11 points to the enhancement of urban infrastructure, which is necessary to support the proliferation of e-mobility in city environments.

On the far right, e-mobility's influence extends to industry, innovation, and infrastructure (Goal 9). Here, e-mobility is seen as a catalyst for technological advancements, driving innovation in EV manufacturing and smart grid technology. This innovation is essential for developing the robust charging infrastructure needed to support a growing fleet of EVs.

Lastly, affordable and clean energy (Goal 7) is tied to e-mobility through the power provided by renewable energy sources. This goal emphasizes the importance of powering EVs with sustainable energy to ensure that the entire ecosystem of e-mobility contributes to the goal of clean and affordable energy (Longo, 2018). The diagram indicates that advancements in battery technology are vital to this process, as they determine the efficiency and effectiveness of both energy storage and the overall performance of EVs.

Overall, this framework not only illustrates the contribution of e-mobility to each SDG but also highlights the synergies between them. It underscores the importance of an integrated approach where advancements in e-mobility support and are supported by progress in renewable energy, sustainable manufacturing, urban planning, and circular economy practices. This integrative perspective is essential for realizing the full potential of e-mobility in the context of sustainable development.

6.4 Key Insights and Contributions

As both a technological innovation and a vital contributor to sustainable development, e-mobility stands at a transformative crossroads. The key insights and contributions of this study on e-mobility, which span across consumer behavior, industry adaptation, policy formation, and sustainable development, are both profound and multifaceted. The rate of consumer adoption of EVs provides a clear insight into the evolving perceptions of and behaviors toward sustainable transportation (Plananska, 2020). Our study reveals that consumers are becoming increasingly aware of the environmental and economic benefits of EVs.

This shift is driven by a combination of factors, including the rising concern for environmental stewardship, the appeal of new technologies, and the tangible benefits of lower operational costs. The data indicate a growing trend of consumers prioritizing sustainability in their transportation choices, which could signal a broader shift toward more environmentally responsible consumer behavior across various sectors.

From an industry standpoint, the transition to e-mobility is not without its challenges, as traditional automakers are compelled to reevaluate and redesign their business models, supply chains, and product lines to accommodate the surge in demand for EVs. This pivot is no small undertaking, requiring substantial investments in new technologies and processes (Rietmann & Lieven, 2019). However, the study highlights that such transformation offers lucrative opportunities for innovation and could potentially lead to a renaissance in automotive design and manufacturing, with sustainability at its core.

The study also underscores the critical role of policy in shaping the e-mobility landscape. Policymakers are tasked with the responsibility of balancing the promotion of e-mobility with the needs of various stakeholders, including automakers, energy providers, and consumers. Our findings suggest that effective policy measures, such as tax incentives for EV purchases and investments in charging infrastructure, have been instrumental in accelerating the adoption of e-mobility (Pan et al., 2021). Moreover, regulatory frameworks that encourage renewable energy integration and set ambitious emissions reduction targets are pivotal in ensuring that e-mobility contributes meaningfully to climate action.

Another significant contribution of this research is the identification of e-mobility as a key enabler of sustainable development. E-mobility intersects with multiple UN SDGs, offering a pathway to achieve several global objectives. By reducing emissions, EVs contribute directly to climate action (SDG 13) and help to create sustainable cities and communities (SDG 11). The shift toward e-mobility also promotes responsible consumption and production (SDG 12) by encouraging the use of vehicles that are more energy-efficient and have a lower total lifecycle environmental impact.

The study further reveals that the global push for e-mobility has spurred advancements in battery technology and charging infrastructure, which have far-reaching implications for the energy sector and beyond. Innovations in these areas not only enhance the performance and appeal of EVs but also have the potential to revolutionize energy storage and distribution systems (Musolino et al., 2019). Such advancements could facilitate the broader integration of renewable energy sources into the grid, contributing to the goal of affordable and clean energy (SDG 7).

The comprehensive analysis provided by this study contributes to the academic discourse on e-mobility by offering empirical evidence on the sector's rapid evolution and its implications for sustainable development. This study provides valuable insights into the complex interplay between technological innovation, consumer behavior, industry dynamics, and policy development. One of the primary insights from this study is the recognition of the speed at which e-mobility is being adopted, which has significant implications for infrastructure development. The need for widespread and accessible charging stations is paramount (Calise et al., 2019). The study contributes to the understanding of infrastructure requirements, suggesting that beyond quantity, the placement and type of charging solutions are crucial for user convenience and can significantly influence consumer adoption rates.

Additionally, the study highlights the economic impacts of e-mobility. The transition to EVs is not merely a replacement of combustion engines with electric motors; it is a complete overhaul of the automotive value chain. This transformation has the potential to disrupt traditional automotive industries while simultaneously giving rise to new market leaders, particularly in the battery and charging equipment sectors (Biresselioglu et al., 2018). The current study's contributions to industry knowledge include mapping the emerging e-mobility value chain and identifying key areas for investment and development.

Furthermore, the study emphasizes the importance of lifecycle analysis in the context of EVs. It contributes to the growing body of knowledge that assesses the environmental impact of EVs, from production to disposal. The study's findings suggest that while EVs have a higher initial environmental footprint due to battery production, their overall impact is significantly lower than that of conventional vehicles when considering the operational phase, especially when charged with renewable energy.

The policy recommendations arising from this study are grounded in a nuanced understanding of the interdependencies between different stakeholder actions and sustainable outcomes (Pavić et al., 2020). The study contributes to policy debates by providing evidence-based recommendations, such as the need for subsidies to lower the economic barriers to EV adoption and the importance of regulatory support for renewable energy to ensure that the true environmental benefits of e-mobility are realized.

Regarding sustainable development, the study advances the argument that e-mobility is a critical component of a more sustainable future. It goes beyond the reduction of emissions and explores how e-mobility can contribute to broader societal goals, such as energy independence, urban planning, and even social equity (Franke et al., 2016). By highlighting case studies where e-mobility has been successfully integrated into public transport systems, the study offers pathways for making sustainable transportation accessible to a wider population.

6.5 Recommendations

6.5.1 For Consumers

The transition to e-mobility is a critical step toward a more sustainable future, and consumers have an essential role to play in this shift. For individuals considering the adoption of e-mobility solutions, a confluence of factors related to affordability, accessibility, and sustainability must be carefully evaluated to ensure informed decisions that align with personal needs and broader environmental goals.

Affordability is often a primary concern for consumers when it comes to adopting new technologies. Historically, EVs have been perceived as cost-prohibitive compared to their ICE counterparts. However, this landscape is rapidly changing, and the total cost of ownership for EVs, which includes the purchase price, fuel costs, and maintenance expenses, is becoming increasingly competitive due to advancements in technology and economies of scale (Abd Alla et al., 2021). Consumers should be aware of the long-term economic benefits of EVs, including lower fuel costs, lesser need for maintenance due to fewer moving parts, and the potential for longer vehicle lifespans. In addition, many governments offer financial incentives such as tax credits, rebates, and grants to offset the initial purchase price of EVs. Consumers are advised to take full advantage of these incentives where available.

Accessibility to charging infrastructure is another critical factor for consumers. The convenience of recharging an EV has improved significantly with the expansion of public charging networks. Prospective EV owners should consider their driving patterns and the availability of charging stations at home, in the workplace, and in public spaces. For those without access to home charging, it is important to research the availability of local charging infrastructure and explore community or workplace-based charging solutions (Kovačić et al., 2022). Innovative solutions such as portable chargers and subscription-based charging services are also emerging, providing more flexibility for EV users.

Sustainability is a driving force behind the move to e-mobility, with many consumers motivated by the desire to reduce their carbon footprint. EVs offer a path to more sustainable transportation, especially when paired with renewable energy sources (Barisa et al., 2016). Consumers considering EVs should be informed about the source of their electricity; in regions where the grid is powered predominantly by fossil fuels, the environmental benefits of EVs are less pronounced. Thus, consumers are encouraged to support and advocate for the integration of renewable energy into the grid, enhancing the overall sustainability of e-mobility.

Beyond personal vehicle ownership, e-mobility encompasses a range of solutions that consumers can adopt. E-bikes, electric scooters, and electric public transportation are all alternatives for those looking for sustainable mobility options beyond cars. Car-sharing services with EV fleets provide another avenue for consumers to experience and support e-mobility without the commitment of ownership (Barisa et al., 2016). These services can also help mitigate the environmental impact of transportation by reducing the number of vehicles on the road and promoting a sharing economy.

6.5.2 For Industries

As industries navigate the transition toward e-mobility, strategic adaptation, and innovation become crucial. This shift presents an array of opportunities and challenges that require industries to rethink their operational models, supply chains, and product offerings. For industries to thrive in an e-mobility-centric market, the following recommendations offer a roadmap for integration and growth within this evolving landscape.

Industries must first recognize the inevitability of the shift to e-mobility and proactively integrate it into their long-term strategic planning. This involves investing in research and development to stay at the forefront of e-mobility technology, including advancements in battery performance, charging solutions, and electric powertrains (Afonso, 2020). For instance, automotive manufacturers can accelerate the development of EV models to meet the growing demand and comply with increasingly stringent emissions regulations.

Furthermore, industries should prioritize sustainability across their operations, aligning with the broader objectives of environmental responsibility. This includes sourcing materials ethically, minimizing the carbon footprint of manufacturing processes, and adopting circular economy principles such as recycling and remanufacturing components (Ala, 2021). The end goal is to minimize the environmental impact of their products throughout their lifecycle, from production to disposal.

Collaboration across the value chain is another key factor for success in the e-mobility industry. Manufacturers, suppliers, energy providers, and infrastructure developers must work together to create an integrated e-mobility ecosystem. For example, automotive industries can partner with energy firms to develop efficient and widespread charging networks, ensuring that infrastructure keeps pace with EV adoption.

6.5.3 For Policymakers

For policymakers, crafting the trajectory of e-mobility adoption is a balancing act of regulatory foresight, economic incentivization, and infrastructural support. Effective policies must be anticipatory, inclusive, and adaptive to guide the transition toward a sustainable e-mobility ecosystem.

A fundamental step for policymakers is the establishment of clear, long-term e-mobility targets and regulatory frameworks. These should aim to phase out ICE vehicles through stringent emissions regulations, while simultaneously promoting EV adoption through incentives such as tax rebates, grants, and subsidies for both consumers and manufacturers (Bi, 2016). Setting minimum quotas for EV production can compel the automotive industry to accelerate their shift toward electric models.

Infrastructure development is equally critical. Policymakers should facilitate investments in charging infrastructure, ensuring accessibility and convenience for EV users. This involves both deploying public charging stations and integrating smart grid technology to manage the increased electrical load from EVs (Bergman, 2017). Urban planning regulations can be revised to include EV-friendly provisions, such as mandating EV charging points in new residential and commercial developments.

Furthermore, policies must encourage the use of renewable energy in conjunction with e-mobility to maximize environmental benefits. Incentives for renewable energy adoption can be coupled with e-mobility policies to foster a holistic approach to decarburization (Bubeck, 2016). Policymakers can also support research and development in next-generation battery technologies and alternative propulsion methods to keep the momentum of innovation.

An inclusive approach to policy development is vital. It is essential to consider the socioeconomic impacts of the transition to e-mobility, ensuring that policies do not disproportionately affect any particular group. Strategies should be put in place to support workforce retraining and reallocation, particularly for sectors that may be adversely impacted by the shift away from fossil fuel-based technologies.

The exploration of e-mobility within this chapter illuminates its multifaceted role in fostering sustainable development. Through rigorous analysis, the study has unveiled how e-mobility intersects with environmental conservation, economic resilience, and social equity, all underpinned by technological innovation.

E-mobility's environmental benefits have been made starkly apparent in this study. By significantly reducing greenhouse gas emissions, EVs directly contribute to the mitigation of climate change, aligning with SDG 13. The study's findings highlight that e-mobility can also ameliorate urban air quality, contributing to healthier cities in line with SDG 11. The implications extend to a broader environmental canvas—promoting biodiversity by reducing pollution, lowering noise levels, and contributing to the reduction of heat islands in urban settings. These are crucial steps in restoring the natural balances that have been disrupted by conventional modes of transportation.

On the economic front, e-mobility is a harbinger of industrial transformation. The shift is stimulating economic growth, with new job opportunities emerging in the renewable energy, vehicle manufacturing, and infrastructure development sectors, resonating with SDG 9. The burgeoning e-mobility market is also a fertile ground for innovation, encouraging industries to invest in the next generation of transport technologies. However, this is not without its challenges. The study acknowledges the need for economic policies that support a just transition, ensuring that the workforce is upskilled and new jobs are created to replace those lost in traditional industries.

In conclusion, policymakers have the instrumental role of steering the e-mobility revolution through strategic legislation, targeted incentives, and robust infrastructure development. By fostering an environment conducive for innovation, ensuring equitable access to technology, and prioritizing sustainability, policymakers can lay the foundation for a future where e-mobility is a cornerstone of transportation and environmental stewardship.

6.6 Future Research Directions

As the landscape of e-mobility continues to evolve, future research must pivot toward addressing emerging challenges and harnessing new opportunities. One critical area is the enhancement of battery technology. Research should focus on increasing energy density, reducing charging times, and improving battery life cycles (Calise, 2021). Exploring alternative battery chemistries and sourcing materials sustainably can also mitigate the environmental impact of battery production.

The integration of e-mobility with renewable energy grids presents another fertile ground for research. Future studies should investigate how best to balance the load on the power grid, particularly with the proliferation of fast-charging stations (Croce, 2019). The potential of V2G systems to stabilize the grid and provide backup energy in times of peak demand is another promising avenue that warrants further exploration.

Understanding consumer behavior and market dynamics remains essential to accelerating e-mobility adoption. Future research should aim to identify the factors that influence consumer acceptance and the barriers to the widespread adoption of EVs (Laurischkat, 2016). Additionally, the socioeconomic impacts of the transition to e-mobility, such as job displacement in traditional automotive and oil industries, require comprehensive studies to develop strategies for workforce transition and economic adaptation.

In summary, the path ahead for e-mobility research is diverse and multidimensional; it spans the gamut from technological innovation to social science and from energy management to policy formulation. By addressing these areas with rigor and foresight, research can pave the way for a more sustainable, efficient, and inclusive e-mobility future.

6.7 Book Summary

In this chapter, we have provided a comprehensive overview of e-mobility's critical role in sustainable development, specifically examining its alignment with key UN SDGs. We summarized the findings of our study, highlighting the environmental, economic, and social benefits of e-mobility and the challenges that must be overcome to realize its full potential.

The integration of e-mobility within the framework of the SDGs was thoroughly discussed, detailing how it supports affordable and clean energy, fosters industry innovation and resilient infrastructure, contributes to building sustainable cities and communities, encourages responsible consumption and production, and is pivotal for climate action.

A visual framework illustrating the interconnected nature of e-mobility's impact across these goals was presented, providing a clear depiction of its wide-ranging influence. Key insights were drawn, emphasizing the novel contributions of e-mobility to the sustainability discourse and the importance of continued innovation and adoption.

Recommendations were articulated for various stakeholders. For consumers, the focus was on the practical aspects of adopting e-mobility, considering affordability, accessibility, and sustainability. For industries, the emphasis was on embracing change and innovation to remain competitive and relevant. Policymakers were guided on how to create conducive environments for e-mobility through appropriate regulations and incentives.

Future research directions were identified, suggesting areas of study that could further enhance the understanding and implementation of e-mobility solutions. These include advancements in battery technology, the integration of e-mobility with renewable energy, consumer adoption, and the socioeconomic impacts of the e-mobility transition. In summary, this chapter has clearly outlined the role of e-mobility in achieving sustainable development, providing actionable insights for stakeholders and a roadmap for future research endeavors.

References

Abbasi, H. A., Johl, S. K., Shaari, Z. B. H., Moughal, W., Mazhar, M., Musarat, M. A., Rafiq, W., Farooqi, A. S., & Borovkov, A. (2021). Consumer motivation by using unified theory of acceptance and use of technology towards electric vehicles. *Sustainability, 13*(21), 12177.

Abd Alla, S., Bianco, V., Tagliafico, L. A., & Scarpa, F. (2021). Pathways to electric mobility integration in the Italian automotive sector. *Energy, 221*, 119882.

Abdellahi, A., Rahimian, S. K., Blizanac, B., & Sisk, B. (2017). Exploring the opportunity space for high-power li-ion batteries in next-generation 48V mild hybrid electric vehicles (0148-7191). SAE Technical Paper.

Abduljabbar, R. L., Liyanage, S., & Dia, H. (2021). The role of micro-mobility in shaping sustainable cities: A systematic literature review. *Transportation Research Part d: Transport and Environment, 92*, 102734.

Adnan, N., Nordin, S. M., Rahman, I., Vasant, P. M., & Noor, A. (2017). A comprehensive review on theoretical framework-based electric vehicle consumer adoption research. *International Journal of Energy Research, 41*(3), 317–335.

Afonso, J. L., Cardoso, L. A. L., Pedrosa, D., Sousa, T. J., Machado, L., Tanta, M., & Monteiro, V. (2020). A review on power electronics technologies for electric mobility. *Energies, 13*(23), 6343.

D. D'Acunto, *The Future of E-Mobility*, https://doi.org/10.1007/978-3-031-65053-6

Ajanovic, A., Haas, R., & Schrödl, M. (2021). On the historical development and future prospects of various types of electric mobility. *Energies, 14*(4), 1070.

Ala, G., Colak, I., Di Filippo, G., Miceli, R., Romano, P., Silva, C., Valtchev, S., & Viola, F. (2021). Electric mobility in Portugal: Current situation and forecasts for fuel cell vehicles. *Energies, 14*(23), 7945.

Alper, E., & Orhan, O. Y. (2017). CO2 utilization: Developments in conversion processes. *Petroleum, 3*(1), 109–126.

Apostolou, D., & Welcher, S. N. (2021). Prospects of the hydrogen-based mobility in the private vehicle market. A social perspective in Denmark. *International Journal of Hydrogen Energy, 46*(9), 6885–6900.

Armand, M., Axmann, P., Bresser, D., Copley, M., Edström, K., Ekberg, C., Guyomard, D., Lestriez, B., Novák, P., Petranikova, M., Porcher, W., Trabesinger, S., Wohlfahrt-Mehrens, M., & Zhang, H. (2020). Lithium-ion batteries—Current state of the art and anticipated developments. *Journal of Power Sources, 479*, 228708.

Ashfaq, M., Butt, O., Selvaraj, J., & Rahim, N. (2021). Assessment of electric vehicle charging infrastructure and its impact on the electric grid: A review. *International Journal of Green Energy, 18*(7), 657–686.

Augurio, A., Castaldi, L., Addeo, F., Mazzoni, C., & Matarazzo, O. (2022). Purchase intention in the Italian e-mobility market. *Journal of Cleaner Production, 373*, 133815.

Axsen, J., & Sovacool, B. K. (2019). The roles of users in electric, shared and automated mobility transitions. *Transportation Research Part d: Transport and Environment, 71*, 1–21.

Axsen, J., Goldberg, S., & Bailey, J. (2016). How might potential future plug-in electric vehicle buyers differ from current "Pioneer" owners? *Transportation Research Part d: Transport and Environment, 47*, 357–370.

Bai, Y., Muralidharan, N., Sun, Y. K., Passerini, S., Whittingham, M. S., & Belharouak, I. (2020). Energy and environmental aspects in recycling lithium-ion batteries: Concept of Battery Identity Global Passport. *Materials Today, 41*, 304–315.

Bansal, P., Kumar, R. R., Raj, A., Dubey, S., & Graham, D. J. (2021). Willingness to pay and attitudinal preferences of Indian consumers for electric vehicles. *Energy Economics, 100*, 105340.

Barisa, A., Rosa, M., & Kisele, A. (2016). Introducing electric mobility in Latvian municipalities: Results of a survey. *Energy Procedia, 95*, 50–57.

Bengler, K., Dietmayer, K., Farber, B., Maurer, M., Stiller, C., & Winner, H. (2014). Three decades of driver assistance systems: Review and future perspectives. *IEEE Intelligent Transportation Systems Magazine, 6*(4), 6–22.

Bennett, R., Kottasz, R., & Shaw, S. (2016). Factors potentially affecting the successful promotion of electric vehicles. *Journal of Social Marketing, 6*, 62–82.

Bergman, N., Schwanen, T., & Sovacool, B. K. (2017). Imagined people, behaviour and future mobility: Insights from visions of electric vehicles and car clubs in the United Kingdom. *Transport Policy, 59*, 165–173.

Berkeley, N., Bailey, D., Jones, A., & Jarvis, D. (2017). Assessing the transition towards battery electric vehicles: A multi-level perspective on drivers of, and barriers to, take up. *Transportation Research Part a: Policy and Practice, 106*, 320–332.

Bi, Z., Kan, T., Mi, C. C., Zhang, Y., Zhao, Z., & Keoleian, G. A. (2016). A review of wireless power transfer for electric vehicles: Prospects to enhance sustainable mobility. *Applied Energy, 179*, 413–425.

Bican, P. M., Caspary, D., & Guderian, C. C. (2023). Cross-border dynamics of IP modularity: International patenting in LEDs and Lithium-Ion secondary battery technology. *Management International Review, 63*(2), 347–376.

Biresselioglu, M. E., Kaplan, M. D., & Yilmaz, B. K. (2018). Electric mobility in Europe: A comprehensive review of motivators and barriers in decision making processes. *Transportation Research Part a: Policy and Practice, 109*, 1–13.

Bissell, D., Birtchnell, T., Elliott, A., & Hsu, E. L. (2020). Autonomous automobilities: The social impacts of driverless vehicles. *Current Sociology, 68*(1), 116–134.

Böckin, D., & Tillman, A.-M. (2019). Environmental assessment of additive manufacturing in the automotive industry. *Journal of Cleaner Production, 226*, 977–987.

Bohn, S., & Braun, T. (2021). Field-configuring projects: How projects shape the public reflection of electric mobility in Germany. *International Journal of Project Management, 39*(6), 605–619.

Bonges, H. A., III., & Lusk, A. C. (2016). Addressing electric vehicle (EV) sales and range anxiety through parking layout, policy and regulation. *Transportation Research Part a: Policy and Practice, 83*, 63–73.

Borras, S. M., Jr., Franco, J. C., Isakson, S. R., Levidow, L., & Vervest, P. (2016). The rise of flex crops and commodities: Implications for research. *The Journal of Peasant Studies, 43*, 93–115.

Bösehans, G., Bell, M., Thorpe, N., Liao, F., de Almeida, H., Correia, G., & Dissanayake, D. (2023). EHUBs—Identifying the potential early and late adopters of shared electric mobility hubs. *International Journal of Sustainable Transportation, 17*(3), 199–218.

Brase, G. L. (2019). What would it take to get you into an electric car? Consumer perceptions and decision making about electric vehicles. *The Journal of Psychology, 153*(2), 214–236.

Bubeck, S., Tomaschek, J., & Fahl, U. (2016). Perspectives of electric mobility: Total cost of ownership of electric vehicles in Germany. *Transport Policy, 50*, 63–77.

Buckley, P. J., & Ghauri, P. N. (2004). Globalisation, economic geography and the strategy of multinational enterprises. *Journal of International Business Studies, 35*, 81–98.

Calise, F., Cappiello, F. L., Cartenì, A., d'Accadia, M. D., & Vicidomini, M. (2019). A novel paradigm for a sustainable mobility based on electric vehicles, photovoltaic panels and electric energy storage systems: Case studies for Naples and Salerno (Italy). *Renewable and Sustainable Energy Reviews, 111*, 97–114.

Calise, F., Fabozzi, S., Vanoli, L., & Vicidomini, M. (2021). A sustainable mobility strategy based on electric vehicles and photovoltaic panels for shopping centers. *Sustainable Cities and Society, 70*, 102891.

Carteni, A., Henke, I., Molitierno, C., & Errico, A. (2020). Towards E-mobility: Strengths and weaknesses of electric vehicles. In *Web, artificial intelligence and network applications: Proceedings of the workshops of the 34th international conference on advanced information networking and applications (WAINA-2020).*

Casals, L. C., García, B. A., & Canal, C. (2019). Second life batteries lifespan: Rest of useful life and environmental analysis. *Journal of Environmental Management, 232*, 354–363.

Castellanos, K., & Heutel, G. (2024). Unemployment, labor mobility, and climate policy. *Journal of the Association of Environmental and Resource Economists, 11*(1), 1–40.

Cheng, X. B., Liu, H., Yuan, H., Peng, H. J., Tang, C., Huang, J. Q., & Zhang, Q. (2021). A perspective on sustainable energy materials for lithium batteries. *SusMat, 1*(1), 38–50.

Clinton, B. C., & Steinberg, D. C. (2019). Providing the Spark: Impact of financial incentives on battery electric vehicle adoption. *Journal of Environmental Economics and Management, 98*, 102255.

Corradi, C., Sica, E., & Morone, P. (2023). What drives electric vehicle adoption? Insights from a systematic review on European transport actors and behaviours. *Energy Research & Social Science, 95*, 102908.

Costa, C. M., Barbosa, J. C., Castro, H., Gonçalves, R., & Lanceros-Méndez, S. (2021). Electric vehicles: To what extent are environmentally friendly and cost effective? Comparative study by european countries. *Renewable and Sustainable Energy Reviews, 151*, 111548.

Croce, A. I., Musolino, G., Rindone, C., & Vitetta, A. (2019). Sustainable mobility and energy resources: A quantitative assessment of transport services with electrical vehicles. *Renewable and Sustainable Energy Reviews, 113*, 109236.

Da Silva Lima, L., Cocquyt, L., Mancini, L., Cadena, E., & Dewulf, J. (2023). The role of raw materials to achieve the sustainable development goals: Tracing the risks and positive contributions of cobalt along the lithium-ion battery supply chain. *Journal of Industrial Ecology, 27*(3), 777–794.

de Kwant, C., Rahi, A. F., & Laurenti, R. (2021). The role of product design in circular business models: An analysis of challenges and opportunities for electric vehicles and white goods. *Sustainable Production and Consumption, 27*, 1728–1742.

De Rubens, G. Z., Noel, L., Kester, J., & Sovacool, B. K. (2020). The market case for electric mobility: Investigating electric vehicle business models for mass adoption. *Energy, 194*, 116841.

Dou, J., & Han, X. (2019). How does the industry mobility affect pollution industry transfer in China: Empirical test on Pollution Haven Hypothesis and Porter Hypothesis. *Journal of Cleaner Production, 217*, 105–115.

Du, J., Ouyang, M., & Chen, J. (2017). Prospects for Chinese electric vehicle technologies in 2016–2020: Ambition and rationality. *Energy, 120*, 584–596.

Dwivedi, Y. K., Ismagilova, E., Hughes, D. L., Carlson, J., Filieri, R., Jacobson, J., Jain, V., Karjaluoto, H., Kefi, H., Krishen, A. S., Kumar, V., Rahman, M. M., Raman, R., Rauschnabel, P. A., Rowley, J., Salo, J., Tran, G. A., & Wang, Y. (2021). Setting the future of digital and social media marketing research: Perspectives and research propositions. *International Journal of Information Management, 59*, 102168.

El Yadari, M., Jawab, F., & Arif, J. (2022). Logistics4. 0 for urban logistics: A literature review and research framework. In *2022 14th international colloquium of logistics and supply chain management (LOGISTIQUA) (pp. 1–7)*. IEEE.

Etxandi-Santolaya, M., Casals, L. C., Montes, T., & Corchero, C. (2023). Are electric vehicle batteries being underused? A review of current practices and sources of circularity. *Journal of Environmental Management, 338*, 117814.

Franke, T., Rauh, N., Günther, M., Trantow, M., & Krems, J. F. (2016). Which factors can protect against range stress in everyday usage of battery electric vehicles? Toward enhancing sustainability of electric mobility systems. *Human Factors, 58*(1), 13–26.

Ghasri, M., Ardeshiri, A., & Rashidi, T. (2019). Perception towards electric vehicles and the impact on consumers' preference. *Transportation Research Part d: Transport and Environment, 77*, 271–291.

Giansoldati, M., Danielis, R., Rotaris, L., & Scorrano, M. (2018). The role of driving range in consumers' purchasing decision for electric cars in Italy. *Energy, 165*, 267–274.

Gionfriddo, G., Rizzi, F., Daddi, T., & Iraldo, F. (2023). The impact of green marketing on collective behaviour: Experimental evidence from the sports industry. *Business Strategy and the Environment, 32*, 5349–5367.

Gruber, H. (2019). Proposals for a digital industrial policy for Europe. *Telecommunications Policy, 43*(2), 116–127.

Gulzari, A., Wang, Y., & Prybutok, V. (2022). A green experience with eco-friendly cars: A young consumer electric vehicle rental behavioral model. *Journal of Retailing and Consumer Services, 65*, 102877.

Haddadian, G., Khodayar, M., & Shahidehpour, M. (2015). Accelerating the global adoption of electric vehicles: Barriers and drivers. *The Electricity Journal, 28*(10), 53–68.

Hagman, J., Ritzén, S., Stier, J. J., & Susilo, Y. (2016). Total cost of ownership and its potential implications for battery electric vehicle diffusion. *Research in Transportation Business & Management, 18*, 11–17.

Hardman, S., Jenn, A., Tal, G., Axsen, J., Beard, G., Daina, N., Figenbaum, E., Jakobsson, N., Jochem, P., Kinnear, N., Plötz, P., Pontes, J., Refa, N., Sprei, F., Turrentine, T., & Witkamp, B. (2018). A review of consumer preferences of and interactions with electric vehicle charging infrastructure. *Transportation Research Part d: Transport and Environment, 62*, 508–523.

Haustein, S., & Jensen, A. F. (2018). Factors of electric vehicle adoption: A comparison of conventional and electric car users based on an extended theory of planned behavior. *International Journal of Sustainable Transportation, 12*(7), 484–496.

He, X., Zhan, W., & Hu, Y. (2018). Consumer purchase intention of electric vehicles in China: The roles of perception and personality. *Journal of Cleaner Production, 204*, 1060–1069.

Higueras-Castillo, E., Kalinic, Z., Marinkovic, V., & Liébana-Cabanillas, F. J. (2020). A mixed analysis of perceptions of electric and hybrid vehicles. *Energy Policy, 136*, 111076.

Higueras-Castillo, E., Liébana-Cabanillas, F. J., Muñoz-Leiva, F., & García-Maroto, I. (2019). Evaluating consumer attitudes toward electromobility and the moderating effect of perceived consumer effectiveness. *Journal of Retailing and Consumer Services, 51*, 387–398.

Hinton, P. R., Brownlow, C., McMurray, I., Cozens, B., & SPSS, E. (2004). Routledge Inc. East Sussex.

Hoarau, Q., & Perez, Y. (2018). Interactions between electric mobility and photovoltaic generation: A review. *Renewable and Sustainable Energy Reviews, 94*, 510–522.

Huang, X., & Ge, J. (2019). Electric vehicle development in Beijing: An analysis of consumer purchase intention. *Journal of Cleaner Production, 216*, 361–372.

Huang, Y., Qian, L., Tyfield, D., & Soopramanien, D. (2021). On the heterogeneity in consumer preferences for electric vehicles across generations and cities in China. *Technological Forecasting and Social Change, 167*, 120687.

Jackson, J. (2023). (Re) coordinating the German Political Economy: E-mobility and the Verkehrswende. *German Politics*, 1–23. https://doi.org/10.1080/09644008.2023.2236557

Jaiswal, D., Deshmukh, A. K., & Thaichon, P. (2022). Who will adopt electric vehicles? Segmenting and exemplifying potential buyer heterogeneity and forthcoming research. *Journal of Retailing and Consumer Services, 67*, 102969.

Jaiswal, D., Kaushal, V., Kant, R., & Singh, P. K. (2021). Consumer adoption intention for electric vehicles: Insights and evidence from Indian sustainable transportation. *Technological Forecasting & Social Change, 173*, 121089.

Jayakumar, J., Nagaraj, B., Chacko, S., & Ajay, P. (2021). Conceptual implementation of artificial intelligent based E-mobility controller in smart city environment. *Wireless Communications and Mobile Computing, 2021*, 1–8.

Jie, W., Yang, J., Zhang, M., & Huang, Y. (2019). The two-echelon capacitated electric vehicle routing problem with battery swapping stations: Formulation and efficient methodology. *European Journal of Operational Research, 272*(3), 879–904.

Jones, T., Harms, L., & Heinen, E. (2016). Motives, perceptions and experiences of electric bicycle owners and implications for health, wellbeing and mobility. *Journal of Transport Geography, 53*, 41–49.

Kalla, A., Mayilswamy, N., Kandasubramanian, B., & Mahajan-Tatpate, P. (2023). Biochar: A sustainable and an eco-friendly material for energy storage applications. *International Journal of Green Energy, 21*(7), 1695–1709. https://doi.org/10.1080/15435075.2023.2259973

Kamran, M., Raugei, M., & Hutchinson, A. (2021). A dynamic material flow analysis of lithium-ion battery metals for electric vehicles and grid storage in the UK: Assessing the impact of shared mobility and end-of-life strategies. *Resources, Conservation and Recycling, 167*, 105412.

Kester, J., de Rubens, G. Z., Sovacool, B. K., & Noel, L. (2019). Public perceptions of electric vehicles and vehicle-to-grid (V2G): Insights from a Nordic focus group study. *Transportation Research Part d: Transport and Environment, 74*, 277–293.

Kline, R. B. (2005). *Principles and practice of structural equation modeling*. Guilford Press.

Kovačić, M., Mutavdžija, M., & Buntak, K. (2022). New paradigm of sustainable urban mobility: Electric and autonomous vehicles—A review and bibliometric analysis. *Sustainability, 14*(15), 9525.

Kraus, S., Jones, P., Kailer, N., Weinmann, A., Chaparro-Banegas, N., & Roig-Tierno, N. (2021). Digital transformation: An overview of the current state of the art of research. *SAGE Open, 11*(3), 21582440211047576.

Krishna, G. (2021). Understanding and identifying barriers to electric vehicle adoption through thematic analysis. *Transportation Research Interdisciplinary Perspectives, 10*, 100364.

Krishnan, R., & Butt, B. (2022). "The gasoline of the future:" Points of continuity, energy materiality, and corporate marketing of electric vehicles among automakers and utilities. *Energy Research & Social Science, 83*, 102349.

Krommes, S., & Schmidt, F. (2017). Business model analysis of electric mobility products and services. *International Journal of Automotive Technology and Management, 17*(3), 316–338.

Kumar, R. R., & Alok, K. (2020). Adoption of electric vehicle: A literature review and prospects for sustainability. *Journal of Cleaner Production, 253*, 119911.

Lashari, Z. A., Ko, J., & Jang, J. (2021). Consumers' intention to purchase electric vehicles: Influences of user attitude and perception. *Sustainability, 13*(12), 6778.

Laurischkat, K., Viertelhausen, A., & Jandt, D. (2016). Business models for electric mobility. *Procedia CIRP, 47*, 483–488.

Lew, S., Tan, G. W. H., Loh, X. M., Hew, J. J., & Ooi, K. B. (2020). The disruptive mobile wallet in the hospitality industry: An extended mobile technology acceptance model. *Technology in Society, 63*, 101430.

Li, S., Tong, L., Xing, J., & Zhou, Y. (2017a). The market for electric vehicles: Indirect network effects and policy design. *Journal of the Association of Environmental and Resource Economists, 4*(1), 89–133.

Li, W., Long, R., Chen, H., & Geng, J. (2017b). A review of factors influencing consumer intentions to adopt battery electric vehicles. *Renewable and Sustainable Energy Reviews, 78*, 318–328.

Liang, Y., Ding, Z., Ding, T., & Lee, W. J. (2020). Mobility-aware charging scheduling for shared on-demand electric vehicle fleet using deep reinforcement learning. *IEEE Transactions on Smart Grid, 12*(2), 1380–1393.

Liao, F., Molin, E., & van Wee, B. (2017). Consumer preferences for electric vehicles: A literature review. *Transport Reviews, 37*(3), 252–275.

Lieven, T. (2015). Policy measures to promote electric mobility–A global perspective. *Transportation Research Part a: Policy and Practice, 82*, 78–93.

Lipu, M. H., Hannan, M. A., Hussain, A., Hoque, M. M., Ker, P. J., Saad, M. H. M., & Ayob, A. (2018). A review of state of health and remaining useful life estimation methods for lithium-ion battery in electric vehicles: Challenges and recommendations. *Journal of Cleaner Production, 205*, 115–133.

Liu, W., Placke, T., & Chau, K. T. (2022). Overview of batteries and battery management for electric vehicles. *Energy Reports, 8*, 4058–4084.

Llopis-Albert, C., Rubio, F., & Valero, F. (2021). Impact of digital transformation on the automotive industry. *Technological Forecasting and Social Change, 162*, 120343.

Longo, M., Foiadelli, F., & Yaïci, W. (2018). Electric vehicles integrated with renewable energy sources for sustainable mobility. *New Trends in Electrical Vehicle Powertrains, 10*, 203–223.

Luca de Tena, D., & Pregger, T. (2018). Impact of electric vehicles on a future renewable energy-based power system in Europe with a focus on Germany. *International Journal of Energy Research, 42*(8), 2670–2685.

MacCarthy, B. L., Blome, C., Olhager, J., Srai, J. S., & Zhao, X. (2016). Supply chain evolution–theory, concepts and science. *International Journal of Operations & Production Management, 36*(12), 1696–1718.

Maggio, G., Nicita, A., & Squadrito, G. (2019). How the hydrogen production from RES could change energy and fuel markets: A review of recent literature. *International Journal of Hydrogen Energy, 44*(23), 11371–11384.

Maghfiroh, M. F. N., Pandyaswargo, A. H., & Onoda, H. (2021). Current readiness status of electric vehicles in indonesia: Multistakeholder perceptions. *Sustainability, 13*(23), 13177.

Mangan, J., & Lalwani, C. (2016). *Global logistics and supply chain management*. Wiley.

Martin, G., Rentsch, L., Höck, M., & Bertau, M. (2017). Lithium market research—Global supply, future demand and price development. *Energy Storage Materials, 6*, 171–179.

Martins, L. S., Guimarães, L. F., Junior, A. B. B., Tenório, J. A. S., & Espinosa, D. C. R. (2021). Electric car battery: An overview on global demand, recycling and future approaches towards sustainability. *Journal of Environmental Management, 295*, 113091.

Mohamed, M., Higgins, C., Ferguson, M., & Kanaroglou, P. (2016). Identifying and characterizing potential electric vehicle adopters in Canada: A two-stage modelling approach. *Transport Policy, 52*, 100–112.

Mohd Yusof, A., Daniel, E. G. S., Low, W. Y., & Ab. Aziz, K. (2014). Teachers' perception of mobile edutainment for special needs learners: The Malaysian case. *International Journal of Inclusive Education, 18*(12), 1237–1246.

Mossali, E., Picone, N., Gentilini, L., Rodrìguez, O., Pérez, J. M., & Colledani, M. (2020). Lithium-ion batteries towards circular economy: A literature review of opportunities and issues of recycling treatments. *Journal of Environmental Management, 264*, 110500.

Muniz, S. T. G., & Belzowski, B. M. (2017). Platforms to enhance electric vehicles' competitiveness. *International Journal of Automotive Technology and Management, 17*(2), 151–168.

Musolino, G., Rindone, C., & Vitetta, A. (2019). Passengers and freight mobility with electric vehicles: A methodology to plan green transport and logistic services near port areas. *Transportation Research Procedia, 37*, 393–400.

Neumann, J., Petranikova, M., Meeus, M., Gamarra, J. D., Younesi, R., Winter, M., & Nowak, S. (2022). Recycling of lithium-ion batteries—Current state of the art, circular economy, and next generation recycling. *Advanced Energy Materials, 12*(17), 2102917.

Nikitas, A., Thomopoulos, N., & Milakis, D. (2021). The environmental and resource dimensions of automated transport: A nexus for enabling vehicle automation to support sustainable urban mobility. *Annual Review of Environment and Resources, 46*, 167–192.

Omahne, V., Knez, M., & Obrecht, M. (2021). Social aspects of electric vehicles research—Trends and relations to sustainable development goals. *World Electric Vehicle Journal, 12*(1), 15.

Palmer, K., Tate, J. E., Wadud, Z., & Nellthorp, J. (2018). Total cost of ownership and market share for hybrid and electric vehicles in the UK, US and Japan. *Applied Energy, 209*, 108–119.

Pan, S., Fulton, L. M., Roy, A., Jung, J., Choi, Y., & Gao, H. O. (2021). Shared use of electric autonomous vehicles: Air quality and health impacts of future mobility in the United States. *Renewable and Sustainable Energy Reviews, 149*, 111380.

Pandey, D. A., Manocha, D. S., & Saini, D. P. (2020). A study on an automobile revolution and future of electric cars in India. *International Journal of Management (IJM), 11*(3), 107–113.

Pavić, I., Pandžić, H., & Capuder, T. (2020). Electric vehicle based smart e-mobility system—Definition and comparison to the existing concept. *Applied Energy, 272*, 115153.

Pelletier, S., Jabali, O., & Laporte, G. (2016). 50th anniversary invited article—Goods distribution with electric vehicles: Review and research perspectives. *Transportation Science, 50*(1), 3–22.

Pichler, M., Krenmayr, N., Schneider, E., & Brand, U. (2021). EU industrial policy: Between modernization and transformation of the automotive industry. *Environmental Innovation and Societal Transitions, 38*, 140–152.

Plananska, J. (2020). Touchpoints for electric mobility: Investigating the purchase process for promoting sales of electric vehicles in Switzerland. *Energy Research & Social Science, 69*, 101745.

Priessner, A., Sposato, R., & Hampl, N. (2018). Predictors of electric vehicle adoption: An analysis of potential electric vehicle drivers in Austria. *Energy Policy, 122*, 701–714.

Pucihar, A., Borštnar, M. K., Kittl, C., Ravesteijn, P., Clarke, R., & Bons, R. (2017). Designing and implementing common market for cross-game purchases between mobile games. In *30TH Bled eConference: digital transformation—From connecting things to transforming our lives*, 531.

Rauh, N., Franke, T., & Krems, J. F. (2015). Understanding the impact of electric vehicle driving experience on range anxiety. *Human Factors, 57*(1), 177–187.

Ravi, S. S., & Aziz, M. (2022). Utilization of electric vehicles for vehicle-to-grid services: Progress and perspectives. *Energies, 15*(2), 589.

Reinhardt, R., Christodoulou, I., Gassó-Domingo, S., & García, B. A. (2019). Towards sustainable business models for electric vehicle battery second use: A critical review. *Journal of Environmental Management, 245*, 432–446.

Requia, W. J., Mohamed, M., Higgins, C. D., Arain, A., & Ferguson, M. (2018). How clean are electric vehicles? Evidence-based review of the effects of electric mobility on air pollutants, greenhouse gas emissions and human health. *Atmospheric Environment, 185*, 64–77.

Rezvani, Z., Jansson, J., & Bodin, J. (2015). Advances in consumer electric vehicle adoption research: A review and research agenda. *Transportation Research Part d: Transport and Environment, 34*, 122–136.

Rietmann, N., & Lieven, T. (2019). How policy measures succeeded to promote electric mobility—Worldwide review and outlook. *Journal of Cleaner Production, 206*, 66–75.

Rongen, T., Tillema, T., Arts, J., Alonso-González, M. J., & Witte, J.-J. (2022). An analysis of the mobility hub concept in the Netherlands: Historical lessons for its implementation. *Journal of Transport Geography, 104*, 103419.

Rosendahl, K. E., & Rubiano, D. R. (2019). How effective is lithium recycling as a remedy for resource scarcity? *Environmental and Resource Economics, 74*, 985–1010.

Ruan, T., & Lv, Q. (2023). Public perception of electric vehicles on Reddit and Twitter: A cross-platform analysis. *Transportation Research Interdisciplinary Perspectives, 21*, 100872.

Ruggieri, R., Ruggeri, M., Vinci, G., & Poponi, S. (2021). Electric mobility in a smart city: European overview. *Energies, 14*(2), 315.

Mesch, G. S., & Dodel, M. (2022). The acceptance of driverless cars: The roles of perceived outcomes and technology usefulness. *American Behavioral Scientist 67*(14), 1736–1754.

Sæther, S. R. (2022). Mobility at the crossroads—Electric mobility policy and charging infrastructure lessons from across Europe. *Transportation Research Part a: Policy and Practice, 157*, 144–159.

Santos, G., & Davies, H. (2020). Incentives for quick penetration of electric vehicles in five European countries: Perceptions from experts and stakeholders. *Transportation Research Part a: Policy and Practice, 137*, 326–342.

Saw, L. H., Ye, Y., & Tay, A. A. (2016). Integration issues of lithium-ion battery into electric vehicles battery pack. *Journal of Cleaner Production, 113*, 1032–1045.

Schwabe, J. (2020). Risk and counter-strategies: The impact of electric mobility on German automotive suppliers. *Geoforum, 110*, 157–167.

Secinaro, S., Brescia, V., Calandra, D., & Biancone, P. (2020). Employing bibliometric analysis to identify suitable business models for electric cars. *Journal of Cleaner Production, 264*, 121503.

Secinaro, S., Calandra, D., Lanzalonga, F., & Ferraris, A. (2022). Electric vehicles' consumer behaviours: Mapping the field and providing a research agenda. *Journal of Business Research, 150*, 399–416.

Shafique, M., & Luo, X. (2022). Environmental life cycle assessment of battery electric vehicles from the current and future energy mix perspective. *Journal of Environmental Management, 303*, 114050.

She, Z.-Y., Sun, Q., Ma, J.-J., & Xie, B.-C. (2017). What are the barriers to widespread adoption of battery electric vehicles? A survey of public perception in Tianjin, China. *Transport Policy, 56*, 29–40.

Skrúcaný, T., Kendra, M., Stopka, O., Milojević, S., Figlus, T., & Csiszár, C. (2019). Impact of the electric mobility implementation on the greenhouse gases production in central European countries. *Sustainability, 11*(18), 4948.

Smith, G., & Hensher, D. A. (2020). Towards a framework for Mobility-as-a-Service policies. *Transport Policy, 89*, 54–65.

Sovacool, B. K. (2017). Experts, theories, and electric mobility transitions: Toward an integrated conceptual framework for the adoption of electric vehicles. *Energy Research & Social Science, 27*, 78–95.

Sovacool, B. K., Kester, J., & Heida, V. (2019). Cars and kids: Childhood perceptions of electric vehicles and sustainable transport in Denmark and the Netherlands. *Technological Forecasting and Social Change, 144*, 182–192.

Sovacool, B. K., Kim, J., & Yang, M. (2021). The hidden costs of energy and mobility: A global meta-analysis and research synthesis of electricity and transport externalities. *Energy Research & Social Science, 72*, 101885.

Stockkamp, C., Schäfer, J., Millemann, J. A., & Heidenreich, S. (2021). Identifying factors associated with consumers' adoption of e-mobility—A systematic literature review. *Sustainability, 13*(19), 10975.

Suman, M. N. H., Chyon, F. A., & Ahmmed, M. S. (2020). Business strategy in Bangladesh—Electric vehicle SWOT-AHP analysis: Case study. *International Journal of Engineering Business Management, 12*, 184797902094148.

Tarei, P. K., Chand, P., & Gupta, H. (2021). Barriers to the adoption of electric vehicles: Evidence from India. *Journal of Cleaner Production, 291*, 125847.

Tarei, P. K., Chand, P., & Gupta, H. (2021). Barriers to the adoption of electric vehicles: Evidence from India. *Journal of Cleaner Production, 291*, 125847.

Tekic, Z., & Koroteev, D. (2019). From disruptively digital to proudly analog: A holistic typology of digital transformation strategies. *Business Horizons, 62*(6), 683–693.

Thompson, D. L., Hartley, J. M., Lambert, S. M., Shiref, M., Harper, G. D., Kendrick, E., Anderson, P., Ryder, K. S., Gaines, L., & Abbott, A. P. (2020). The importance of design in lithium ion battery recycling—A critical review. *Green Chemistry, 22*(22), 7585–7603.

Tian, Z., Hou, W., Gu, X., Gu, F., & Yao, B. (2018). The location optimization of electric vehicle charging stations considering charging behavior. *SIMULATION, 94*(7), 625–636.

Tian, Y., Zeng, G., Rutt, A., Shi, T., Kim, H., Wang, J., Koettgen, J., Sun, Y., Ouyang, B., & Chen, T. (2020). Promises and challenges of next-generation "beyond Li-ion" batteries for electric vehicles and grid decarbonization. *Chemical Reviews, 121*(3), 1623–1669.

Tlili, O., Mansilla, C., Frimat, D., & Perez, Y. (2019). Hydrogen market penetration feasibility assessment: Mobility and natural gas markets in the US, Europe, China and Japan. *International Journal of Hydrogen Energy, 44*(31), 16048–16068.

Turienzo, J., Cabanelas, P., & Lampón, J. F. (2022). The mobility industry trends through the lens of the social analysis: A multi-level perspective approach. *SAGE Open, 12*(1), 21582440211069144.

Turner, C., Di Tommaso, M. R., Pollio, C., & Chapple, K. (2020). Who will win the electric vehicle race? The role of place-based assets and policy. *Local Economy, 35*(4), 337–362.

Ullah, I., Liu, K., Yamamoto, T., Zahid, M., & Jamal, A. (2021). Electric vehicle energy consumption prediction using stacked generalization: An ensemble learning approach. *International Journal of Green Energy, 18*(9), 896–909.

Van Fossen, J. A., Chang, C.-H., Ford, J. K., Mack, E. A., & R. Cotten, S. (2022). Identifying alternative occupations for truck drivers displaced due to autonomous vehicles by leveraging the O*NET database. *American Behavioral Scientist 67*(14), 1693–1715.

Varghese, A. T., Abhilash, V., & Pillai, S. V. (2021). A study on consumer perception and purchase intention of electric vehicles in India. *Asian Journal of Economics, Finance and Management 3*(1), 272–284.

Vassileva, I., & Campillo, J. (2017). Adoption barriers for electric vehicles: Experiences from early adopters in Sweden. *Energy, 120*, 632–641.

Virmani, N., Agarwal, S., Raut, R. D., Paul, S. K., & Mahmood, H. (2022). Adopting net-zero in emerging economies. *Journal of Environmental Management, 321*, 115978.

Virshup, A. M., Punwong, C., Pogorelov, T. V., Lindquist, B. A., Ko, C., & Martinez, T. J. (2009). Photodynamics in complex environments: Ab initio multiple spawning quantum mechanical/molecular mechanical dynamics. *The Journal of Physical Chemistry B, 113*(11), 3280–3291.

Voskoboynik, D. M., & Andreucci, D. (2022). Greening extractivism: Environmental discourses and resource governance in the 'Lithium Triangle.' *Environment and Planning e: Nature and Space, 5*(2), 787–809.

Wang, N., Tang, L., & Pan, H. (2019). A global comparison and assessment of incentive policy on electric vehicle promotion. *Sustainable Cities and Society, 44*, 597–603.

Wang, T., Luo, H., Zeng, X., Yu, Z., Liu, A., & Sangaiah, A. K. (2020). Mobility based trust evaluation for heterogeneous electric vehicles network in smart cities. *IEEE Transactions on Intelligent Transportation Systems, 22*(3), 1797–1806.

Wu, G., Inderbitzin, A., & Bening, C. (2015). Total cost of ownership of electric vehicles compared to conventional vehicles: A probabilistic analysis and projection across market segments. *Energy Policy, 80*, 196–214.

Xu, X., Lin, Y., Wang, F., Yang, S., & Zhou, Z. (2019). A hybrid observer for SOC estimation of lithium-ion battery based on a coupled electrochemical-thermal model. *International Journal of Green Energy, 16*(15), 1527–1538.

Yang, C., Li, P., Yu, J., Zhao, L. D., & Kong, L. (2020). Approaching energy-dense and cost-effective lithium–sulfur batteries: From materials chemistry and price considerations. *Energy, 201*, 117718.

Ye, F., Kang, W., Li, L., & Wang, Z. (2021). Why do consumers choose to buy electric vehicles? A paired data analysis of purchase intention configurations. *Transportation Research, 147*, 14–27.

McConnell, V., & Leard, B. (2021). Pushing new technology into the market: California's Zero Emissions Vehicle Mandate. *Review of Environmental Economics and Policy, 15*(1), 169–179.

Zhang, X., Bai, X., & Shang, J. (2018). Is subsidized electric vehicles adoption sustainable: Consumers' perceptions and motivation toward incentive policies, environmental benefits, and risks. *Journal of Cleaner Production, 192*, 71–79.

Zhao, Y., & Guo, J. (2020). Development of flexible Li-ion batteries for flexible electronics. *InfoMat, 2*(5), 866–878.

Zhou, Y., Wang, M., Hao, H., Johnson, L., Wang, H., & Hao, H. (2015). Plug-in electric vehicle market penetration and incentives: A global review. *Mitigation and Adaptation Strategies for Global Change, 20*, 777–795.

Zijm, H., & Klumpp, M. (2016). Logistics and supply chain management: developments and trends. In : Zijm, H., Klumpp, M., Clausen, U., Hompel, M. (eds.), *Logistics and supply chain innovation: Bridging the gap between theory and practice* Springer, Cham. https://doi.org/10.1007/978-3-319-22288-2_1

Index

D. D'Acunto, *The Future of E-Mobility*, https://doi.org/10.1007/978-3-031-65053-6

The manufacturer's authorised representative in the EU is Springer Nature Customer Service Centre GmbH, Europaplatz 3, 69115 Heidelberg, Germany. If you have any concerns regarding our products, please contact ProductSafety@springernature.com

Printed and bound by CPI Group (UK) Ltd, Croydon, CR0 4YY

30/09/2026

02225595-0004